THE STORY OF PADUCAH

The Story of Paducah
(Kentucky)

By
Fred G. Neuman

author of "The Story of Irvin S. Cobb". etc.
and Revision by Catherine Neuman Adams

With an introduction by
Irvin S. Cobb

Original Printing
Young Printing Co.
1927

Revised Printing
Image Graphics
1979

Copyright, 1927, by
FRED G. NEUMAN

Copyright, 1979, by
CATHERINE NEUMAN ADAMS

Copyright, 2000, by
CATHERINE NEUMAN JONES

Library of Congress Control Number: 00-131145
ISBN 0-615-11775-9

To Our Grandsons
David Michael Jones
Frederick Stanley Jones
Of Whom We Are Justly Proud

Reprinted in Honor and Memory of
My Mother and Father
CATHERINE and FRED G. NEUMAN

PREFACE

In collecting and preparing material for this volume it was the purpose of the author to present a faithful history of Paducah. Much time was spent in searching the old files, studying the old historical accounts and consulting the old authorities. Facts were gleaned wherever they could be found; traditions were sifted. The story was written with an eye looking toward the perpetuation of the splendid record of the forefathers.

Thanks are due scores of residents and former citizens for courtesies extended while the chapters were in preparation. No one showed the slightest irritation or impatience, though homes were invaded and family circles traversed.

Despite his busy life, Mr. Irvin S. Cobb found time to read the typewritten pages, make corrections and supply new sidelights. That he should dignify the book with a foreword is a source of genuine gratification.

Mr. V. Blaine Russell was especially helpful in making a careful revision of the manuscript, incident to which were many valuable suggestions which have been incorporated in the text. The author is indebted to Mr. W.G. McFadden for a number of photographs, and to Mr. Robert Wilkins for several drawings. Mr. Al E. Young is largely responsible for the arrangement of illustrations and other details of typography.

The months employed in planning and executing the work would have been insufficient had not the author been assisted by his wife who copied the sheets, read proof and rendered other fine services.

FRED G. NEUMAN

Paducah, KY, November, 1927

PREFACE

In preparation of this the second printing of the *Story of Paducah* inserts are included that had been placed in the margins of his book by the author himself shortly before his death in 1953. The first six chapters had been compiled by Mr. Neuman with the expectation of bringing out another edition. Otherwise the book reads the same as the original. An effort has been made to include events since 1927. There was so much that happened within fifty-two years that I found it an impossible task.

So many of the first printing were lost in the flood that there was a real need for the revision.

This book is compiled in memory of one who dearly loved Paducah and all the persons who dwell therein, Mr. Fred G. Neuman, my former husband. This volume comes forth hoping it will supply information needed, and bring an added appreciation for our lovely city, and heartfelt thanks to those who brought it from an early beginning to the place we love to call home.

Many thanks to those who gave information and a very special thanks to my loving daughter, Catherine, and her husband, Malcolm Jones, who gave inspiration and were helpful in so many ways.

CATHERINE NEUMAN ADAMS

Paducah, KY, 1979

TABLE OF CONTENTS

	Page
Foreword, by Irvin S. Cobb	XV

CHAPTER I
Jackson Purchase 17

CHAPTER II
Chief Paduke 24

CHAPTER III
Early Exploits 29

CHAPTER IV
Settlement and Founding 35

CHAPTER V
McCracken County; Wilmington 44

CHAPTER VI
Paducah Platted; Becomes County Seat 51

CHAPTER VII
Corporate Town—1830-1856 61

CHAPTER VIII
Third Class City—1856-1902 70

CHAPTER IX
Second Class City—1902 85

CHAPTER X
Places of Historic Interest 99

CHAPTER XI
Sports and Amusements 112

CHAPTER XII
Along the River Front 128

CHAPTER XIII
Wars and the Warriors 142

	Page
CHAPTER XIV	
Means of Transportation	159
CHAPTER XV	
Educational Factors	169
CHAPTER XVI	
Cemeteries; Fire Departments; Telephones	178
CHAPTER XVII	
Sphere of Religion	186
CHAPTER XVIII	
Sphere of Religion (Continued)	203
CHAPTER XIX	
Irvin S. Cobb	219
CHAPTER XX	
Noted Paducahans	235
CHAPTER XXI	
Home-Coming Week, 1913	257
CHAPTER XXII	
A Golden Period	260

FOREWORD

BY IRVIN S. COBB

I call it an honor to be asked to write a brief introduction for this book, and I accept the assignment with pleasure and with pride as well.

Not that the book needs any introduction, any preliminary praise. It has merits which advertise themselves. It has in it truth, sincerity, an honest affection by the writer for the place of his nativity, an honest and painstaking presentation by him of the story of his home-town.

I am proud because my friend Fred Neuman chose me for this most congenial task, I am honored because I have my share, and more than my proper share of mention, in these pages. And I am pleased because I have here an opportunity publicly to testify to the high regard in which I hold the author.

All Paducahans--native-borns who have removed elsewhere, the present residents of the community, the residents who will come afterward--owe this man a debt of gratitude for his successful efforts to assemble the historical facts, both written and the previously unwritten, the lore and the traditions, of a town which all of us love very dearly. The task was one of his own choosing and most competently he has performed it. In collecting and preserving the story of the past generations he has rendered a patriotic service to generations yet unborn. Others may differ with me, but I, for one, regard Fred Neuman as Paducah's most useful citizen. Certainly devotion to civic ideals scarcely can rise to a higher level than the level upon which his feet are placed.

IRVIN S. COBB

THE STORY OF PADUCAH

CHAPTER I

JACKSON PURCHASE

Situated at the confluence of the Ohio and Tennessee rivers, twelve miles below the Cumberland and forty-seven miles above the Mississippi, Paducah[1] the largest city in western Kentucky, lies at a latitude of 37 degrees, 5 minutes, and at a longitude of 88 degrees, 36 minutes, based on Greenwich.[2] The city received its name in honor of Chief Paduke, who reigned over a small tribe of Chickasaws known around the mouth of the Tennessee River as the Paducahs.

At least, "Paduke" as a name for the chief and "Paducah" as the name for the sub-tribal division over which he ruled, have come to be commonly accepted. Recent discoveries, however, prove that both names were, in a measure, corruptions of the same word of the Chickasaw language.

When General William Clark (1770-1838), the founder of the city, christened the town he followed the spelling and pronunciation of a name frequently encountered by him in the ever-famous Northwest Expedition of the Lewis and Clark party, of which he was one of the two leaders. "Paducah" was the generic title which the Comanche Indians had for themselves, "Comanche" being a word of Spanish derivation. Those savage tribesmen of the plains through whose domain the explorers passed, undoubtedly called themselves "Paducahs" and not "Comanches." The name appears in at least fifteen early chronicles.

From the fact that General Clark afterward used the word for the name of the infant settlement here in Kentucky a legend arose, some years ago, that old chief "Paduke," or "Paducah," might have been a Comanche who followed Clark as his patron back to the eastern banks of the Mississippi. Through the efforts of Irvin S. Cobb, a native of Paducah, there was unearthed in 1926 what, almost surely, is the genesis of the name. Mr. Cobb, who always took a deep interest in the early history of his home town, was proud that he was instrumental in clearing up a mystery of more than local interest. He was an authority on Indian lore.

According to Mr. Cobb's contention, the name of Paducah--and incidentally of the old chief--was derived from a compound word in the Chickasaw tongue meaning "wild grapes hanging," or, more properly, "place where the grapes hang down." This word, as spelled by the whites in their effort to catch the slurring accents of the Indians, is "Pakutukah," or "Pak'tukah," which seemingly is an abbreviation.

The former spelling was given by the Rev. H.B. Cushman,[3] the historian of certain southern tribes who spent practically his entire life from childhood to death among the red men in Tennessee, Mississippi and Louisana. He was a missioner to the Indians as his father and mother before him were.

It was Mr. Cobb's theory either that the site where the city stands was called "Pakutukah," or, if the condensation is preferred, "Pak'tukah," because of the number of wild grape vines found here, or that the head of the resident sub-tribe was himself called by one of the abbreviated forms of the same word, meaning, probably, "Wild Grape." Wild grape vines are still plentiful in the willow and sycamore fringes of Owen's Island, opposite the site of the Indian chief's wigwam, the heavy growth being spared by the woodsman to hold the tract against the river currents.

In translating the name into English, General Clark naturally followed the spelling of the similarly sounding word of the Comanche language with which he was acquainted. Even those most familiar with the Indian tongues would be likely in such cases to become confused; a good many of them did become confused, as conflicting statements in pioneer records attest.

But, in two modified forms "Pakutukah" as a name for a spot where grapes abounded is still preserved in northern Mississippi,

THE STORY OF PADUCAH 19

and is a plausible explanation that "Paducah" is but a third modification of the same word.

When the Chickasaws ceded their lands to the United States through the Jackson Purchase, white men gained control of the territory between the Tennessee river and the great Mississippi, east and west, stretching from the Ohio river down to the northern boundary of the state of Mississippi. This deal, effected in 1818, embraced what is known as southwestern Kentucky and western Tennessee, including eight counties in Kentucky and twenty in Tennessee.

The Jackson Purchase as it relates to Kentucky includes Ballard, Calloway, Carlisle, Fulton, Graves, Hickman, McCracken and Marshall counties, approximately 2,100 square miles. In Tennessee, the area is 6,000 square miles. The whole territory involved 8,100 square miles, the major portion of which is in Tennessee; yet for many years now, reference to the Purchase, as it is commonly called, has erroneously narrowed in speech and often in the press to the section only in Kentucky.

By sale of the land, the Chickasaw Nation of Indians relinquished all its title and claims in favor of the United States of America.

Nature could scarcely have endowed the red men with more desirable hunting grounds than those of the Purchase district before the coming of white civilization. It was an ideal Indian country, a veritable hunting paradise. Here the warriors pushed through entangling cane and dense forests of hickory, oak, walnut and sycamore, or followed birch-lined and willow-hung creeks in search of wild game which inhabited the woods. Here roamed the bear and the deer, the fox and the wolf. Here in plenteous number was the raccoon and the squirrel. Here, too, was the panther, for it was wild country and only deer paths led into the deep woods. Benevolent streams afforded fish. When the red man lifted his bow and arrow skyward the dart found its billet in wild ducks and geese.

Tents bloomed under every tree on top of the hill from what is now Norton Street to Island Creek. Often the interlacing boughs of sycamore and oak formed the only awning of the tent that sheltered some hardy son of the forest. The red men were dwarfed by the dense growth of trees, the silvery water, and the blue-gray sky.

This vast domain, with its peace and contentment, was not to be enjoyed by the Chickasaws forever; now and then they found themselves annoyed by white adventurers — traders, trappers and backwoodsmen who pulled upstream and downstream in pirogues. These strangers increased at the turn of the nineteenth century. It was evident on every hand that the palefaces, as the Indians called the white men, envied the natives and desired the wooded plateau and its verdant valley. With each visit the white men carried back glowing stories of the land, picturing its character and possibilities in extravagant terms.

The government in 1816 commissioned General Andrew Jackson, fresh from his defeat of the Creek Indians, and Governor Isaac Shelby of Kentucky, then in the last year of his second term, to make overtures for the large tract, wisely choosing General Jackson for the major role owing to the fear and respect he instilled in the Indians. Jackson's prominence is recognized by its designation as the "Jackson Purchase," although it is now frequently called the Purchase district or simply the Purchase. Governor Shelby had distinguished himself in the Battle of King's Mountain and as a state executive, but "Old Hickory," as Jackson was nicknamed in token of his physical toughness, seemed better qualified for the immediate task through experience with the Indians.

Authorized to treat with the red men for sale and evacuation of the territory, the commissioners succeeded only after two years of deliberation. The Indians wanted time to "think through" the plan and advise with their tribesmen. The Chickasaw chiefs and warriors, in full council assembled, agreed to the compact October 19, 1818.[4] It was later confirmed by President James Monroe and ratified by the United States on January 7, 1819.

The deal consumated, the Chickasaws began preparations for

THE STORY OF PADUCAH 21

migrating to the state of Mississippi. Without haste and in good order, they reluctantly left their old haunts, departing with a sigh as they looked again upon the vast domain they knew and loved so well. It was a great procession of flatboats, dugouts, canoes and other crude means of river transportation that moved slowly downstream.

The Paducahs, stemming from the Chickasaws and living at or near Pekin, the future site of Paducah, joined the cavalcade in that frosty autumn. A few stragglers remained and others came from time to time, a remnant of Paducahs still lingering at the site and being on friendly terms with the white settlers nearly a hundred years after the treaty was signed.[5]

Previous to sale of the Jackson Purchase, Virginia and the Confederation sought to reward General George Rogers Clark (1752-1818) for valuable military services rendered at Kaskaskia, Vincennes and other points under British control. It was in 1778, during the American Revolution, that the red-headed general led an expedition in flatboats down the Ohio river from above Pittsburgh.

Skillfully manning their craft over the falls at Louisville, the frontiersmen pushed downstream with their leader. At Fort Massac, twelve miles below the mouth of the Tennessee river, they abandoned their boats. Then began an arduous march through swamps and dead forests to Kaskaskia and Cahokia, both of which were captured without bloodshed. Vincennes was next taken, and the vast northwest thus won by General Clark and his band of heroic volunteers. For this magnificent victory, John Randolph, of Roanoke, called George Rogers Clark the "Hannibal of the West."

Years later the federal government wished to show further appreciation of General Clark's great services and gave him two tracts of land by patents bearing the date of September 15, 1795. These tracts contained 73,962 acres and were located in southwestern Kentucky, at the concourse of the Ohio and Tennessee rivers. General Clark had gazed at the wooded area on his

22 THE STORY OF PADUCAH

expedition in 1778.

One of these grants contained 37,000 acres and was located in what is now McCracken county. It embraced nearly a fifth of the county and included the present site of Paducah, then called Pekin, a small clearing at the foot of Broadway.

Records define the boundaries as follows:

> Beginning at three maples, two ashes and a hackberry on the banks of the Ohio river, at the mouth of the Tennessee river, running thence south 16 degrees, west 1,280 pole, cross a creek to two white oaks and three maples standing on the banks of the creek that empties into the Ohio, at the lower end of the island at the mouth of the Tennessee; thence north 74 degrees, west 5,598 poles, crossing a fork of Massac creek at 1,850 points, another at 2,340 poles, a branch at 3,000 poles, and another at a 3,396 poles, passing a corner, five black jack saplings, in the head of a hollow at 3,840 poles to a white oak and hickory by a small drain, corner to George Smith, running thence west, 2,166 poles to two maples and a cottonwood tree standing on the Ohio river, at the lower side of a small creek, and the fifth below Massac, running thence up the Ohio, binding thereon, 8,640 poles to the beginning.

General George Rogers Clark lived and died near Louisville. Following his death February 13, 1818, proper distribution of his estate in southwestern Kentucky became a subject of consideration for several years, or until April 20, 1823, when F.B. Bullett conducted a ballot at Louisville whereby the land was divided among the late soldier's brother and sisters, and their heirs. In this way the immediate land upon which Paducah stands fell into the hands of General William Clark, youngest brother of the Revolutionary hero.

General William Clark was prominently identified with the early development of Paducah. He gave the hamlet that name--Paducah--changing it from Pekin when he visited it in 1827. He was widely known as an explorer and a governor of the Louisiana Territory. He was red-headed, red-faced, never stern nor silent, got along well with both white men and Indians, and kept everybody in good spirits with his cheerful chatter.

Although known chiefly in national history for his expedition with Meriweather Lewis to the far west in 1804-1806, General William Clark occupies an important niche in the early annals of Paducah, for, besides bestowing that name upon the infant

THE STORY OF PADUCAH

village, he laid out its streets. He died at St. Louis in 1838, twenty years after his famous brother passed away, and was buried there in Bellefontaine Cemetery. The funeral services were among the most impressive that city has ever known.

---

[1] Paducah, Texas, the capital of Cottle county, was named after Paducah, Kentucky, at the suggestion of J.R. Neff, who moved from the Kentucky city by that name in 1883 and settled in the Lone Star state. Cottle county was organized in 1892 and the townsite laid off by R. Potts, owner, who favored Mr. Neff's recommendation. Mr. Neff was living there at the time and bought a large number of lots from Mr. Potts. Paducah, Texas, was incorporated February 12, 1910. The population in 1940 was 2,677.

[2] Figures of latitude and longitude are at a fairly representative spot, approximately Seventh and Washington streets, or the McCracken county court house.

[3] As an old man Reverend Mr. Cushman wrote his book, "*History of the Choctaw, Chickasaw and Natchez Indians,*" in which he incorporated the fruits of seventy years of direct contact with the aborigines. This book, which is now out of print, is accepted by ethnologists everywhere as one of the most accurate and dependable works dealing with the original Americans. Among students it is quoted as an authority.

[4] "The stipulation of this treaty were made in Monroe county, Mississippi, on the banks of the Tombigbee river, on the road between Aberdeen and Cotton Gin port, about ten miles from the former place. The magnificent oak under whose branches General Jackson and his staff stood, side by side with Chinnuby and his chiefs, is fast fading away."-Redford in *The History of Methodism in Kentucky.* (Vol. II, p. 494).

[5] One of the last of the Paducah tribe of Indians in these parts was recalled in a letter written January 8, 1946, by V. Blaine Russell, columnist on the Vicksburg (Miss.) Evening Post who spent his younger days in Paducah. Mr. Russell wrote: "The last of the original tribe of Paducahs left on the scene used to sit on the metal bases of the building at the northwest corner of Second and Kentucky Avenue. That was about the year 1900. He was always there on market days with a splintwood basket on his arm. In it he had dried apple pies, fried in half-moon shape, for sale at a nickel each. He would never say a word. I distinctly recall that he was very old when I was a boy passing the corner. He was short in stature, long hair to his coat collar--he dressed in white man's apparel. His skin was a wrinkled brown, his features typically Indian. I recall he was a bit stoop-kneed, as Indians often are, and walked so straight-toed or Indian fashion, we boys called it pigeon-toed."

CHAPTER II

CHIEF PADUKE

There was one outstanding personality among the Paducah Indians--Chief Paduke, towering Atlas-like above the common range. With his bronzed companions the giant roamed the wilds for many miles around Pekin, where his wigwam stood. The Paducahs were especially numerous along the Tennessee River bank opposite Owen's Island. Their camping grounds, however, were scattered all through McCracken county, as mounds and other evidence testify.

Indian relics found on the banks of Clark's River where it flows into the Tennessee, indicate that that section was popular as a rendezvous. Mounds long since discovered in the vicinity of Eden Hill suggest the burial of relics and other treasures there. Several mounds stood back of the William Rottgering property at the edge of the city limits on the Cairo Road. Findings of Col. Fain W. King's excavations there in September-October, 1939, were turned over to the Paducah Junior College.

Gooseneck Hill, at the foot of South Tenth street, was a slight elevation surrounded by Cross Creek, except for a narrow neck of land on the west, and was next in choice to the grove where Chief Paduke's wigwam stood overlooking the river. Graveyard Hill, a ridge on which the Franklin Junior High School was erected in 1926, had fourteen mounds and as late as 1910 was noted as a depository for tomahawks, arrowheads and flint rocks, bringing to mind the days of the grand sachem and his tribe.

Chief Paduke was a picturesque and stately figure; he was tall and massive, with his weight mathematically distributed over his several limbs. His physique was imposing and easily claimed him as the choicest representative of the sub-tribe of Paducahs. He towered above his braves like the pyramid of Ghizeh above the desert. His fellow tribesmen often called him Chief Paduke.

THE STORY OF PADUCAH 25

The husky, full-chested body and sunburnt visage were broad, clearly-cut, and of reddish-brown hue. The forehead was broad and excessively high for one of his race, making the intellectual portion symmetrical and well fashioned. Black eyes were sunk deep under heavy brows. Abundant hair hung in plaited braids over either shoulder, held in shape by circlets of wampum.

Chief Paduke's address was easy and agreeable, quite unusual for a gutteral language; his step firm and graceful. Natural powers of endurance and vigilance had been developed by life in the wilderness. Often, before the sun pinked the tip of Owen's Island, the smokey-eyed chief and his warriors were tracking to earth a deer, closing in on the exhausted buck and felling it with a long spear.

When in the autumn of 1818 the Government acquired the Purchase territory, Chief Paduke and most of his tribe made ready their canoes to start down the river to the State of Mississippi, where the Northern Chickasaws were migrating. They also bargained for a flatboat and a number of squaws boarded it. Tents and other possessions were piled on the flatboat.

As the chief was making ready to depart, he was advised of a visit which General William Clark was planning to make to Pekin and the camping grounds the following summer. This information interested Chief Paduke, as he was a great admirer of General Clark, and the chief thought to himself that he would surprise the explorer and meet him there. Chief Paduke meant to pay General Clark personal homage.

In less than a year the summer of 1819 had come and Chief Paduke, accompanied by ninety braves, set out to greet Clark at Pekin. Dauntless and determined, the warriors paddled upstream. It was a stiff pull, but they made good progress. The ninety braves served as a proud escort.

But, meanwhile, General Clark changed his plans and did not visit the site. He was, of course, unaware that Chief Paduke contemplated such a trip, for the sub-tribal head had indeed kept it a secret, planning the visit in the nature of a surprise. The General is said to have stated later that had he known of Chief Paduke's good intentions, he would not have disappointed the red man.

Eight years later when he did visit Pekin, General Clark recalled the touching incident and renamed the place Paducah in honor of the chieftain, but too late for the noble redskin to know of it.

Disappointed at the General's failure to come, the chief visited the scenes of his ancestors and in the latter part of July began the return trip downstream. It was a dry year and the river was at a low ebb.

Chief Paduke complained of feeling ill, but felt equal to the voyage. The midsummer sun blazed overhead and the water reflected its heat. Mosquitoes swarmed everywhere. Chief Paduke suffered a chill and high fever as his frail craft moved downstream.

At a point a short distance above the Mississippi river, the chief's comrades turned their canoes toward the Kentucky bank and carried the stricken warrior ashore. They procured medicinal roots, herbs, barks, berries and leaves, which were compounded and faithfully administered by the native medicine man. But this weird mixture failed to stay the malady. The chief passed away the next morning in the arms of his comrades, among them Bone Shirt, Broken Leg and Tanglefoot. "He die!" they moaned. Like a spent stag, his chase was ended.

It was then decided that their leader's remains should be brought back to Pekin, where he had reigned so nobly. Bringing

CHIEF PADUKE'S GRAVE UNDER THE LARGE SYCAMORE TREE
WHERE HIS WIGWAM STOOD

the body to the old camping site, the braves paddled to the foot of what is now Husbands Street; his wigwam had stood under a large sycamore tree in a royal grove on the hill. The grieved comrades carried the body there to the spot he loved so well.

With careful hands the body was laid upon the ground, facing the east or rising sun. There was the customary ceremony befitting a stricken leader. The body was then covered with sod. Before they lifted glaze-dimmed eyes and turned from the mound, his comrades placed hewed logs around it.[1] Thus another member of a much-abused race had departed for the Happy Hunting Ground.

Tradition says that Chief Paduke died on the morning of July 28, 1819. He must have been about 63 years old, yet in no particular had age shown itself in stooping shoulders or dim eyes.

A bronze marker in the sidewalk on the east side of South Third street fifty feet north of Husbands street, determines the resting place of the chief. It reads:

"Two Hundred Feet East of This Spot Was Buried the Indian Chief Paduke, in 1819, for Whom the City Was Named."

The burial site became the gathering place for the red men who came from distances to pay homage to the memory of the beloved chief.[2] Col. James B. Husbands, an early historian of Paducah, writes: "Chief Paduke was a great favorite among his people, who were in the habit of visiting the place of his remains for several years after his death."[3]

In the early part of April, 1874, an unsuccessful effort was made to find the remains of the chief by a committee of citizens who wished to disinter the body and bury it in a more prominent locality. But fifty-five years had elasped since the great son of the forest was laid to rest and chemical processes of the soil had obliterated all trace of his mortal being.

A heroic statue of Chief Paduke was unveiled and presented to the city May 19, 1909, by the Paducah Chapter of the Daughters of the American Revolution. Mrs. E.G. Boone, then regent of the chapter, suggested the fountain-statue, and the $3,000 necessary

28 THE STORY OF PADUCAH

for its erection was raised by public subscription. It represents Lorado Taft's conception of the Indian chief. The statue stood at the northwest corner of Fifth and Broadway until June 3, 1937, when it was set in the esplanade at Nineteenth and Jefferson streets.

In a poem entitled "To the Statue, Chief Paduke," written in 1927, the poet, Mrs. Mary Lanier Magruder, expressed both sentiment and truth. The lines read:

The paleface daughters set his image here,
   Cold, white and passionless, with patient art
Beneath the summer suns, through autumn sere,
   Or spring's gay burgeoning in the city's heart.
He waits and listens, looking into space,
For some dim phantom of his vanished race.

Serene he sits and gazes into space,
   Beyond our present to his peopled past.
A half ironic smile upon his face,
   At life that flows so frenziedly and fast;
At all our feverish waste and haste that must
So soon be ended--in a little dust!

And we, whose greed deprived him of his own,
   And made him exile from these happy lands,
See his revenge incarnate in this stone,
   Whereby the sculptor's art and cunning hands.

CHIEF PADUKE STATUE   Through years that will obscure, our little frame,
Have made immortal Chief Paduke's fair name.

---

[1]A few years before her death at the age of 90 in 1923, Mrs. Elizabeth Smedley, native resident, described Chief Paduke's grave as she remembered it in 1843, when she was 10 years old. "We children had weird thoughts as we approached the burial spot several blocks north of Island creek," Mrs. Smedley said. "Third street was but a narrow road which led past it, the scene being a slight hill. It filled us with superstitious fear. We thought the place was haunted and in our childish vision often imagined we saw Chief Paduke's spirit or ghostlike appearance."

[2]"Capt. John (Jack) Lawson, pioneer resident, told me that for years after most of the tattered remnant of Indians vanished from these parts, a delegation of them returned annually to hold some sort of powwow. This would tend to confirm the oft-repeated tale that Paduke's followers revisited the burying place of their people." Irvin S. Cobb in "Sidelights on Paducah," The Sun Democrat, March 14, 1943.

[3]Williams' Paducah Directory (1859), Sketch of Paducah, p. 2.

CHAPTER III

EARLY EXPLOITS

Three parties of sturdy pioneers breasted the rivers at Paducah, or Pekin as it was then called, previous to the Jackson Purchase and withdrawal of the friendly Indians. Forty years before the memorable treaty was completed in 1818, General George Rogers Clark and 180 crack riflemen aboard flatboats landed at the island opposite the Paducah Indian village. Within two years Colonel John Donelson arrived on the so-called flagship "Adventure", leading a daring expedition down the Tennessee River and up the Cumberland. Thirty-two years after Donelson's voyage, while the red men were still in their glory at Pekin, the steamer "New Orleans" made port. Those were exciting events in the wilderness country.

CLARK'S EXPEDITION

General George Rogers Clark enlisted volunteers above Pittsburgh and brought his party down the Ohio River for services against the British in Illinois. He augmented his forces at Louisville, and left there June 24, 1778. "The whole of our force, after leaving such as was not judged competent to the expected fatigue, consisted of only four companies," General Clark notes in his Memoir.[1] As they climbed into their pirogues and started their long trek, the militiamen in outward appearances resembled bedraggled Indian traders, being dressed in what they could find in hurried preparation.

General Clark's small army reached the mouth of the Tennessee River June 28, and landed at the foot of Owen's Island.[2] "As I intended to leave the Ohio at Fort Massac, three miles below the Tennessee, I landed on a small island at the mouth of that river in order to prepare for the march," the Memoir says. The journey from Louisville was made in four days, relays of oarsmen pulling day and night to cover the distance in the shortest possible time.

Shortly after landing, the party sighted a boat with half a dozen hunters, who on coming nearer were hailed and forced to land. The backwoodsmen proved friendly and joined General Clark's band to Fort Massac, a few miles downstream on the Illinois shore, where the boats were hid in a creek and the overland march begun.

DONELSON'S VOYAGE

No fabled Jason ever led his adventurers in search of the Golden Fleece on a journey beset with more hardships and greater danger than Colonel John Donelson headed when his party left eastern Tennessee and came by way of the Tennessee River to where Paducah stands, and then ascended the Ohio River twelve miles, thence up the Cumberland to the present site of Nashville, their destination. Colonel Donelson kept a diary, a thrilling record of a thousand-mile voyage on uncharted waters.

Thirty families made the trip in addition to thirty-two men engaged to manage and propel the boats, and defend the party. The flagship, "Adventure", with Colonel Donelson aboard, led the flotilla of thirty-odd boats—canoes, dugouts and flatboats—none of them with less than two families aboard. The "Adventure" was a barge-like craft, virtually a large scow, having broad square ends and a flat bottom. The boat was covered, and accomodated thirty persons and a quantity of supplies.

Colonel Donelson's pretty daughter, Rachel, was among the party on the "Adventure". A few years later this wilderness beauty became the wife of General Andrew Jackson.

Starting from a point on the Holston River in December, 1779, the colonists endured continuous hardships through the cold winter. They reached Pekin on April 20, 1780. Fearing the Indians would give them trouble, they landed on the Illinois shore. There they debated the wisdom of ascending the swift Ohio a distance of twelve miles and then facing the Cumberland, which was pouring its waters into the "River of Many Whitecaps," as the early missionaries called the Ohio. Colonel Donelson's journal reads:

THE STORY OF PADUCAH 31

We arrived at the mouth of the Tennessee on Monday, the 20th (April), and landed on the lower point, immediately on the bank of the Ohio. Our situation is truly disagreeable. The river is very high and the current rapid. Our boats are not constructed for the purpose of stemming a rapid stream, and we know not what we have to do, or what time it will take us to reach our destination.

The scene is rendered more melancholy as several boats will not attempt to ascend the rapid current. Some intend to descend the Mississippi to Natchez; others are bound for the Illinois River.

The crude fleet moored opposite Pekin through the remainder of the day and night. Bent on pushing up the Ohio and taking the Cumberland in stride, Colonel Donelson overcame opposition to his plan and carried all but two boats against the current early the next morning. They passed before long out of the Ohio into the mouth of the Cumberland at what is now Smithland. Then slowly they gained the towering hill where Kuttawa now stands, on past the bluffs around the present site of Eddyville; between the sheer precipices beyond in what is now Trigg county, and past Rockcastle and Dover.

No doubt the wondering eyes of redskins gazed from the tops of the high banks with what must have been the same feeling that filled those who had seen Columbus land nearly 300 years before.

The voyage upstream was extremely difficult, slow-moving and laborious. Tired but joyous, the emigrants reached their destination after many exciting experiences.

FIRST STEAMBOAT LANDS

Another and greater wonder was in store for the Indians at Pekin. As daylight was breaking on December 7, 1811, Chief Paduke and his bedaubed warriors were awakened by a distant roar. A number of them hurriedly left their tents along the river front and jumped into their hollowed-out gum-log canoes, not forgetting bows and arrows. Others, with their squaws and papooses, lined the tableland ranging all the way from Island creek to what is now Broadway. Smoke curling in the sky and a sound which grew nearer, and nearer, created a scare never to be forgotten. It was the steamer "New Orleans" on her maiden trip, the first steamer to ply the Ohio and Mississippi Rivers.

Early in the year 1811, Captain Nicholas J. Roosevelt, the

great-uncle of Theodore Roosevelt, arrived at Pittsburgh for the purpose of introducing steam navigation in that part of the country. He built the steamer "New Orleans", a large craft modeled after the historic "Clermont" which Fulton had launched just three years before on the Hudson River.

The steamer "New Orleans" was 116 feet long with a 20-foot beam. She had a paddle wheel and was painted a blue-gray; her name was lettered on each side. The crew consisted of a captain, a pilot, an engineer, and six hands. There was also aboard a large Newfoundland dog, Tiger. When the boat traveled with the current she moved about nine miles an hour.

Leaving Pittsburgh on her initial voyage down the Ohio River, the queer-looking vessel departed October 20 with a grand send-off. Much doubt was expressed by those ashore whether the steamer would reach her destination--New Orleans--after which she was named. Captain Roosevelt served as chief pilot. Mrs. Roosevelt was a passenger.

Delayed at the falls at Louisville for a month, the "New Orleans" did not continue her course down the winding, snag-strewn Ohio until December 3. A rise in the river then afforded safe passage over the falls. Meanwhile, during the layover at Louisville, the Roosevelts' baby was born.

STEAMER NEW ORLEANS AS SHE APPEARED ON LANDING HERE IN 1811.

The next stop of any consequence was Pekin, the only Indian village where the "New Orleans" made port. Hearing the roar of the engines and hiss of escaping steam, and seeing the smoke billowing over the tops of willows on Owen's Island, many of the superstitious red men believed that Ishkoodah, the comet, had fallen into the river, causing the confusion. Children of the natives screamed and hid in the forest. As the steamer rounded the island, the churning paddlewheel and glare of engine fires added fear to their trembling hearts.

"Wait!" commanded Chief Paduke, tall and defiant. The smokey-eyed chief noticed Captain Roosevelt standing on the bow. Chief Paduke gathered his warriors around him when he saw the captain's smile was warm and friendly, waving greetings to the Indians.

At length the strange visitor made port, docking at the foot of what is now Broadway. In the early days a small bluff at that point made it popular with the pioneer trader, and the woodpile in the small cleared area gave it the appearance of an ideal landing site.

The "New Orleans" landed at Pekin early Saturday morning, December 7, 1811. Off the boat stepped white men with sunshine in their faces.

Finding the Paducah Indians friendly, Captain Roosevelt invited them aboard. Chief Paducah and his stalwart braves inspected the strange craft, but even after repeated explanations they could not understand what made the paddlewheel turn. They stood amazed as Captain Roosevelt set the engine in motion and the paddlewheel turned without manual labor.

Before departing downstream that afternoon, Captain Roosevelt bargained with the chief for a supply of wood on the river bank. The pile of wood had interested Captain Roosevelt before the boat made shore. Several strings of beads, a number of gaudy calicoes, with gew-gaws and other cheap articles, as well as a quantity of whiskey, or "fire-water," as the Indians called it, was given in exchange for the fuel.

Hulbert in "The Ohio River," page 331 says: "The New Orleans' engine was fired with coal, but the bunkers were soon exhausted. The woods were soon called upon to give up their beech and sycamore to feed the hungry firebox."

As the "New Orleans" prepared to leave, squaws scrambled for decorative or medicinal shrubs which they presented to Captain and Mrs. Roosevelt. Some of the braves piled into canoes and paddled out alongside the steamer, playfully racing the ship which soon left them in the distance. Both red men and white men waved lustily as long as they were visible to one another.

The steamer reached her destination without mishap and was greeted with a tremendous ovation. Even in these later days of modern steamboats, a journey by river from Pittsburgh to the Gulf is a considerable trip.

---

[1] Thomas D. Clark, "A History of Kentucky," page 70.

[2] The lower part of Owen's Island lies opposite Kentucky Avenue. "Tradition says General Clark and his riflemen came across the Tennessee river and moored their craft at the foot of Kentucky Avenue. A marker there reads: "At the foot of this street General George Rogers Clark and his followers landed in 1778 on their way to Fort Massac, Kaskaskia and Vincennes."

CHAPTER IV

SETTLEMENT AND FOUNDING

In the latter part of 1817 white men from North Carolina, South Carolina, Virginia and Tennessee, learning the Indians planned sale of the territory in southwestern Kentucky, began visiting the section at the mouth of the Tennessee River with a view toward bettering their condition. It was understood the Indians considered withdrawing, realizing it was only a question of time until white settlers would control the ramping wilderness. Some of these trail blazers came overland, crossing the rivers and streams in various ways, all hazardous; but mostly they floated down the Ohio, Tennessee and Cumberland Rivers in broadhorn or flatboats.[10]

For three years these explorers traversed Pekin-now Paducah- and adjacent territory. With the passing of the winter of 1820, at least four families decided to make Pekin their permanent home the following year. As the spring of 1821 approached, James Davis, of Harrison County in northeastern Kentucky, set out for the site, accompanied by his wife and four sons, Robert S., Issac, Jacob, and James, Jr.

Davis and his sons constructed a sturdy, ample flatboat and, launching it in a small stream which flowed into the Licking River, proceeded to Newport and then pushed into the Ohio River for the swing downstream. The father and sons served as the crew. The wife and mother prepared the meals, a large supply of provisions having been loaded on before the craft cut loose from its moorings. A horse, cow, and several hogs shared the flatboat. The family looked forward to making a home for themselves out of the solitudes. Their faces were alight with hope and wonder.

When the Davis family arrived, James and William Pore were constructing a round-log cabin, sixteen feet square, at the southeast corner of what is now First and Broadway, the first house built at Pekin. That was in April, 1821. With their crude implements the Pores had gnawed down trees for wood with which to build their cabin.

The elder Davis and his sons lost no time building a hut that would afford shelter. They pulled their flatboat ashore, dismantled it and used the material to construct a two-room hut at the northwest corner of First and Broadway. Even the boat's nails were salvaged, as they were a scarce item. Trees were felled for the corner posts, and the shanty hurriedly took shape. The Pores and others on the ground helped their new neighbors throw the hut together. A small group of red men looked on in amazement.

At that time there were but four white families in Pekin, a mere handful of dwellers--the two Pores, the Davises, Dr. Jonathan D. Martin and the Charles Fergusons. They formed the nucleus for a hardy pioneer settlement.

From then on settlers became more numerous. Inspired by the love of adventure and lured by the surroundings, a score came within a few months after the first hut took form. Under their strong arm the immediate forest disappeared and the ground yielded increase of human needs. The few Indians lingering in these parts were friendly and not to be feared, but the villagers had to drive back the timber wolf, the panther and the bear. It was a wild country.

Among the early adventurers was Captain Valentine Owen (1803-1874), who breasted the Ohio River at Louisville in a canoe and made the voyage alone. That was in 1822, when a river journey was beset with many dangers. He was only 19 years old. He was a grandson of Colonel Brackett Owen of Revolutionary days and a nephew of Abram Owen, who fell at Tippecanoe. Captain Owen set up a ferry and prospered at the new site, acquired much land which Indians tilled for him, and in 1830, a year before his marriage, built a two-story frame house on the west side of First street between Washington and Kentucky Avenue. Some of Captain Owen's land is still owned by his grandchildren and great-grandchildren. In his earlier days he leased additional land for corn crops. Miss Anna Brack Owen, a granddaughter, prizes the following indenture which was found among Captain Owen's papers:

> An indenture was made on the 9th day of May, 1829, between William Clark, of Missouri, and Valentine Owen, of McCracken County, State of Kentucky.
> William Clark leased to Valentine Owen a tract of land on the Ohio River below the mouth of Island Creek, for the term of one year. In consideration of the lease, Valentine Owen agreed to put up a good log cabin, corn crib, stable and to enclose the cleared land with a good fence, and deliver possession of all premises to William Clark at the expiration of the lease.
> (Signed) WILLIAM CLARK,
> VALENTINE OWEN,
> ROBERT FLETCHER.

As the months passed and word spread of colonization of Pekin, many pioneers with their families stopped for a look at the village and most of them stayed. New settlers included Captain John F. Harris, Albert Hayes, John Haynes, Braxton Small, James S. Long, Frances A. Harrison, Rodney Case, John Fields and John Rollins, most of them bringing their families with them. Flatboats piled high with household goods, supplies and livestock, became more numerous.

Meanwhile other log cabins and shacks dotted the banks of the Tennessee River reaching from Island Creek, or Tennessee River Creek as it was then called, to the newly-built three-room cabin which the James Davises had constructed overlooking the Ohio River at the present site of Riverside Hospital. More than half of the twenty-odd abodes of sorts at Paducah in July, 1826 were built out of flatboats which brought their occupants to the pioneer village; the others were constructed of freshly-hewn logs.

The foot of Broadway was recognized as a commercial site, affording easy access to both the Ohio and Tennessee Rivers; and, this convenience was sought by the first merchant, who established a storehouse there. Articles of food and clothing were sold, the currency often being the pelts of wild animals. This pioneer store, erected in 1826, was of frame construction. It had a clay-wall basement and was situated on the river shore near the northeast corner of First and Broadway. Pekin was then only an outpost, a trading place where hunters and trappers came to exchange their trophies for other products.

The coming and going of these itinerants brought about need of an inn. Those who came to the infant village and were obliged to stay overnight had to find lodging in private homes until John Fields erected an inn, a log structure, at the northwest corner of First and Broadway, the James Davises meanwhile having moved their cabin from that site farther north along the riverfront. Fields bought the lot, 47 by 173 feet, for $12, building the inn at the corner. It was opened in 1830.

But before this, as the summer of 1826 waned, Albert Hayes built a three-room house near the southeast corner of First and Broadway. The house was quite attractive for those days and bore the name "Fox House," after an adventurous fox hunter who occasionally stayed overnight. This was the first frame house in the village, aside from more than a dozen shanties built out of the hulls and sides of flatboats which has borne newcomers to the site. Here General William Clark made his headquarters when he visited the settlement in 1827.

Flatboats, keelboats and small scows multiplied in the rivers, and the steamboat, new on the scene, lent further encouragement to emigrants. Major Charles Ewell (1758-1830), a native Virginian and patriot of 1778, came to the village by steamboat December, 1826. He lived in a small house in the "woods" at what is now 325 North Sixth Street. Like many other pioneer residents, Major Ewell sleeps in Oak Grove Cemetery. John Haynes (1759-1838), also a soldier of the Revolutionary War, came to Pekin the same year (1826) and, with William Enders (1806-1881), erected the first brick house in 1828, the year the Enders family settled in the town. It was located on the west side of First Street between Broadway and Jefferson Street. After a few years this house was used as an inn and as such was known as the Indian Queen, in token of its diminutive size and neat appearance. Haynes is buried on a lonely hill off the Clinton Road ten miles from Paducah.

THE STORY OF PADUCAH 39

William Enders and three of his brothers, Robert, Henry and Demarcus, accompanied their father, Dr. Jacob Enders (1775-1841), a physician, from Virginia to the new town. They came aboard a wood-fired steamboat. The elder Enders is buried in Mt. Kenton Cemetery. The Enders brothers engaged in the merchantile business for many years.

George Woolfolk (1793-1843), a lawyer of Shelbyville, Ky., was induced by William Clark and other property owners to come to Pekin in 1825 to look after their interests. He, too, came down by steamboat and, after clearing titles, returned to Shelby County, but six years later came back to the town with his wife and son, Robert Owen Woolfolk (1818-1874), and located on South Second Street.

Other pioneers also visited the place and returned later to make it their home. Among them was the valiant pathfinder, Chiles Terrell (1779-1851), who came overland from Virginia in 1826 with his son, J.H. Terrell, then 11 years old. He surveyed a large portion of the land in McCracken County. There were no stagecoach lines in that early day and the journey, attended by many perils, was made on horseback over an area in which there were but few trails. Often the route was only an animal path. A month was required each way. They later moved to Louisville and eventually boarded a steamboat there to cast their lot at the mouth of the Tennessee River.

Not all the settlers had to come long distances. James C. Calhoun (1811-1886) came from Livingston County with his widowed mother in 1828. He was first a salesman in a merchantile house, then followed steamboating, and in 1842 became sheriff. Abel Sullivan (1782-1871) and his wife were living in Muhlenberg County, but located in Paducah in 1831 and opened a store. He was a native of North Carolina.

One of the largest and most interesting families to locate at the place was James Walters (1769-1836) and his wife, Mary Walters (1778-1860), and their four daughters and three sons. He was a prosperous merchant at Leesburg, Virginia, but wishing to follow the trend of times, took his family to Pittsburgh, Pennslyvania, bought a keelboat there which he loaded with merchandise, and boarding a steamboat with his family, had the shallow covered barge towed to the new western settlement. That was in 1828, a year after the town of Paducah was laid out. He bought a lot near the northeast corner of First and Kentucky Avenue and built a brick store there, stocking it with wares brought down from Pittsburgh. The building had entrances from both First Street and Front or Water Street on its side nearest the river. It was an ideal business site.

In the history of the community there has probably never been a more attractive family than the Walters household. The daughters were Elizabeth, Lydia, Grace and Mary, all young women renowned for their beauty; the sons were Enoch, John and James, witty and handsome.

The river trip to Paducah was a long and tedious one. It seemed like an endless journey. Daily the family talked about their new homestead, and they were eager to reach it and get established. On the last day before reaching their destination, the girls played a then-popular fortune game to relieve the boredom. When it was Elizabeth Walters' turn to ask about the future, the answer was that the first man to come up the gangplank at Paducah would be her husband. They laughed but thought nothing of the prediction.

At noon the next day the steamer pushed her cargo barge around the island at the town and swung in to the cleared landing area at the foot of Broadway. Standing on top of the hill was young Captain Valentine Owen who, seeing the new boat come into port, went down and stepped aboard to ask if he could be of any service. Curiously enough, three years later he and Elizabeth Walters were married. The prophecy was then recalled with much merriment.

One day, a few weeks after the family moved to the site, Grace Walters, then 17 years old, visited the Indian grounds on South Third Street in company with her parents. She was the state's fairest flower, the acknowledged belle of Kentucky, and a sweeter expression, an eye more kind, a smile more truly genial, and a handshake more cordially warm, no young woman ever possessed. One of the Indians, observing the beautiful girl, approached and raised her veil. Catching the light of her violet eyes, he exclaimed, "Prit-tee!" She received the compliment as flattery, although the red man really beheld a maiden for whom troubadours sang and errant knights would gladly have died. She became Mrs. Braxton Small (1811-1882). A modest shaft in Oak Grove Cemetery marks her grave.

Lydia Walters became Mrs. William Enders (1813-1888); their home was at Fourth and Clark Streets. Mary Walters, youngest of the girls, married Nimrod Long, who became president of a bank at Russellville, Ky.

It took courage and faith to set out for a new and unseen country, but the pioneers ventured with all the confidence of an army general. Captain Charles Carroll Pell was typical. Born in New York State he migrated west and in the spring of 1830 came prospecting down the Ohio River from Evansville on a flatboat, and located at Paducah. He steered the craft himself. Aboard it was a supply of provisions for himself and also enough hay to feed his favorite horse over a period of weeks. The saddlebags were kept on the horse; they looked innocent enough but contained $10,000 in gold, a large fortune in those days. No one suspected he had all this money; certainly not in pouches slung carelessly over his steed. Establishing himself in the community, Captain Pell built a three-room log house on the east side of Second Street near Kentucky Avenue. His wife moved to the town when the crude structure was completed. Captain Pell loved horses, but was by nature a river man and invested most of his savings in a large sidewheel steamboat which operated out of port.

No more conspicuous figure in the early days landed at the foot of Broadway than Captain John (Jack) Lawson (1805-1901). Born in England, he had come to America in 1829 to operate the first locomotive on her trial trip in this country and later the same year found his way to Paducah. He engaged in river interests and acquired a fleet of steamboats, but his chief claim to fame was his pioneering instinct which manifested itself in his railroad connection. He settled here and lived the remainder of his long life in the community.

Irvin S. Cobb was intimately acquainted with Captain Lawson. In Lawson's later days, when Mr. Cobb was a Paducah newspaperman, the patriarch reminisced and, writing in "**Sidelights on Paducah**" on March 14, 1943, Mr. Cobb said in part:

> When I talked to Captain Lawson, he was nearly a hundred years old. He told me that when he first came to the junction of the Tennessee River with the Ohio, there was little here except a wood-landing, a primitive ferry, and a cluster of houses, mostly cabins, and that dense canebrakes covered the flat lands where the older parts of Paducah now cluster. The wild grape vines, from which the Chickasaw name of the spot was derived, made veritable jungles in the low grounds and along the water courses.
>
> Captain Lawson said that the early inhabitants then depended for their fruit almost altogether upon native products--so-called 'Injun' peaches, persimmons, pawpaws, berries, frost-grapes, wild crab apples and wild goose plums. No cultivated orchards had come into bearing yet. There were plenty of nuts, though-- pecans, hazelnuts, black walnuts, big river-bottom hickory nuts and scalybarks.

With the rivers as the only means of transportation and the steamboat coming into its element, it was natural that early business houses should be located near the streams. All pioneer commercial interests were at the top of the hill and most of the town's residents lived close by. First Street, or Main as it was originally known, was the principal thoroughfare, and mercantile establishments sought its advantage.

Front or Water Street, now forgotten, was popular in the early days. This block-long street, extending from old Court Street, now Kentucky Avenue, to Broadway, ran parallel with First Street about 50 feet closer to the river. One-story buildings facing First Street had basements which opened to trade on Front Street from the riverside below; from the river these appeared to be two-story structures.

One of the most pretentious buildings in the town was a tavern called the Rising Sun, built by Captain Valentine Owen in 1831. From the riverside it looked like a three-story building, but on First Street there were only two stories. It was located at the nor-

THE STORY OF PADUCAH 43

theast corner of First and Kentucky Avenue, then Court Street. Its prominence on a corner gave it the appearance of being the tallest building in Paducah and therefore the first to greet the morning rays, hence the name Rising Sun, which was painted in bold letters above the upper windows overlooking the river.

[10] As early as 1807 the location was recognized as a townsite by Christian Schultz, the explorer, who notes in "Travels on an Inland Voyage Through the States of New York, Pennsylvania, Virginia, Ohio, Kentucky and Tennessee" (Vol. II, page 2); "About one mile below the mouth of the Tennessee is a very fine site for the establishment of a town; but this part of the state is yet entirely unsettled, and the Indian title probably not yet extinguished. Some years must elapse before any considerable improvements can take place." Dr. Donald Davidson also makes reference to the explorer's observation in "The Tennessee" (Vol. II, page 214).

CHAPTER V

McCracken County; Wilmington

McCracken County was taken from Hickman County of the early days, becoming the seventy-eighth county in Kentucky. The General Assembly authorized its establishment December 17, 1824, although the bounds were described and approved three years before. The Kentucky Geological Survey in 1928 gave its area as 264.38 square miles.

The county was named after Captain Virgil McCracken, who lost his life in the Battle of the River Raisin, twenty-two miles south of Detroit, January 22, 1813, in the second war with England. He was the son of Captain Cyrus McCracken, an adventurer, killed November 4, 1782, in an expedition against the Piqua towns.

Captain Virgil McCracken represented Woodford County in the Kentucky House of Representatives during the 1810-1811 session. The next year he organized a company of riflemen, and after training them for military service led the band northward to what proved one of the most heroic trials Kentuckians ever experienced. They became the target of both the British and Indians under Colonel Henry A. Proctor in southern Michigan, where Captain McCracken fell mortally wounded.

Embodied in the act creating McCracken County were articles providing proper organization of the county. Section 2 authorized "selection of nine justices, a sheriff and a coroner, the justices to meet at the house of Isaac Lovelace on the third Monday of January (the 17th), 1825, to choose a county clerk." Braxton Small (1795-1865) was named county clerk and held the office continuously for thirty-three years.

An article empowered Jonathan Shelton, Charles Plummer, W. Titsworth, James Ashby and George Lovelace to serve as commissioners in locating the seat of justice in Town 6 north, Range 2

THE STORY OF PADUCAH 45

west. Another section warranted "laying out of a town on said site." Section 4 said the commissioners should be "granted $2 per day for such services." It was agreed that Hickman County should continue jurisdiction over "New McCracken" until the latter fully adjusted itself.

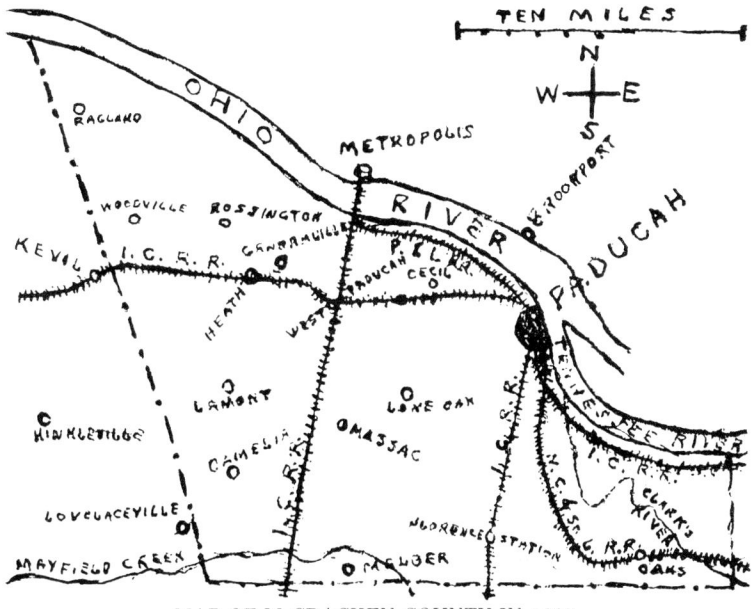

MAP OF McCRACKEN COUNTY IN 1927.

It was a bleak January day when the commissioners assembled for their first meeting, but that did not interfere with the attendance nor hinder the work at hand. There was much to do and following friendly greetings, a word about the weather and prospects of the meeting, the commissioners settled down to business. Records of the meeting read in part as follows:

At Issac Lovelace's, in the county of McCracken, in the year of our Lord, 1825, Isaac Lovelace, Jacob King, Philip Williams, Arthur P. Thompson, George Adams, Joseph Daniel, Samuel Hunsaker, William Hazard and Jesse Doolin severally produced commissions from his Excellency Joseph Desha, governor of the Commonwealth of Kentucky, appointing them justices of peace for the county of Mc-Cracken, agreeable to the provisions of an act of the assembly establishing the county of McCracken on the southwestern side of the Tennessee River, approved December 17, 1824. Whereupon Ebenezer Kellough, Esq., justice of the peace, in and for the county of Graves, administered to said Isaac Lovelace, et al, the several oaths required by law, whereupon county court was held for the county at the place and on the times aforesaid.

Mr. Small's name was proposed as clerk and carried without a dissenting vote. He was administered the oath of office by Mr. Lovelace. Other offices were created and appointments made. James Martin, father-in-law of Jonathan D. Martin, was declared sheriff, and Hiram Hall deputy clerk.

In the course of business, a recommendation was sent to Governor Joseph Desha in behalf of William S. Davis and Joseph Lovelace as county surveyors. Constable districts were set aside and three constables named to police them.

The home of Luke Swetman, located at the site of the seat of justice, was declared the future meeting place of the commissioners and court. The Swetman home was at Wilmington, which was platted as a town two years later, only a few months before Pekin was renamed Paducah and laid out as a town. The court met for the second session March 21, 1825 and voted to pay Mr. Swetman $2 rent for each meeting at his home. Sessions were held there until October 15, 1827.

The first deed recorded was that of Andrew Frazer, of Livingston County, to William M. Darby, for "lot No. 59 in the town of Pekin and County of McCracken." It was made a matter of record at a regular meeting June 18, 1825, and represented the transfer of title to the lot and what was on it--a two-room log house.

Owing to scarcity of ordained ministers in McCracken County, it was necessary for certain authorized persons to perform marriage ceremonies, Philip Williams thus officiated at the first wedding, March 24, 1825, uniting in marriage Duncan Henderson and Mrs. Sarah Glenon, a widow. The license was dated March 21, the couple searching three days for someone invested with authority to perform the ceremony. Luke Swetman also held such power, but he could not be located.

The town of Wilmington, six miles west of Paducah, was laid out in January, 1827, covering 102 acres and calling for 108 lots.

Four streets ran north and south--East, Water, Main Cross and West; and four the opposite directions--Clark, Main, Jefferson and South. The public square was ideally located in the center of the town. A plan for a courthouse was reported October 12, 1829. The contract was awarded Frederick Harper.

Within five months the new structure graced the public square. It was of frame construction. The building committee inspecting it March 8, 1830 reported that "said courthouse is finished and completed in a manner and form by the plan thereof designated."

Previously, however, James Martin was awarded a contract for $398 to "well and truly build and complete a log jail in a workmanlike manner by November 1, 1827."[11] The contract was carried out to the letter and of the eight buildings that stood in Wilmington the log structure was the last to be torn down many years after the ill-fated place was abandoned in 1832.

On a visit in Paducah in 1925, Irvin S. Cobb recalled the site of Wilmington jail as he saw it forty years before. He visited Wilmington as a small boy and on viewing a large hole was told by an old farmer that "this was the jail cellar." It was then a crude dugout and the only sign of the ancient bastile save a few crumbling logs.

The summer following completion of the courthouse witnessed the first "county-wide" dance in West Kentucky annals. It was decided to celebrate with a notable outdoor affair; an invitation was extended to one and sundry. And both young and old gathered on the moonlit courthouse grounds to enjoy the Virginia reel and kindred dances.

All night the roses heard
   The flute, violin and bassoon;
All night the casement jasmine stirred
   To the dancers dancing in tune.
Till a silence fell with the waking bird
   And a hush with the setting moon.

Those attending the social event liked to picture it in their minds many years afterward. Lovely young girls with hair brushed back from tender temples and snowy necks enhanced by necklaces, were never to be forgotten. Nor were their gracious smiles as they played the dangerous artillery of brilliant eyes on hapless frontier cavaliers. Long after the fiddle and bow were gone, hearts ravishing the wild strains of irresistible witchery spoke happily of that memorable summer evening at Wilmington in 1830.

Forty-two lots ranging in price from $2 to $32 each, the total amounting to $458.62½, were sold in Wilmington in January, 1827. Purchasers included Luke Swetman, Philip Williams, Braxton Small, James Martin, Andrew Newman and Major Charles Ewell. Another sale of lots was held in May and among the in-

JOHN W. POLK,
Clerk.

HOLLAND G. BRYAN,
Attorney.

McCRACKEN COUNTY OFFICERS IN 1927.

vestors at that time were Captain Valentine Owen, A.W. Naylor and Martin J. Fletcher. Like previous purchasers, they had hopes in the future of the infant town. Most of the purchasers, however, had homes at Paducah and only half a dozen houses were erected at Wilmington before the county seat was moved to Paducah.

Examination of old and tattered Wilmington records reveals that Isaac Lovelace signed the first court papers and John Hardin attached his signature to the last filed at the primitive courthouse. The first mortgage was executed August 12, 1830 by Francis A. Harrison for $689.66 in payment for lots Nos. 5, 43 and 44 in Paducah.

Despite its ambitious launching, Wilmington was soon found to be inconvenient as the county seat, and December 10, 1831 the General Assembly passed an act authorizing the seat of justice moved to Paducah. Incidentally, the name of the future capital was misspelled in the order, which read as follows:

Whereas, it is represented in this general assembly that it would be greatly to the interest of the people of McCracken to remove their seat of justice from Wilmington to the town of Paduca therefore,

Be it enacted by the general assembly of the Commonwealth of Kentucky, that as soon as the people of Paduca shall, by subscription or otherwise, raise and secure to the county court of said county the sum of $600, which shall be appropriated in aid of building the necessary public buildings in said town of Paduca, and provide a house to hold court in; it shall then be the duty of the county and circuit court clerks, to cause all the public papers and records belonging to said courts to be removed to Paduca within twenty days thereafter; which shall be and remain the permanent seat of justice for said county, and the county and circuit courts shall be held in said town.

Braxton Small brought the county records to Paducah in a skiff during the high water of 1832. The river reached flood proportions and practically submerged Wilmington.

The following January, Mr. Small was named commissioner to dispose of the county's estate at Wilmington. The recent flood militated against sale and the property brought only $945.

The fate of Wilmington was pathetic, almost tragic. That a town could exist within a few miles of Paducah and pass so swiftly seems incredible. But it is an old story--the story of Nineveh, the cities of Persia, the high places of Edom, the temples and heroes of Greece. Wilmington is of the past entirely, and with old Massac Creek flowing nearby the scene suggests a description by Goldsmith--

No more thy glossy brook reflects the day,
But choked with sedges, works its weedy way;
Along thy glades, a solitary guest,
The hollow-sounding bittern guards its nest;
Amidst thy desert walks the lapwing flies.

Commemorative of McCracken County's hundredth birthday, a four-day Centennial Celebration was held beginning June 25, 1925. The idea originated with Mrs. C.E. Purcell, who served as chairman, and a parade, pageant and pyrotechnical display were featured. In the presence of a large crowd a two-acre tract of land at old Wilmington was set aside by the county as a park. The log jail, restored for the occasion, stood on its original site. A boulder was unveiled near the roadside where the village once flourished, the inscription on it reading:

WILMINGTON

First Capital of McCracken County

1825-1832

A naval transport for use in World War II was built on the west coast and named McCracken, in honor of the county of which Paducah now is the capital.

---

[11]Martin was required to make bond. The original document, six by eight inches in size and scribbled in longhand, is owned by Fred G. Neuman.

CHAPTER VI

PADUCAH PLATTED; BECOMES COUNTY SEAT

General William Clark platted the site at the mouth of the Tennessee River and renamed it Paducah on May 26, 1827. Its incorporation as a town dates from January 11, 1830.

Before General Clark came to the site and as far back as the Indians could remember, the clearing at the foot of what is now Broadway was known as Pekin. It was probably bestowed by white men, adventurers and traders from eastern parts of Kentucky who regarded it as "the other side of the earth," quite as remote as an area in China.

It was the explorer's first visit and he was fascinated by its location and Indian background. He came from his home in St. Louis. Upon reaching the village, General Clark learned of the late Chief Paduke's friendly gesture a few years before, when the old warrior came to the site to pay his respects to the explorer. The compliment was a signal one and General Clark, deeply touched by it, renamed the place "Paducah" in honor of the grand old sachem. He visited Chief Paduke's grave and stood with bared head for some moments in respect to the old warrior.

Work of laying out streets and designating lots was carried on over a period of two weeks, during which time General Clark roomed and boarded at 106 South First Street, overlooking the river. Brass lettering in a concrete slab at the southeast corner of First and Broadway reads: "A Few Feet South of Here Stood the First Frame House Where General William Clark, Founder of Paducah, Stayed When He Platted the Town, May 26, 1827."

The plan confined the infant town to twelve blocks of twelve lots each, fronting 57½ feet and in depth 173 feet exclusive of a 12-foot alleyway. There were also twenty-four smaller lots lying along the river.

Cross streets, running north and south, cut off the western

boundary at what is now known as Fourth Street. A sidewalk marker at the southwest corner of Fourth and Broadway indicates the line and says: "Here Ended the Western Boundary of the Town of Paducah as platted in 1827." Jefferson Street on the north and Clark Street on the south limited the boundaries in those directions. Total area was one-tenth of a square mile, including Clark, Jefferson and Fourth Streets.

The town was laid out with the rivers as its base. This is borne out by maps of the city which show the numbered streets flanking the rivers, more or less paralleling them from one end of town to the other. The rivers have been used for the base or bottom of maps instead of the south, which is customary in general engineering practice.

As a result of the streets paralleling the rivers, the city lies at a bias and confusion sometimes results as to north and south, east and west. The numbered streets in the downtown or older section run, roughly, N. 36 06' W. (heading north) or S. 31 06' E. (heading south).

There were only nine streets in the original plat, including a blocklong street extending from Broadway to Kentucky Avenue on the levee. This short business thoroughfare was known as Front or Water Street and passed out of the picture after a score of years. Main Street, now First, was laid out as the principal street. It was more than thirty years before Broadway took on aspects as the leading commercial lane. Second Street was Market, Third was known as Locust and Fourth was called Oak Street.

Running opposite were the following streets, beginning at the south side boundary: Clark, Washington, Court (now Kentucky Avenue), St. Louis (now Broadway), and Jefferson. Clark Street, like Clarks River, was named in honor of General William Clark, who owned large tracts of land in and around the town. Court Street was given that title in 1832 owing to the presence of the county building at the junction of Second Street. St. Louis Street received its title from the fact that General Clark lived there, but it was soon changed to Broadway. None of these titles was officially given until May 28, 1841.

Third Street, as it is now known, extended all the way to Island Creek, but was "nothing more than a cow path," as one pioneer resident described it. Indeed, at its southern reaches it was hardly more than a trail made by the feet of Indians.

GENERAL WILLIAM CLARK

The original plan set aside space for streets as wide as the present paved thoroughfares. There was little resemblance, however. Trees were cut down following surveys, and stumps that remained in the roadways for several years made the streets little more than winding highways--dusty dirt roads that dodged obstructions and followed the path of least resistance.

There were no brick sidewalks. Even the long planks or wooden sidewalks, the first hint of conveniences, were missing until 1832, when muddy footpaths were forsaken and pedestrians took to improved conditions. In the early days, everybody walked.

Mindful of the rich soil around Paducah for producing garden products, General Clark set aside an area on South Second Street for a public market. Thus a large space was assigned for a building or center where all might trade and swap. Nine years later a small frame structure was erected and a market house became a mecca for thrifty purchasers. Occasionally the mixture of city and country folk was so large that traffic jams occurred.

Although Second Street bore the name Market in token of the trading center, the wide portion ran south from Broadway only a block and a half, the remainer being uniform in width to other streets. Space was only allotted west of the market site for hitching purposes, as great a convenience to the farmer with his horse and wagon as parking space to the motorist now.

It is interesting to note prices paid at the time for real estate within the town limits, the large site at the northwest corner of First and Broadway fetching only $12. The lot ran into an alley on First Street and half a block on Broadway, the same as that across the street which sold for $11. Equally large lots over town were bought for $10, and land on the outskirts was obtainable at 25 cents an acre and in some instances only 10 cents. however, it should be remembered that money had a much greater purchasing value than at the present time.

In 1828, a year after the plat was made, property owners at Paducah numbered twenty-five. A large part of the real estate was still in custody of General Clark. Other prominent holders were Captain Valentine Owen, George A. Flournoy, John C. Enders, Robert Enders, and Major Charles Ewell. A bronze marker there is self-explanatory; "Here in His later years Lived and Died Charles Ewell, Patriot of the Revolutionary War."

The first white child born in Paducah was John F. Davis, who arrived June 12, 1830, just two months after his parents moved into their new home at the northeast corner of Second and Clark Streets. The first recorded birth of a girl was that of Adelaide Small, born December 23, 1831 at 315 Kentucky Avenue. Her parents were Braxton Small, county clerk, and the former Miss Grace Walters, the renowned beauty. Their marriage March 1, 1831, was the first recorded here, the ceremony being performed by the Rev. Lewis Goad, G.M.--gospel minister.

After the town of Paducah was named the future county seat in 1831, a committee composed of Braxton Small, George A. Flournoy and Milton Perry was appointed to draft plans for a two-story brick courthouse at Second and Kentucky Avenue. Specifications called for a building not to exceed thirty-six feet either way. Jesse Yandell, contractor, put up a building of those proportions, furnishing it throughout and turning in a bill for $3,049, for which prompt payment was made. A log jail was built in a ravine at 218 South Third Street. Workmen excavating there November 28, 1945 for foundation for a new business structure found remains of the old jail.

THE STORY OF PADUCAH 55

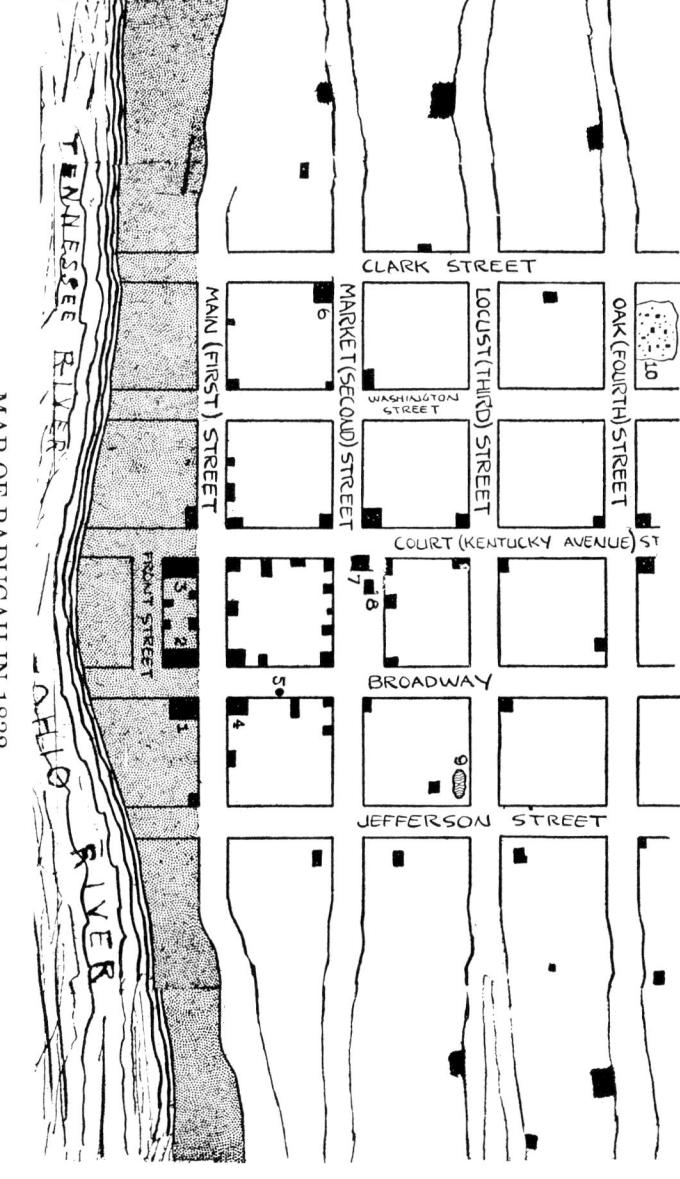

MAP OF PADUCAH IN 1832.

1. First store building in town. 2. First frame house. 3. Rising Sun, three-story frame hotel. 4. Tavern, the site for which was bought for twelve dollars. 5. Public well. 6. Birthplace of John F. Davis, first child born in the town. 7. Courthouse. 8. Jail. 9. Pond popular with fishermen. 10. Old cemetery, the town's first burial plot.

Entrance to the county building was from the east side. The brick structure was square and sat in the middle of Market (Second) Street and extended out into Kentucky Avenue, which acquired the name Court in consequence of the county building's prominence. The name was officially changed to Kentucky Avenue in 1903.

Among suits filed in the old Second Street courthouse was one which involved a house in the middle of the street where Ninth and Jefferson Streets intersect. The controversy arose a short time before the courthouse was abandoned. At that time the western boundary was Ninth Street. The owner of the house contended that General William Clark, who was said to have owned the ground on which it stood, was not on the scene at the time of building to dispossess him of property. On the other hand, Attorney J. Wyatt Jones, representing General Clark's interests, exhibited maps sustaining claim to the land.

The dispute was finally settled, the Clark interests gaining their point, but Hickory Street, as Ninth was then known, was dubbed "Contest" as a result of the litigation. In 1876 the name was changed to Churchill Avenue in honor of Colonel Samuel B. Churchill, a resident of Louisville who bestowed many kindnesses on the city, including a liberal donation toward construction of a new courthouse in 1856. He at that time owned considerable property here.

Lawyers who on various occasions pleaded cases in the Second Street courthouse included Colonel A.P. Thompson, who lost his life in the Battle of Paducah; Oscar Turner, member of Congress (1878-1884); L.S. Trimble, who served in Congress (1865-1871); James B. Husbands (1805-1885), L.D. Husbands (1823-1907), Richard S. Ratcliffe (1817-1878), Q.Q. Quigley (1828-1910), J.M. Bigger and W.H. Jones.

Braxton Small performed the duties of county clerk from 1825 till 1858, or ten years before his death August 2, 1868. In his younger days Mr. Small was an ardent fisherman and often carried the county's documents under his hat while fishing, believing they were as safe there as in the primitive courthouse at Wilmington.

For a quarter century the county building at Second and Kentucky Avenue served its purpose, but as the town grew it became quite inadequate and larger quarters were urgently needed. With a view to remedying the situation, the county in 1857 purchased a whole square from Braxton Small bounded by Washington and Clark Streets north and south, and Sixth and Seventh Streets east and west. The site was chosen and deal made by a committee composed of John H. Terrell (1815-1876), James C. Calhoun (1811-1886) and L.D. Husbands. Contract for the building, a two-story red brick, was awarded to John F. Hendren, of Louisville. It represented an expenditure of $27,830. The building was later painted a dull gray. Calhoun and Husbands then disposed of the abandoned courthouse property for $30,501.86.

When contract was let for the new courthouse, objection was raised on the part of some citizens over putting it "so far out." Paducah, which had just been incorporated as a third class city, lacked settlement in that neighborhood and residents felt justified in criticizing what was termed a move "too far westward." However, objection was overruled and in time adjacent territory was dotted with houses.

The jail was of log construction, similar in design to that near the river but of larger proportions. It proved insecure and was replaced with a brick structure in 1868. This answered all purposes until 1882, when it was cleared from the site and a safer building put up at a cost of $19,500.

Construction of a still larger and more modern courthouse began in the summer of 1941 and was completed with opening on October 25, 1943 of the handsome structure of colonial type which now graces the grounds. The building cost $330,000. It was the biggest undertaking of its kind the county ever attempted and a federal grant of $114,999, plus labor by the Works Progress Administration, was of material help. A new jail matching architectural lines of the courthouse was also constructed. The entire project meant realization of a dream by County Judge Brady M.Stewart, who worked tirelessly toward its successful completion.

Many lawyers of note held court or practiced in the courthouse which was razed in 1941, among them Vice President Alben W. Barkley, who was chosen county attorney in 1905 and served in that capacity until he went to Congress in 1913; Circuit Judge William S. Bishop, the prototype of Irvin S. Cobb's beloved "Judge Priest"; Colonel John K. (Honest John) Hendrick (1849-1921), former congressman; Judge L.D. Husbands, chosen circuit judge in 1897 at the age of 74 years; Judge William M. Reed (1848-1926), three times circuit judge; and Circuit Judge Joe L. Price (1878-1949), who presided for more than 20 years. Many stories are related of these and other members of the Paducah bar.[12]

On one occasion when Vice-President Barkley, then county attorney, was running for re-election, word came that one of his closest friends was supporting the rival candidate. Knowing the family for many years and having befriended the man many times, Mr. Barkley hastened around to see him. The man admitted he might support the opposition. Choking with indignation, the county attorney recited the many courtesies done in his friend's behalf.

"Surely," asked Mr. Barkley, "you remember all these things?"

"Yeah," replied the man. "But what have you done for me lately?"

During Judge Reed's career as a practicing attorney he had among his admirers two brothers of Marshall County. One of them committed a crime which landed him in prison. The offender had been in confinement just long enough to learn that he did not like it, when his brother, who had unbounded confidence in Judge Reed's legal ability, hurried over to the latter's office. He exclaimed in all good faith:

"Judge, you'll have to go up thar and git Henry out of the penitentiary. Why he's plum' dissatisfied!"

THE STORY OF PADUCAH 59

Back in Colonel John K. Hendrick's day it was the custom of Kentucky governors to bestow the honorary title of "colonel" on men of rank over the state. It was given to "Honest John" in his thirties. Years later, another chief executive of the state was in Paducah and sat in the lobby of the Palmer House with a group of friends, Colonel Hendrick included. They were mixing lively banter with their conversation. Suddenly the governor asked: " 'Honest John,' just what does the 'Col.' in front of your name mean?" Never at a loss for an answer and as frank as red ink, Hendrick replied: Just like the 'Hon.' in front of yours--it doesn't mean a thing!"

Judge Bishop was typical of the rugged but sagacious barristers and jurists of this section at the tail end of the last century. He was a man of many parts--shrewd, simple, kindly, witty and gentle.

It seems a gangling young blacksmith decided it would be easier making speeches before juries than bending mule shoes and shrinking wagon tires, and applied for a license to practice law at the local board from a committee of which Judge Bishop was chairman. Judge Bishop opened the inquiry and asked about the applicant's reading. The candidate confessed he had "never heard tell of" Blackstone nor Coke. He further admitted that he was not familiar with the Constitution of the United States nor the Bill of Rights of the State of Kentucky.

"Henry," pressed Judge Bishop, "suppose you tell us just what books--what authorities--you have studied since you were seized with the desire to be a member of our bar?"

"I tell you, Jedge," he said, "I read one big book called *'Revised Statutes of the State of Kentucky'* might nigh through, an' I kin remember part of what it says."

"My son," stated Judge Bishop, adjusting his glasses, "the trouble with you is that the next legislature is liable to meet to repeal everything you know!"

---

[12]For stories of lawyers who practiced in the brick courthouse in its later years, see the chapter "Some Great Lawyers of Kentucky," by D. Henry Hughes, in proceedings of Kentucky State Bar Association, 1930," pp.55-57

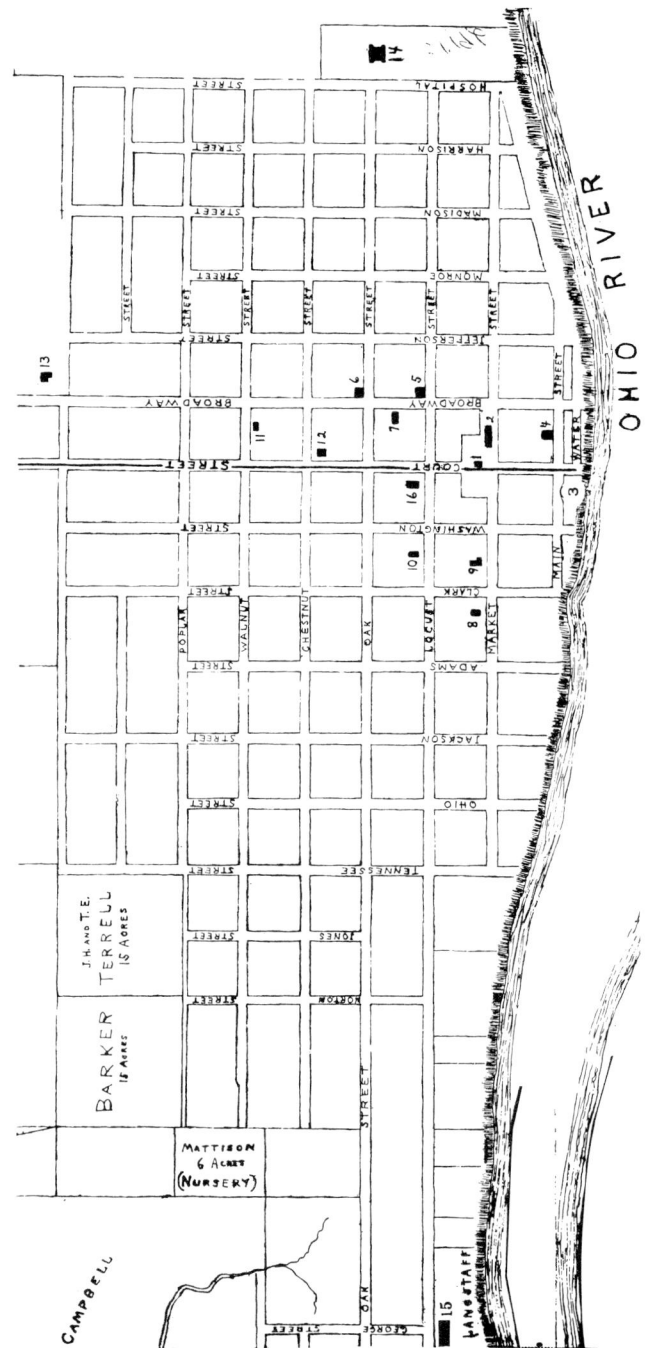

MAP OF PADUCAH IN 1856.

1. Courthouse. 2. Market House. 3. Marine ways. 4. Branch Bank of Louisville. 5. Commercial Bank of Kentucky. 6. Broadway Methodist Church. 7. First Baptist Church. 8. First Christian Church. 9. Grace Episcopal Church. 10. Cumberland Presbyterian Church. 11. St. Francis de Sales Catholic Church. 12. Female Seminary. 13. Paducah Male University. 14. Marine Hospital. 15. Site of old Langstaff mill. 16. First Presbyterian Church. Note on railroad track on Kentucky Avenue to river.

CHAPTER VII

CORPORATE TOWN--1830-1856

After the village was incorporated as the town of Paducah on January 11, 1830, there was some delay, nearly half a year, before Dr. Robert Fletcher recorded the plan. Acting as agent for General William Clark, he made a record of it June 18, 1830.

The first election for town trustees occurred the following year, May 2, 1831, at the home of George Dunn on Broadway. Population in 1830 was 105.

Francis A. Harrison received the highest vote and through this honor was declared chairman. Other members of the Board of Trustees named at the same time were George Dunn, Dr. Robert Fletcher, Robert Enders and Thomas J. Flournoy. These five officers constituted "The Chairman and Board of Trustees of Paducah". Assembling for their first business session three days after being chosen, they appointed Reuben Laughlen, clerk and assessor; James C. Calhoun (1811-1886), collector, and Valentine Owen, overseer of streets.

Minutes of the initial meeting stated that all persons were "required to move their fences and houses out of streets" and that all keel-boats were prohibited from landing in front of the town, which at that time extended only four blocks along the river. Henry Burnett addressed the members on property values, appraising various locations and pointing out the worth of land adajacent.

The value of taxable property, real and personal, including negro slaves, was $29,270 for the year 1831. Poll tax was fixed at 50 cents and taxes levied for all purposes 18¾ cents on the $100. The tax rate increased to 20 cents in 1838, and less than ten years later reached 50 cents, but in 1850 dropped to 34 cents. Steady advances followed, until $2.64 was reached in 1927. Poll tax jumped to $1.25 by 1841; in 1927 it was $1.50.

Modest as these early taxes seem now, a number of property owners sometimes found it difficult to meet them. Instances appear in the clerk's records where poorer property holders performed various tasks, including grave digging, to liquidate taxes. At a regular meeting July 10, 1847, the clerk made note that a man "was allowed $2 on his claim for digging a grave and that said amount was to go to his credit for taxes due by him to the corporation".

Location of a public well was among questions which came before the town fathers, and after much dispute the well was sunk on the north side of Broadway between First and Second Streets. This afforded drinking water without the customary trip to the river with buckets, proving a great convenience to residents of the infant town. Unfortunately a number abused the privilege and trustees in session July 11, 1834 issued the following edict--somewhat severe, but conducive of good results:

Whereas, it is represented to this Board that persons drawing water at the public well are in the habit of starting the windlass and letting the bucket run down with great velocity by which the bucket is frequently broken, and the corporation put to considerable expense for remedy thereof;

Resolves, that if any person shall hereafter let the said bucket run down with greater velocity than by holding and turning the windlass with the hand, he or she, if a free white person, shall be subject to a fine of four dollars for each offense; if a slave or free negro, he or she shall for each offense receive on his or her back ten stripes well laid on by the supervisor.

Records indicate a fair revenue from assessments on drays, carts and oxen, and "dogs over one to a family", beginning with the year 1833. Five years later the primitive business establishments were paying the following licenses: Dry goods stores, $50; taverns with liquor, $40; groceries and victualing house, the latter an early term for restaurants, $25; and coffee houses, which were saloons or places for the sale of liquor, $40.

A survey in 1851 showed 373 white males over 21 years of age qualified to vote, each paying $1.25 poll tax. Meanwhile licenses and taxes had been increased to meet the need of improvements and a substantial revenue from all sources was being realized by the middle of the century.

The first Board of Health, appointed June 17, 1833, consisted of Dr. Samuel A. Withers and Dr. Joseph Merrell. At a called meeting of the trustees in December, 1848, consideration was given propriety of building a hospital "to take care of anyone who may stop at this place with cholera". This project took immediate form in erection of an institution formally opened for the reception of patients in the spring of 1849.

Town trustees were chosen annually. Meetings were held in homes of the members, in stores, and in offices of attorneys when representatives of the legal fraternity were on the Board. Rent was paid for use of the "meeting room". The Board usually met at night and required the host to furnish fuel in winter and candles for light, the latter being the only means of illumination.

At the general election March 12, 1849, David A. Watts was chosen chairman, with the following strong Board to support his thorough business program, the personnel having been increased by two; William Enders (1809-1881), William F. Norton, James Campbell, John W. Crockett, Adam Rankin (1802-1856), born at Henderson, Kentucky and came to Paducah from Louisville in 1845 to open a branch bank, and James B. Husbands.

Shortly before the town became a city, the following officers were installed as elected March 12, 1855; Board of Trustees-- Braxton Small, chairman; James B. Husbands, W. Thornberry, Dr. Reuben Saunders, W. Thompson, A.S. Jones (1818-1872), Gabriel Kay; George Smedley, police judge; J.W. Sauner, marshal; J.W. Cobbs, clerk; M.W. Cole, treasurer; David C. Peters, assessor.

Soon after incorporation the town outgrew its swaddling clothes and extended itself. General Clark's plat marked the western boundary at Fourth Street, but in 1833 there was added, by an amendatory act of the Legislature, the territory from Fourth Street out to Ninth Street, the north and south boundaries remaining unchanged. This western addition was called the "First Addition to Paducah", early deeds and records designating property transfers in the district after this manner. General Clark's original boundaries were known as "Old Town", that territory lying between the river and Fourth Street, and between Clark and Jefferson Streets.

Three years later another amendatory act embraced the territory from Clark to Tennessee Streets and from the river west to Ninth Street, which was known as "Upper Town". A little later in the same year, 1836, the Legislature passed still another amendatory act which annexed to the town of Paducah all that section below Jefferson Street north to Clay Street, and from the river west to Ninth Street, and this addition was termed "Lower Town". Still another addition, the last to the early town of Paducah, was made in 1841, when that area lying between Tennessee and Husbands Streets and bounded by the river on the east and Seventh Street on the west, became a part of Paducah. This was known as "First Addition to Upper Town".[1]

One of the early needs recognized by town officials was a market house, a place where farmers could meet and bargain with town and county folk in disposing of their farm products. The community endorsed the project from the outset and urged the trustees to definite action. They resolved April 16, 1836, that a market house should be built and finished by August 6 of the same year, and by that date a frame structure sixty feet long and thirty-three feet wide stood completed on Second Street, between Kentucky Avenue and Broadway. Cost of construction was $464.50

Market hours were from four o'clock in the morning till seven in the evening. No one was permitted to buy more than enough for one family, eliminating chances of resale or further profit. A fine of five dollars was imposed for selling on Sunday. Walter B. Padgett, first market master, received ten dollars a month. A new market house was built in 1850, measuring 32 feet in width and 132 feet in length, equal distance from Broadway and Kentucky Avenue. In 1905 a brick market was erected by George Katterjohn after the plans of W.L. Brainerd, at a cost of $25,000.

It ceased being a market house for the sale of produce in 1960

THE STORY OF PADUCAH 65

MARKET HOUSE

and has instead become a cultural center and is called the Market House Museum. The building was renovated in 1965 and divided into three sections; the Art Guild using north end facing Broadway; the center houses the historical museum and the south end "The Little Theater." Great interest is manifested in each of them.

Dr. Ben Bradford, a playwright and actor in his own right, writes and directs many of the plays. Local talent and other make up the Market House players and Little Theater Group.

While the town was level in a general way, ridges scattered here and there and the presence of small ponds offered hindrances in the plan of improvements, particularly in regard to streets. Hills disappeared as the town grew, but as late as 1843 a shallow pond stood in Kentucky Avenue between First and Second Streets. A foot bridge was completed the same year over a small body of water at Fourth and Kentucky Avenue. Fishing proved a popular sport near the southeast corner of Third and Jefferson Streets, where a good-sized pond yielded choice catches of perch, catfish and occasionally green bullfrogs whose legs were delicacies.

Front Street, just below First Street, and running parallel with the river, was the first to have brick sidewalks. This street ran south from Broadway just one block, and was sidewalk paved only on the west side. The paving, eight feet wide, was put down at the expense of property owners and completed November 1, 1835. At a meeting August 24, 1837, the Board of Trustees passed a resolution making it unlawful for anyone to "drive a cart, wagon or other carriage, or ride a horse or other animal on the sidewalks", under $10 penalty. Both sides of Broadway from the river to Third Street were paved with brick in 1841.

In the early summer of 1837 the trustees employed Eli Houston, a blacksmith, to make implements for use in grading and improving the streets. Winding roadways over town now began to take the semblance of avenues. J.H. Slee was given the contract on July 16 1847, for paving Broadway from the wharf across Second Street, the center of Broadway to be macadamized twenty feet wide "in a workmanlike manner". The contract included ten-foot sidewalks on either side. As the task proceeded, the workers sang songs of the day--"Old Dan Tucker," "Woodman Spare That Tree," "A Life on the Ocean Wave" and "Stop Dat Knocking at My Door."

On April 16, 1849, the Committee on Internal Improvements was authorized to advertise for proposals for graveling all the streets, but the bids proved too high and only a part of the project was carried out at the time. P.G. Meath signed a contract in June the next year to macadamize Broadway from Second to Third Street. Contract to grade Jefferson Street was awarded July 23, 1852, to H.M. Brown, the stipulations saying he was to do the work "at his sole cost and expense, from low water mark back 1,880 feet, at 22 cents per cubic yard for all cuts in same and 16 2/3 cents per cubic yard for all fills".

Galloping a horse on the streets was prohibited by an ordinance drawn up in 1837, the penalty for this offense being five dollars.

THE STORY OF PADUCAH 67

In addition to unnecessary excitement, such behavior created a whirl of dust.

The town's first banking institution was established August 16, 1837, bearing the name "Exchange Bank of Paducah". Controlled by the town, with Braxton Small as treasurer, the bank served as the community's lone monetary institution until the Commercial Bank of Kentucky and the Branch Bank of Louisville, established in 1845 by Adam Rankin, both antedating the Civil War, were established. Owing to heavy duties in other capacities, Mr. Small held the treasurership of the Exchange Bank only a short term, and was succeeded by James Brown.

The Commercial Bank of Kentucky was located at the northwest corner of Third and Broadway. L.M. Flournoy was president, and James L. Dallam, cashier. James Campbell headed the Bank of Louisville Branch, and S.B. Hughes served as cashier. The bank's home is still standing, a brick structure at 117 South First Street.

General William Clark's plat of Paducah in 1827 called in part for names of the Town's streets, but these titles and those of streets in extended area were not formally adopted until May 28, 1841, when the trustees in regular session passed ordinance giving titles to these and additional streets. It read:

Be it resolved, That the streets in Paducah running up and down parallel with the rivers Tennessee and Ohio be named as follows: Beginning at the rivers and running back in succession as follows: first, Water (or Front) Street; second, Main Street; third, Market Street; fourth, Locust Street; fifth, Oak Street; sixth, Chestnut Street; seventh, Walnut Street; eighth, Poplar Street; and ninth, Hickory Street.

And that the streets running out from said rivers be named as follows: Beginning at the street running out between lots Nos. 12 and 13, by the courthouse shall be named Court Street, then in succession with the streets down the river as follows: first, Broadway; second, Jefferson; third, Monroe; fourth, Madison; fifth, Harrison; sixth, Hospital. Then commencing above Court Street the streets shall be named as follows: first, Washington; second, Clark; third, Johnson (for Colonel Richard M. Johnson); fourth, Jackson; fifth, Ohio; sixth, Tennessee.

None of the cross streets mentioned now bears the name officially given in 1841, the designations having been changed to their present form in 1886, when houses were numbered and free mail delivery begun. Water, or Front Street, no longer exists, now forming part of the levee. Hospital Street, named after the old Marine Hospital which stood at its east end was changed to Clay Street and Johnson is now labeled Adams Street, leaving only ten original designations.

Oak Grove Cemetery was formally declared a burial ground when the town bought the site in 1847. It had then been used as a cemetery ten years, remains of the deceased being scattered over the area in haphazard fashion.

The town's earliest cemetery was located on the west side of Fourth Street between Washington and Clark, and was outside the town limits when first used for interment purposes. After the town acquired the new site the remains of those buried in the Fourth Street Cemetery were disinterred and laid to rest in Oak Grove.

Until the railroads began bidding for trade at Paducah in 1853, and for nearly a half century afterward, the rivers afforded the principal means of commerce. It thus became evident to town officers that a suitable levee was necessary for proper handling of freight. The first ordinance to this effect was passed March 20, 1842, the town appropriating $1,000 for construction of a wharf extending half a block up the river from Broadway and an equal distance down. Ferry service across the Ohio River was established February 15, 1838.

Fire hazards were recognized by town officers at a meeting December 3, 1835, when William W. Lay was asked to buy "four fire hooks and two ladders", which, coupled with buckets furnished by citizens during a blaze, constituted the first fire-fighting equipment Paducah ever knew.

An election for the last town officers was held March 10, 1856, resulting in W. Thornberry being named chairman of the Board of Trustees, and the following chosen to serve with him: L.D. Roberts, T.H. Glenn, Q.Q. Quigley, A.S. Jones, Charles C. Smedley and J.Q.A. King. They came together for the last regular session May 2 the next year, when graveling of sidewalks was ordered on Second Street from Broadway to Monroe Street.

THE STORY OF PADUCAH 69

The Board opened the street "back of town" (Ninth Street) April 16, 1857, and officially called it Contest Street. At the same session a contract was let for improvement of Third Street from Jefferson south to Tennessee, the specifications declaring it should be "graded, rounded and shaped, curbed and guttered, graveled one foot in depth, and sidewalks either paved with brick or graveled at the option of property owners".

Taps for the Board of Town Trustees were sounded at a called session May 7, 1857. City officers chosen a few days before were formally declared elected, and the same day the mayor and Board of Councilmen met and took over the reins of government.

¹See Burgess Scott's page in Sun-Democrat.

CHAPTER VIII

THIRD CLASS CITY--1856-1902

Such steady growth was manifested by the town of Paducah that in less than three decades it became a third class city. The residents approved the new order by a handsome vote--209 to 35.

Passing the Kentucky Legislature on March 10, 1856, the bill making Paducah a third class city was next submitted to the people. Notices of a referendum appeared during July 1856, in both the Paducah Democrat and American Sentinel, local newspapers, and the proposition was voted upon August 25 of that year. It was ratified by a good majority and new government was formally inaugurated May 7, 1857. In seventy-one years, or since its incorporation as a city, Paducah's destiny has been guided by fourteen mayors.

It was mainly through the efforts of Q.Q. Quigley that Paducah entered upon the city plan. He came here in 1848, just entering his twenties. Taking up the study of law, he succeeded in that profession. Recognizing the benefits Paducah would derive from city classification, he drew up a charter in 1856, carried it before the State Legislature and procured its passage, and brought it to a vote among those whom it affected. Adoption of the franchise gave Paducah additional territory and overnight it spread north, south and west, yielding a substantial increase in population. Four years later (1860) the population was 4,590.

Mr. Quigley lived to see the city grow and prosper, and witnessed its transfer to the rank of a second class city in 1902. His body rests in the northwestern part of Oak Grove Cemetery. The slab marking the six feet of soil which has been honored as the resting place of his body, bears this inscription--a testimonial of his love and affection for Paducah:

Q.Q. Quigley, a Lawyer of Ability and Integrity. He had the interest and progress of the city at heart, and framed and procured the first charter.

THE STORY OF PADUCAH 71

Complete revision of municipal control was necessitated when the change took effect, in 1857. The franchise called for a full quota of city officers and a Board of Councilmen--two from each of the six wards into which the city had now been divided. It meant selection of officers to carry on the city's business. A provision in the charter provided for the first city election May 4, 1857. The Honorable Jesse H. Gardner was elected to the highest office, that of mayor, receiving 210 votes above the rival.

JESSE H. GARDNER.   JOHN W. SAUNER.

Mayor Gardner was born in Clark County, Kentucky, September 23, 1817, and removed to Calloway County with his parents. He did then, without much thought, what now would be classed as an athletic achievement, when he walked to Paducah at the age of twenty-two years to obtain employment. His first work was felling trees on Owen's Island. Prospering by honest toil, he clerked in Captain G. Castleman's store and then engaged in the mercantile business for himself in 1846. He soon served the town as a trustee and proving his ability in public office as well as private enterprise, the mayoralty was tendered him and he accepted.

72   THE STORY OF PADUCAH

Retiring from this latter office in 1859, Mr. Gardner became secretary-treasurer of the New Orleans and Ohio Railroad, and helped organize the First National Bank of which he was a director and served as vice president until his death, March 1, 1886. He was buried in Oak Grove Cemetery, a twenty-foot shaft on Ivy Avenue marking the grave.

City officers chosen with Mayor Gardner under the new setup included M.W. Cole, treasurer; William F. Swift, assessor; Charles H. Bonnin, clerk; Q.Q. Quigley, attorney; George Smedley, police judge; J.W. Sauner, city marshal. Councilmen elected were: First Ward, A.G. Lee and D.A. Given; Second Ward, George A. Allen and J.C. Walden; Third Ward, Gabriel Kay and William Enders; Fourth Ward, W.G. Bullitt and Daniel Fourshee; Fifth Ward, T.J. Atkins and J.K. Leeman; Sixth Ward, George Langstaff and W.H. Slack.

The first caucas was held May 7, 1857. Gardner's Hall, located on the east side of South Second Street between Broadway and Kentucky Avenue, served as councilmanic chambers until a site for City Hall could be purchased and a building erected.

Additional posts were created and officers appointed. Henry S. Lewis was named railroad tax collector; John W. Sauner, tax collector, in connection with his duties as marshal; George Dunn, market master; Henry F. Dunn, wharfmaster; and James S. Long, (1812-1895) sexton. Four policemen constituted the law-enforcement body--W.L. Fuqua on day duty, and W.W. Adkins, W.J. Wheelis and A.H. Noble at night. Dr. D.A. Maxwell (1825-1885) was appointed city physician. With this personnel the first city administration set about its tasks.

One of the prime needs by the Council was a city building. The city acquired a site at 124 North Fourth Street and erected a two-story brick structure on it. The lower floor served as the court room, the upper as a council chamber and clerk's office. A lockup at the rear of the ground floor lent an air of threatening authority to the City Hall.

An ordinance passed in April, 1858, authorized opening Broad-

BIRD'S-EYE VIEW OF PADUCAH IN 1873.

way from Ninth Street to the city limits. A survey was promptly made and the street extended. About the same time the council appropriated $100 for construction of a plank walk on Third Street from Tennessee Street to the section known as "Jersey".[1]

Despite confusion owing to the complete turnover of town government to city control, Mayor Gardner's administration was characterized by sound judgment which reflected itself in beneficial measures on every hand. The new franchise gave Paducah greater opportunity for development. The assessed value of property within the corporate limits when Paducah changed to a city was $714,300.

The Honorable John W. Sauner became the city's second mayor at the May 2, 1859 election by 187 majority, and was re-elected in 1861 for another two-year term. He then retired from office but was recalled in 1867, and at the expiration of another two years, was again returned, retiring from the mayoralty in 1871 after serving eight years in all, or four terms.

Mayor Sauner was born at Nashville, Tenn., May 31, 1824. He came to Paducah as a barefooted boy at the age of twelve, learned the trade of carpenter, proved his worth as a citizen by energy, industry and good sense, and at the age of thirty-five received the highest gift at the hands of its citizenry. Death overtook him at the age of sixty-six, July 17, 1890, and he sleeps on Rest Avenue in Oak Grove Cemetery.

Street and other public improvements marked Mayor Sauner's administrations. Police protection was strengthened, streets graveled and repaired, property values increased, and every department placed on a sound and stable basis. The population continued to grow.

Mayor Sauner's second term was marked by the first years of the Civil War, and it was during this period that General U.S. Grant visited the city and handed Mayor Sauner his proclamation to the people, with the request that the mayor have it printed for distribution. The mayor obeyed orders but not from anything akin to fear. He saw as a sensible man that his citizenry was over-

THE STORY OF PADUCAH 75

whelmed and did the most gallant thing a faithful leader of a community could do under the circumstances.

Property appraisals completed March 3, 1868, fixed value of property on First Street for some distance north and south of Broadway at $100 per front foot, well above the 1927 evaluation. By this time business houses had been seeking Broadway locations, and the assessor's scale showed relative values per front foot then as follows: First to Third, $200; Third to Fourth, $150; Fourth to Fifth, $100; Fifth to Sixth, $75; Sixth to Seventh, $50; Seventh to Ninth, $40; Ninth to city line, $20 and $10. In 1927 the front foot valuation of property on Broadway between Second and Third was listed at $325 and corner lots $375.

Born in Wurttemberg, Germany, October 1, 1816, the Honorable John G. Fisher, who was to become the third mayor of Paducah, immigrated to America at the age of eighteen, and located in Philadelphia where he learned the trade of baker. Four years later he moved to Paducah and operated a bakery. He served the town as trustee and the city as tax collector, and was chosen to head the city government in 1863. After a two-year term he was re-elected. In 1875 he accepted the office for the third time, another two-year term, making six years in all. His death occurred November 17, 1896, and he was buried in Oak Grove Cemetery, on Rest Avenue. A granite stone seven feet high marks the grave.

Mayor Fisher's incumbency was especially trying, for his inauguration came during the last years of the Civil War, and his second administration began just as the war ceased. Disrupted and torn by the bitter conflict, with business paralyzed and conditions generally in a state of quandary, Paducah needed a leader and found him in Mayor Fisher, who met all tasks bravely and successfully guided the city through its darkest days.

The Battle of Paducah (1869) occurred during Mayor Fisher's first administration, and throughout his first term the city was occupied by Federal soldiers, as in the case of his predecessor's last term. Despite military excitement and a contracted treasury,

76   THE STORY OF PADUCAH

the city realized many worthy improvements.

JOHN G. FISHER.   MEYER WEIL.

The Honorable Mayor Weil, the fourth mayor, was born in Hohenzollern, Prussia, June 29, 1830, immigrating to America in 1847. He lived in several West Kentucky towns before locating in Paducah in 1863, where he opened a merchantile store, soon turning his attention to tobacco and the brokerage business. Conspicuous for his rugged honesty, he was chosen mayor in 1871, and again in 1873. Two years intervened and he was recalled to the office (1877), serving with such distinction that in 1879 his name on the ballot practically foreclosed re-election. He served four terms, or a total of eight years. He later represented McCracken County in two State assemblies. His death came April 13, 1891, and his grave on Mercy Avenue in Oak Grove Cemetery bears an imposing memorial.

While several noteworthy accomplishments are credited to Mayor Weil's administrations, the signal achievement lies in restoration of Paducah's credit, which was at a low ebb following the Civil War. With wonderful financial ability, Mr. Weil accomplished much under reconstruction-day handicaps.

Despite limited funds, a new hospital known as the City

Hospital was erected in March, 1872, at 1280 South Fifth Street, adjoining Mattison's Garden. This represented an outlay of $3,317.63. Children thoughtlessly playing and thereby creating a nuisance on the wooden bridge leading from Sixth Street to the hospital, forced the Council to forbid "foot-races or playing" on the structure. The rule proved effective, but often the clop-clop of horses' hoofs, the rhythm of ox-teams, and the thud of cattle and sheep annoyed patients.

As a member of the Kentucky Legislature Mr. Weil distinguished himself by his pithy remarks in impromptu speech. On one occasion when excitement was running high over a bill proposing reduction of the tax rate, in an unguarded moment one "high tax" orator, pointed to the danger of a deficit. Instantly Mr. Weil was on his feet. "That's just where the trouble is" he thundered. "We don't want money in the treasury: we want a deficit. Who ever heard of any State treasurer running away with a deficit?" This clever retort won the House and added to his reputation for quick, pungent speech.

The fifth mayor, the Honorable Charles Reed, was a veteran of the Civil War, serving first with General Lloyd Tilghman and later participating in the sanguinary Battle of Shiloh and the lesser conflicts at Corinth and Harrisburg, as well as the Battle of Paducah. He was born in Paducah, November 4, 1842, and attended school until twelve years of age, when he was apprenticed at the tobacco trade which he followed until joining the Confederate ranks at nineteen. At the close of the war he engaged in the wool business for a time, and then assumed management of the Richmond House and later the Palmer House. Death claimed him October 28, 1908, and his remains were placed in a vault at Oak Grove Cemetery.

Elected to the highest office at the hands of Paducah's citizenry in 1881, Mayor Reed immediately inaugurated a series of measures calculated to advance the city in no small way. A paid fire department was established in 1882, substituting the valiant though inadequate volunteer fire-fighters.

In 1887 the fire department boasted two stations, one at No. 726 South Third Street and the other (Central) at No. 124 North Fourth Street. Equipment consisted of a supply truck carrying hooks and ladders, two fire engines and five hose reels. A report that year mentions the fire plugs and "a dozen or more capacious cisterns located in different parts of the municipality", both of which were sometimes called upon to quench fires.

CHARLES REED.   JOSEPH H. JOHNSON.

Mayor Reed's initial term was so fruitful that he was re-elected in 1883, again in 1885 and still again in 1887, serving four successive two-year terms in all. During this time numerous thoroughfares were opened and fresh gravel placed on worn streets. The City Hall was built in 1883 at a cost of $20,000, the third story being added in 1909. It took the place of the old city building on North Fourth Street and represented a handsome brick structure. The basement served as jail quarters.

The city hall formerly at Fourth and Kentucky Avenue was razed and the space is now a city parking lot. A new city hall at 300 Washington Street was erected in January 1965, covering a full city block, cost approximately $1,500,000. It was designed by the internationally famous architect, Edward Durell Stone, New

CITY HALL
ERECTED IN JANUARY 1965

York City. It is a show place because of its unusual design.

Two notable improvements realized in 1886 added to the comfort and happiness of the community. The water works were completed that year, consisting of an engine house and a stand-pipe twenty-two feet in diameter and 175 feet in height, which still stands. The company laid twelve and a half miles of mains and in addition to supplying residents with purified water, connected with 159 double-nozzled fire hydrants. The gas plant was also completed and streets illuminated by 300 gas lamps set on nine-foot lamp- posts at intervals along the thoroughfares. "Night life" had not arrived and street lamps were only faint blobs in the darkness.

Work on the old stone postoffice was started in 1882 and completed in 1885. Honorable Oscar Turner who served six years as congressman (1878-1884) got the appropriation from Congress to build the $145,000 structure. It was twice enlarged.

Free city mail delivery began July 1, 1886, requiring appointment of four carriers--John W. Baynham, Pete Derrington, Ed Bonds and W.P. Hummel, the latter since 1888 a member of Hummel Brothers, insurance agents. Upon accepting the routes, they went to a local tailor to have measurements taken for uniforms which in due time came from Washington. The suits were of heavy material for winter use, and the carriers had to suffer the error through the remainder of summer, being obliged to wear the coat with the trousers to complete the official uniform.

Cross Streets were renamed when free mail delivery was established. Until then (1886) what is now known as First Street was Main; Second, Market; Third, Locust; Fourth, Oak; Fifth, Chestnut; Sixth, Walnut; Seventh, Poplar; Eighth, Hickory; Ninth, Churchill Avenue or Contest Street; Tenth, Pine or Mocquet Street; Eleventh, Cedar; Twelfth, Girard; and Thirteenth, Cypress.

Although he served only one term as chief executive of his adopted city, the Honorable Joseph H. Johnson bore the mantle of office with honor to himself and credit to Paducah. He was

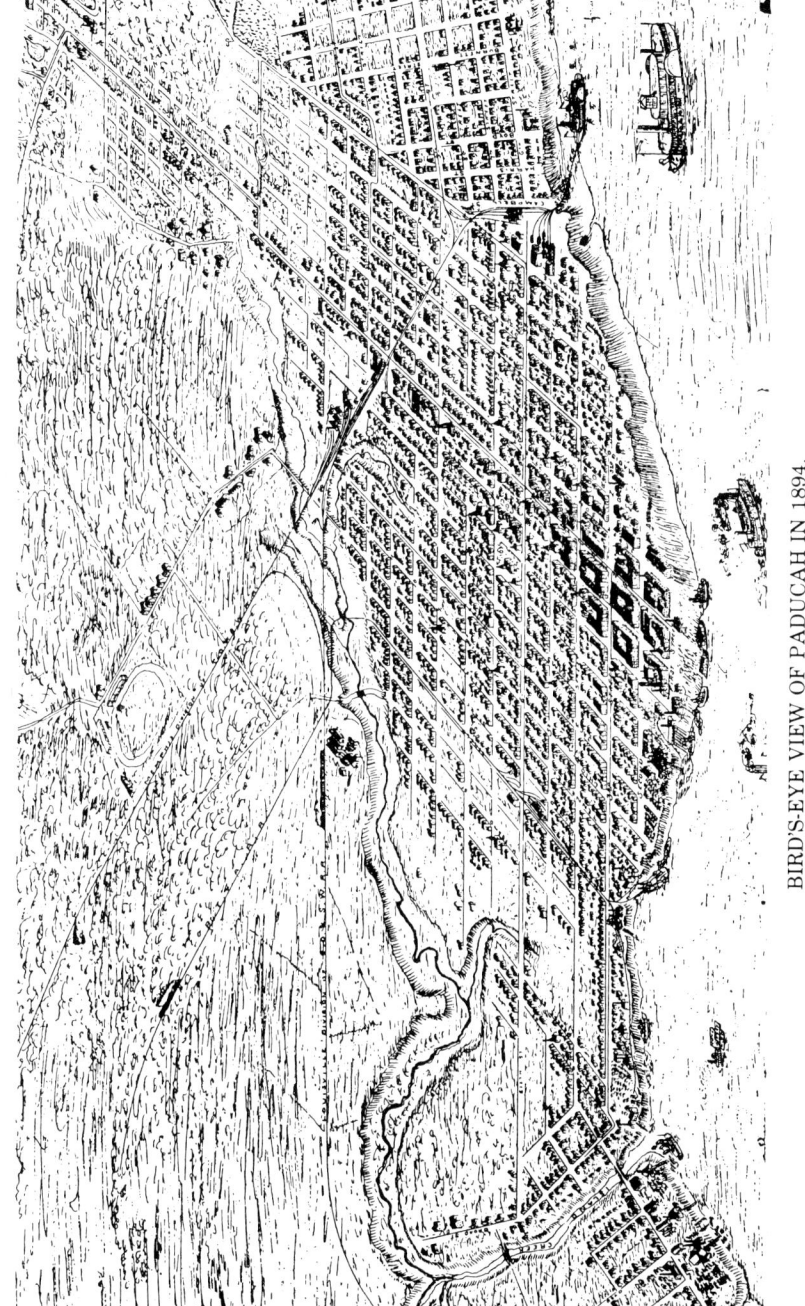

BIRD'S-EYE VIEW OF PADUCAH IN 1894.

82 THE STORY OF PADUCAH

born in Pittsburgh, Pa., July 8, 1829. After attending school there, he became a machinist. At twenty-seven he came to Paducah, interested himself in steamboats, and later operated the Johnson Foundry and Machine Company at Second and Tennessee Streets. He represented his ward as a councilman and served twelve years on the School Board. A modest stone on Magnolia Avenue in Oak Grove Cemetery, points his last resting place and records the date of his death--December, 2, 1902.

A progressive spirit pervaded the city's official life during Mayor Johnson's administration, evincing itself in many ways. He entered office in 1889 and served two years. An outstanding event about this time was the city's $100,000 subscription toward the Paducah, Tennessee & Alabama Railroad, now the Nashville, Chattanooga & St, Louis Railway. Other progressive movements marked the period.

DAVID A. YEISER, SR.   JAMES M. LANG.

The eighth mayor, the Honorable James M. Lang served the four-year term intervening Mayor David A. Yeiser, Sr.'s incumbency, and headed the city government from 1897 through 1901, while Paducah was still in the third class rank among cities.

THE STORY OF PADUCAH 83

Born at Paducah, July 15, 1857, he attended public and private schools in his native city. As a young man he was a member of the Board of Health and later the Board of Education, serving ten years on the latter. In 1913 the governor tendered him the appointment of county judge following election of Judge Alben W. Barkley to Congress, and he occupied this position until retiring in January, 1926.

Street lights and the water system were extended to Mechanicsburg and Rowlandtown, and also westward during Mayor Lang's administration, insuring adequate police and fire protection in these sections. Lang Park became a public center. With the aid of the Rev. G.W. Perryman, pastor of the First Baptist Church, Mayor Lang obtained the Carnegie Library for Paducah, and the beautiful site on which it stood was selected by him and at his instance purchased by the city.

For the first time in its history the city realized a hard-surface thoroughfare, when Broadway from First to Fifth was paved with brick at the city's expense. The first concrete sidewalks were laid on either side of the improved street. What were then considered suburban streets received graveling, such as North Tenth to the city limits, and North Fourteenth, Harahan Boulevard and North Sixteenth, and the western reaches of Monroe, Madison and Harrison Streets. By constructing a fill through an almost impassable hollow, the Littleville section, including the Union Station was linked with the city proper.

Outstanding railroad bonds were refunded at a lower rate of interest and the $20,000 indebtedness on the City Hall was cleared. The Second District sewer was entirely constructed in the years 1898-1899. Yet with these improvements the average tax levy was only 97½ cents for city purposes and all licenses stood at a low figure--a distinct compliment to the manner in which Mayor Lang's administration carried on the city's affairs. Lang died May 18, 1933; was buried in Oak Grove Cemetery.

The community still had a rustic flavor in the tardy 1890's. Visitors referred to it as "a country town" or "a southern country town." The descriptions were correct; there were many wooden sidewalks and no paved streets. Unimproved areas, such as gaping hollows, greeted the eye on all sides. Cattle foraged in the streets. But hanging over the town was a sense of the future, of destiny, of becoming. It was a belief in progress. Rapid development now set in. Village conditions were no longer tolerated. So great was the expansion, that the city in 1902 passed from third class to second class rank. The change came none too soon.

---

¹The name "Jersey", as known in Paducah, conjures up many memories among old-timers. The designation is not heard much nowadays, but there is hardly a man of over thirty years of age who will not recall the bitter boyhood rivalry between all Jersey boys and lads from the northern sections of the city. Jersey, or Jersey City, as it was sometimes called, extended from a point just north of George Street to Island Creek and ran westward from the river to Sixth Street.

CHAPTER IX

SECOND CLASS CITY--1902-

Determined that Paducah should receive recognition as a second class city, local officials prevailed upon the government to take a special census in June, 1901. This enumeration revealed 21, 457 inhabitants, which met requirements of the State constitution with reference to population. Sanctioning the bill March 22, 1902, the Legislature thus declared Paducah a second class city on that date. The Honorable David A. Yeiser Sr., was mayor when the act passed the State body, and while half of his incumbency fell under the old charter, the whole is treated in this chapter for the sake of clarity.[1]

No citizen occupied the mayor's post longer than Mayor Yeiser, the seventh mayor, who was chosen on five occasions and served a total of thirteen years. Born at Danville, Kentucky, October 13, 1845, he came to Paducah at the age of seventeen and procured employment in a drug store, later establishing himself in that business. Chosen mayor in 1891, he served continuously until 1897, and taking up the duties again in 1901 he held the office until retiring in 1908. He died September 3, 1925, and sleeps in Oak Grove Cemetery.

Lasting improvements came with Mayor Yeiser's government of public affairs. Among these was the laying of the first sewer system, tending to eliminate disease. Two hundred arc lights were substituted for the old lamp-posts crowned with gas lamps, affording better street lighting. Three new fire stations were built, the Washington School erected, and two small parks added to the city's property. The city limits were also extended west to Twenty-fifth Street, the extension becoming legal November 28, 1894.

Hard surface streets found a champion in Mayor Yeiser. Third Street from Kentucky Avenue to Broad Street was paved in 1905, at a cost of $75,617. The next year Kentucky Avenue was paved with brick from First to Fourth, and bitulithic from Fifth to Ninth. Jefferson Street received brick from Second to Fifth at this time, and bitulithic from Fifth to Ninth.

Contract for reconstruction of Broadway from Fifth to Ninth was let in the fall of 1904, but the work was not received until late in 1906. The four blocks cost $18,735. At the close of 1906 the city had 48 miles of gravel and 4.18 miles of paved streets.

BROADWAY LOOKING WEST FROM THIRD STREET IN 1900, BEFORE THE AUTOMOBILE MADE ITS ADVENT THERE.

A white stone levee at the river front between Jefferson Street and Kentucky Avenue was laid in 1895 at a cost of $30,000. Construction of the present brick market house at a cost of $25,000 was undertaken in 1905, and Riverside Hospital completed the same year, at an outlay of $30,000. The hospital was opened in July, 1905, with Miss Frances E. Farley, superintendent.

City officials co-operating with Mayor Yeiser in promoting the community's welfare in 1895, included D.L. Sanders, judge; Charles K. Wheeler, attorney; John T. Donovan, treasurer; E.G. Boone, tax collector; W.L. Patterson, clerk; James W. Wilcox, engineer; Gus G. Singleton, police chief; James J. Wood, fire chief. A glance at the roster nine years later, in 1904, shows Judge Sanders still on the bench; T.B. Harrison, attorney; John J.

THE STORY OF PADUCAH 87

Dorian, treasurer; E.H. Puryear, solicitor; Henry Bailey, clerk; James Collins, police chief.

Phenomenal success also attended the directorship of the ninth mayor, the Honorable James P. Smith, who took up the duties at the age of thirty-three. He was born in Paducah November 14, 1874. Graduating from the Paducah High School in 1891, he studied further in St. Louis and then returned to his native city where he associated himself with his father in the wholesale grocery business. Chosen mayor in the November, 1907, election, he went into office January next (1908) and served four years. He was the youngest mayor in the city's history.

Mayor Smith's regime stressed importance of better fire protection and the second year (1909) fire losses were cut to $27,198. A site was bought on Kentucky Avenue for the Central Fire Station and the building erected at a cost of $19,000, and the No. 5 Station at Tenth and Clay was also built, both valuable adjuncts in reducing fire hazards. A combination police and fire box call system was installed throughout the city. Salaries of firemen and policemen were increased.

Another floor was added to the City Hall in 1909. An elevator was installed and new equipment furnished offices, the total cost, including the third floor addition, amounting to $15,284.

The faulty wooden bridge across Island Creek at Fourth Street was replaced with a handsome concrete bridge, and Cross Creek was spanned with a steel structure. The latter made possible a short route from southern reaches of town to Union Depot, the railroad passenger station, at Union and Caldwell Streets.

Besides adding a tract of land to Oak Grove Cemetery west of the entrance, a receiving vault and reception room were built. Improvements were noted at Riverside Hospital, where a fire escape was installed and a nurses' home provided. Health standards were raised, and a tuberculosis sanitarium and smallpox hospital established, while a visiting nurse was engaged by the city and organized charity begun.

South Tenth Street was transformed into an attractive

88 THE STORY OF PADUCAH

thoroughfare, with a spacious lawn in the center, and renamed "Murrell Boulevard". Several miles of concrete sidewalks were laid, part in Mechanicsburg, and the block map system adopted for uniform taxation. At the same time the State was prevailed upon to pass a law giving property owners ten years to pay for

JAMES P. SMITH.   THOMAS N. HAZELIP.

street and sidewalk improvements. In addition to other purchases, the city stables were bought. The city presented the U.S. gunboat Paducah with a $1,500 silver service set.

Saloon licenses were increased from $150 to $500, netting a substantial sum for the city's treasury. Meanwhile banking arrangements were bettered. A floating debt of $40,013.03 was paid in full, and approximately $25,000 remained in the general tax fund at the close of 1911.

An interesting feature of Mayor Smith's administration was the fact that all improvements were made out of the regular tax levy. No bonds were issued. On the contrary, outstanding bonds were reduced and the city's financial condition improved.

During the next four years the Honorable Thomas N. Hazelip headed the city government, the tenth citizen so honored. Born April 6, 1877, at Munfordsville, Kentucky, he attended athe

THE STORY OF PADUCAH 89

public schools and Ogden College at Bowling Green, and then studied law. In 1905 he located in Paducah. Six years later he was elected chief executive of his adopted city, and administered the affairs of that office in a creditable manner. Mayor Hazelip went into office January 1, 1912. Under the Commission Form of government he was chosen Commissioner of Property in 1917, serving two years. In 1922 he was appointed United States Marshall, Western District of Kentucky.

From the outset, Mayor Hazelip favored improved fire-fighting equipment, and placed in service a four-cyclinder motor car November, 1912. This was used by Fire Chief James J. Wood. Shortly afterward a La France truck was bought, the first motor-driven truck in the department. But all through 1912 horse-drawn combinations responded to alarms, 259 of which were registered for the year. At the close of 1912 seventeen horses were in service at the five fire stations.

Street paving also received attention, ordinances passing the upper and lower Boards for bitulithic on two most popular promenades, Broadway and Jefferson, from Ninth to Fountain Avenue. As the flood of 1913 receded it left some of the gravel streets in bad repair, loose gravel washing away and holes in instances making passage dangerous, but with proper attention the streets were soon placed in excellent condition.

The city realized a saving of $60,000 by starting a sewer fund from general revenues, and this and other economical measures gave impetus to thrift.

At the beginning of 1913, the second year of Mayor Hazelip's administration, the city's official personnel read as follows: Maurice McIntyre, clerk; Don P. Martin, treasurer; David A. Cross (1868-1913), city judge; Roscoe Reed, city attorney; Henley Franklin, police chief; L.A. Washington, city engineer; and A.Y. Martin, city solicitor.

Mayor Hazelip moved to Louisville where he lived twenty-two years. He died there November 12, 1950 and was buried there.

While the Honorable Ernest Lackey occupied the Mayor's office less than a year, the months were filled with material progress. Like three of his predecessors, the eleventh mayor was a native Paducahan. He was born June 8, 1867. After attending the public schools, he traveled as a salesman, and then engaged in real estate and insurance. For seven years he served as an alderman. In 1915 he was elevated to the mayoralty and entered that office January 1, 1916, but in June the Kentucky Court of Appeals decided

CITY OFFICIALS IN 1908.

Top row, reading left to right—August Budde, George W. Walters, Lige Cross, Ed Dalton, Judge David A. Cross, Ed. D. Hannan, president Board of Alderman; Mayor James P. Smith (seated), Ernest Lackey, Dr. H.P. Sights, Miss Creemens, John J. Dorian, Miss Sophia Kirkland, Alex Kirkland, ——, Ed Miller, Miss Katie Nunnemaker, Tom Orr.

Middle row—James Campbell, James McCarthy, C.L. Van Meter, Al M. Foreman, president Board of Councilmen; Pat Lally, C.C. Duvall, R. Richardson, Fred Kreutzer, B.W. Cornelison, Al E. Young, R.J. Wilson, T.H. Clayton, W.L. Bowers, Frank J. Mayer, T.E. Ford.

Lower row—Dr. P.H. Stewart, E.W. Baker, Harry R. Hank, Virgil Sherrill, Maurice McIntyre, W.T. Miller, George Oehlschlaeger, Lucian E. Durrett.

against the election. However, Governor Stanley re-appointed Mayor Lackey to serve through the November election, and he carried forward a progressive program until November 10, 1916.

The administration let the contract for paving Broadway with resilient bricks from First to Fifth Streets, an experiment which eliminated much of the noise attending heavy traffic. The contract for bitulithic paving of Jefferson Street from Ninth to Fountain Avenue was also awarded, although this work was not begun until 1917. Contracts for concrete sidewalks were awarded and carried out in several parts of the city during 1916.

All remaining horse-drawn rigs in the fire department were relegated and motorization undertaken. A motor car was also supplemented for the police patrol, with its clanging bell and team of spirited horses. There was a sort of heart-pang attached to disposing of the faithful horses that had, in all kinds of weather, at all hours, responded as readily as the men themselves to the alarms of fire.

About this time the Morals Commission, a committee of representative citizens bent on renovating the city, urged remedial measures in that direction. The plea fell on receptive ears, for Mayor Lackey's administration not only tightened laws against vice but established a hospital or home where unfortunates received protection and were given another opportunity.

Real estate in Paducah for assessment purposes in 1916 was $9,225,884, with a 60 per cent valuation. The tax rate was $1.85 per hundred.

Mr. Lackey was again elected mayor in November, 1927, to take office January 1, 1928. He was chosen to serve four years.

Mr. Lackey died March 7, 1941.

An administration altogether admirable was that of the Honorable Frank N. Burns, a young attorney who sprang into prominence as the twelfth mayor. Born at Clifton, Tenn. August 11, 1879, he came to Paducah at the age of eleven years, attended the public schools, studied law, practiced in Chicago, and returned to Paducah in 1908, where he built up a strong legal business. He served as an alderman, Commissioner of Public Safety, and from November 10, 1916, to January 5, 1920, was chief executive, serving a little more than three years. He was chosen railroad commissioner in November, 1919, and was acting in that capacity when death came May 30, 1925. The body was taken to Los Angeles, California, where it was placed in the Englewood Mausoleum.

92 THE STORY OF PADUCAH

Construction of the Tennessee Street trunk line sewer occurred during Mayor Burns' administration. In 1917 Broadway and Jefferson from Ninth to Fountain Avenue were paved with bitulithic, although contract for the Jefferson Street stretch was awarded during the previous administration. Gravel streets underwent overhauling, new and compact material being used.

ERNEST LACKEY.   FRANK N. BURNS.

An incineration plant was perfected and a modern nurses' home established at Riverside Hospital, and also a contagion hospital for children. Riverside Hospital received the latest equipment for a bacteriological laboratory, stimulating scientific investigation and study. A concrete speaker's stand was built at Oak Grove Cemetery.

Despite the changing conditions brought about by the World War, the administration held fast to its program of development and maintained a high standard of efficiency. Municipal coal and milk depots were kept by the city during the war. The City Hall became a veritable clearing house for reports of Government agencies.

When the Eighteenth Amendment to the Constitution went into effect January 16, 1919, fifty-six licensed saloons were affected. The prohibitory measure was accepted with good grace and the bar-rooms transformed into other business establishments.

Assessed valuation of property in the city in 1920 was $14,000,000, based on 60 percent on real value. The tax rate was $2.21 for city and school.

Fruitful in many ways was the four-year term of the Honorable F.W. Katterjohn, chief magistrate from January 5, 1920 to January, 1924. He was born in Louisville, November 13, 1860, but at the age of ten years came to the city of which he was destined to be mayor. Receiving a working education in the public schools, he learned the contracting business and built some of the largest commercial houses in Paducah. His administration, the thirteenth, was purely a business one, characterized by major projects requiring wide knowledge and constant attention.

The crowning achievement was the movement to girdle the entire city with sanitary improvements, Mayor Katterjohn introducing an ordinance to this effect. On November 8, 1921, the city endorsed a $600,000 sewer bond issue by a vote of 2,854 as against 1,182 opposed. Active work began in August, 1922, with Henry A. Pulliam as chief engineer.

Street improvements of a permanent nature included concrete paving of Fifth from Kentucky Avenue to Washington, and Washington from Third to Fifth Streets. The same material was used in paving Third, Fourth and Fifth Streets from Jefferson to Monroe, and Monroe from Second to Fifth, thus completing hard surfacing of streets adjacent the business district. Considerable work was done on gravel streets and several were extended.

At the time of Mayor Katterjohn's administration the Commission Form of government was in vogue. Working in conjunction with the mayor who headed the Department of Public Affairs, were: R. Wynn Tully (1868-1927), serving his second term as Commissioner of Finance; Claude C. Pace, Commissioner of Public Safety; L.A. Washington, Commissioner of Property, and

94 THE STORY OF PADUCAH

Henry A. Pulliam, Commissioner of Public Works.

Mayor Katterjohn died August 28, 1939 and was laid to rest in mausoleum in Oak Grove Cemetery.

One of the most successful administrations on record was that of the Honorable J.N. Bailey, a practicing physician who shared the office with his professional duties. Born at Elk Creek, Mo., March 13, 1883, he attended the graded schools and did special high school and normal work, later studying medicine. During the World War he served as a first lieutenant. Coming to Paducah from Fredonia, Ky., in February, 1919, he followed his chosen profession, but answering a community call he ran for mayor in November, 1923, and was elected the fourteenth chief executive. Assuming the duties of that office January 7, 1924, less than five

F. W. KATTERJOHN. J. N. BAILEY.

years after taking residence in Paducah, Mayor Bailey served one term for four years.

An ambitious street program featured Mayor Bailey's supervision, including paving and extension of leading thoroughfares. Contracts for seventy blocks of sheet asphalt were awarded in 1926 and 1927, and all of the work completed during that time. Total cost of paving ran to $376,397, exclusive of sidewalk con-

THE STORY OF PADUCAH 95

struction.

The Union Station route, long a reproach to the city, was included in this schedule as were eight blocks on Bridge Street and five on Clements. Guthrie Avenue was given a hard surface and South Sixth Street, from Washington to Broad, was similarly paved. Two blocks on Fountain Avenue, from Broadway to Monroe were also paved, as were two on Jefferson, from Fountain Avenue to Nineteenth Street. A total of two miles was hardsurfaced in 1926, giving the city 12.5 miles of all-weather streets at the close of that year. At the end of 1927 there were 18 miles of paved streets.

Trimble Street was changed in name to "Park Avenue", on May 2, 1927, following receipt of a petition from residents on that thoroughfare. Later in the year it was paved from Tenth Street to Fountain Avenue.

Creation of a Planning and Zoning Commission in September, 1925, was a worthy accomplishment. This body inspected every plat of subdivided property within the city and also extended its scope three miles beyond the corporate limits. As a result, this territory was so divided that the streets now connect properly with those long in service.

With both the Board of Councilmen and Board of Aldermen approving an ordinance October 23, 1926, annexing a large territory, work of the Planning and Zoning Commission received hearty co-operation. The ordinance, however, did not become effective until March 18, 1927, when suburban property south and west, embracing approximately two and three-fourths square miles, was taken into the city. This gave Paducah an area of 8.96 miles.

Right of way for extending pivotal thoroughfares was purchased and streets joined where links had long been needed. The city's growth in part necessitated these cuts and extensions, which included five blocks on Kentucky Avenue and opening of Jackson Street. Traffic signals were placed at principal downtown street intersections, and a traffic ordinance covering their use was passed September, 1925, reducing accidents at the intersections.

Construction of a concrete bridge over Island Creek at Sixth Street was completed in October, 1927, the new structure taking the place of a wooden bridge which was pronounced unsafe. The Fire Department received a 750-gallon triple combination pumper and a service truck, while the Paducah Carnegie Public Library through a larger appropriation served the citizens better than at any time since its establishment.

Passage of a bond issue March, 1926, made possible a relief sewer in District No. 2, thereby eliminating the overflow and practically perfecting sewerage in that section. Sewer laterals were built in District No. 3 at an expense of $546,972. Storm water sewers were built in 1927 from Ninth Street to the river on Madison, Harrison, Clay, Clark, Adams, Jackson and Ohio Streets.

It was natural that the mayor, a physician, should attempt higher health standards. Soon after his installation, Mayor Bailey and his colleagues appointed an all-time health officer. Through a standardized milk ordinance adopted November, 1925, infant immortality took a drop of 20 per cent the next year. Riverside Hospital was standardized May 1, 1927, following a series of improvements and was recognized by the American College of Surgeons as having full equipment for all surgical work. A new operating room was added and fully equipped, including a sterilizing outfit and X-ray. Acquisition of an obstetrical department with nursery was among other improvements. More than $40,000 was spent on these and other betterments.

By a count of 5 to 1, the city gave thumping approval November 2, 1926, to return to Commission Form of government, effective January 1, 1928. An election was held November 8, 1927, and the following commissioners were named: Ernest Lackey, mayor; Ross Rutter, finance; Rumsey Bradshaw, works; George A. Hannin, property; and Jack Nelson, safety.

Parks and recreational centers of a city are vital contributions to the health and well-being of the people, and nothing in this particular was overlooked. Extensive improvements were made at Bob Noble Park and other playgrounds, popular in both winter and summer.

---

¹Mayor James M. Lang's administration, which came between Mayor Yeiser's terms of office, and while Paducah was still rated as a third class city, is noted in the preceding chapter.

MAP OF PADUCAH IN 1920.

CHAPTER X

PLACES OF HISTORIC INTEREST

Scattered about the city are many places of historic interest, some of which though weather-beaten still tell their story, while others less fortunate are almost forgotten. In rare instances bronze tablets mark the spots, but some of them are left to conjecture--faint memorials that evoke a breath of pity at the passing of fame and coquetry of fate. Alas, it is hard for present generations to realize the existence of places that held front rank a few years ago.

Although Paducah is now (1927) the second largest manufacturing center in the State, it held a position equally envious in the olden days. Years ago a mammoth rolling mill stood on South Second Street near Clark, manufacturing nails and kindred wares. Long after this plant disappeared the Kentucky Iron Company was operating a huge iron furnace at Third and Norton Streets.

The Plain City Foundry and, later, the Johnson Foundry and Machine Company ran south nearly a block from Second and Tennessee Streets. These large foundries suffered destruction by fire in 1868 and 1902, respectively.

At one time there were five flour mills, including the John L. Allard Mill (1814-1893) at N.E. First and Washington. Mr. Allard was a man of generous impulse and kept a barrel of flour at the mill door for the poor, who were always welcome. They came by the score. The same liberal spirit was manifested in later years by Dr. Don Gilberto, (1836-1911) who, meeting a farmer bound for market with a wagonload of watermelons, bought the whole lot and ordered them delivered to the Friendly Home for Children. Nobody ever knew who did this gracious deed.

Wholesale grocers prospered in the earlier days, doing practically all business by river. Their annual business from 1850 through 1858 increased from $50,000 to $1,000,000. This was carried on by six wholesale stores and four commission houses.

Wholesale trade in all lines amounted to $9,000,000 in 1887.

The river bank from Washington to well above Island Creek boasted a couple of lumber mills every quarter mile. Pioneering in this field, the Langstaff-Orm Lumber Company dates back to 1858, but the mill was really founded in 1840 when John Orm started sawing logs, employing the old pit process. This consisted of a long saw manned by two men, one of whom stood in the pit while the other was above. It was considered a good day's work for two workmen to saw out 180 feet by this method. The first Langstaff mill located at the mouth of Island Creek, later at Second and Adams, quit business in 1939.

Another large concern of ante-bellum days was the R.H. Bennett planing mill, occupying a site on the east side of Third Street between Norton and George. George Meyers also started operating a saw mill above Island Creek before the Civil War. Fourth Street in that section parallels the river and was more than a half a century called "Meyers" in token of the large industry.

More than a hundred men worked at the Paducah Furniture Factory, established in 1870, which occupied a large two-story brick planing mill and three-story frame finishing plant adjoining, the buildings and lumber yards nearby covering five acres on the east side of Third Street between Tennessee and Norton. Paducah also boasted a chair industry which lent employment to many hands. Steamboats under construction or repair contributed toward making the harbor one of the busiest spots along inland waters.

Among early business establishments was the drugstore operated by G.F. Hendren on South First Street between Broadway and Kentucky Avenue, and the grocery store of Rodney Case at 118 South Second Street. Mr. Hendren lived in a stately home just beyond Eden's Hill, which was guarded by northern soldiers during the Civil War in the erroneous belief that Major Thad Gipson was in hiding there. Loeb and Bloom, wholesale liquor dealers, faced the river front. The dry goods store of Captain

John F. Harris was conducted on Broadway between Third and Fourth Streets. He married Rebecca Calhoun August 27, 1833. Watts, Givens and Company, prominent bankers and commission merchants, were located at the southeast corner of First and Broadway.

Another early industry was a mattress factory at the northeast corner of First and Jefferson Streets. During the Battle of Paducah (1864) part of the roof was blown off by cannonading from gunboats. Ed Hale's tobacco warehouse stood on the northwest corner.

John Q.A. King, a prominent lawyer, lived at the southwest corner of Seventh and Madison, and Q.Q. Quigley, another well known barrister, made his home at the northwest corner of Fourth and Monroe. Colonel A.P. Thompson, also an attorney, lived at the southeast corner of Seventh and Monroe Streets previous to the Civil War. Benjamin H. Wisdom, (1819-1896) who came to Paducah at the close of the War Between the States and acquired a vast fortune through sound real estate investments here and elsewhere, resided at 912 Jefferson Street until his death, having built the house which still stands.

Associated with the early business life of the town was the name of Henry Enders, dealer in real estate and insurance. He resided in a two-story house that stood on the site at 409 Broadway. The Enders household was distinguished by three lovely daughters whose charm, grace and exquisite beauty elicitated state-wide comment.

South Second Street was in the olden days one of the aristocratic sections of town. It was then known as Market Street, and some of the finest homes were situated on either side from Broadway to Clark Streets. Others who had homes in this section were J.G. Cole, Robert Enders, William Enders, Abel Sullivan, Bradford Barber, Captain Joyce, Dr. Brownell, Dr. Lay, and Francis A. Harrison (1800-1844), the first postmaster.

Mrs. Robert Shanklin conducted a millinery store in a two-story frame house on Broadway near the northwest corner of Second

Street, just before the civil conflict began. At this time Greenbaum and Kaskel's Clothing Store, a leading establishment of this kind, was located on the south side of Broadway between First and Second Streets.

A few doors west from Second Street, on the north side of Broadway, was a one-story frame where Ferd Hummel Sr., had his gunshop, to which Federal soldiers occupying Paducah brought their firearms for repair. When the Confederates came to the city they raided part of his stock, but Mr. Hummel had foresight enough to carry the most valuable pieces to his home on the north side of Jefferson, between First and Second Streets, where they were hidden behind false walls. Mr. Hummel was an expert gunsmith with an inventive turn of mind. After the Civil War he moved to 109 N. Fourth where he conceived the idea of the bolt movement for rifles.

Captain Joseph H. Fowler's home, which stood at 619 Kentucky Avenue, was headquarters for Colonel Stephen G. Hicks during his stay in the city. Captain Fowler, who was one of the most prominent steamboat owners in the country, served as clerk on the first wharfboat which landed here in 1850.

The S.B. Hughes home, torn down in 1921, stood back a distance from the sidewalk at 613 Broadway. General Sol Meredith and his staff used this as headquarters while stationed here. General E.A. Paine had his headquarters at 420 Broadway.

THE OLD LLOYD TILGHMAN HOME AT THE NORTHEAST CORNER OF SEVENTH AND KENTUCKY AVENUE.

Prominent among landmarks is the two-story brick house at the northeast corner of Seventh and Kentucky Avenue. This was the residence of General Lloyd Tilghman and his noble wife, Mrs. Augusta Tilghman. They came to Paducah in 1852, and for a time lived near Third and Elizabeth Sreets, but later moved into their new home. He left it to join the Confederate cause when the State's neutrality was broken. The gallant officer never returned, meeting death near Vicksburg in 1863.

There is a marker at the southeast corner of Sixth and Ohio Streets indicating where Colonel Edward C. Murray lived, famous in the annals of American history as builder of the Merrimac. This 4500-ton pachyderm carried eight heavy guns and seven small ones, and inflicted considerable damage at Hampton Roads before meeting the Monitor of only 987 gross tonnage, in a memorable battle, March 9, 1862. Colonel Murray's vessel was pyramidical, the sloping sides plated with iron four inches thick. He was born in the District of Columbia, January 10, 1826. He died in Paducah in 1895. The tablet at 700 S. 6th Street reads:

<blockquote>
Here lived Colonel Ed Murray
Builder of the Merrimac Which Fought the Monitor
At Hampton Roads, March 9, 1862
</blockquote>

Antedating the Civil War was the old home place of the Honorable Linn Boyd at 1710 Kentucky Avenue. It was a handsome two-story brick, built for Mr. Boyd in 1853, shortly before he retired from Congress. The exterior suggested the Colonial period, and large rooms with high ceilings lent dignity to the interior. The ballustrade was made of walnut, representing the genius of a famed wood-worker who came from Pennsylvania by horseback for this special work. Mr. Boyd planted the oaks surrounding the home at the time of its construction. A storm many years later destroyed them.

Vivid recollections cluster about the old Braxton Small home, which was situated near the southeast corner of First and Kentucky Avenue. This was the birthplace of Adelaide Small (1831-1887), the first girl born in the town, and also the scene of her wedding to Dr. Philip Thornberry of Louisville, one of the most brilliant events in Paducah's pioneer annals. The house was built on pillars and stood several feet above the ground.

An accident at the time of the Small-Thornberry nuptial vows caused an interruption. Elaborate plans had been made and the guests crowded into the halls and parlors. The folding-doors were left closed until the bridal party took their respective positions, Maria, a privileged family servant taking her place on the back parlor hearth. At this moment part of the superstructure gave way and Maria's head sank to the floor level, while the piano, one of the few uprights in town, lunged forward to the consternation

FERD HUMMEL, SR.   JOHN (JACK) B. SLEETH.
PROMINENT PADUCAH INVENTORS.

of fleeing guests. After assurances of safety the remaining guests were calmed.

Sharing in the earlier reminiscenses was Captain Valentine Owen's two-story frame residence on the west side of First Street between Washington and Kentucky Avenue, an imposing structure built by Captain Owen in 1830, the first two-story residence in the city. This was the birthplace of Mrs. Angeline Owen Woolfolk, and likewise where she was married in 1861 to George W. Woolfolk. The wedding supper on this occasion consisted of everything from roast turkey and pig to dainty cake and wine, served without regard to courses. It was necessary to remove the partition between the dining room and kitchen to make space for the long festive board, which fairly groaned with good things to eat. Mrs. Angeline Owen Woolfolk was born November 1, 1834, and attained the greatest age of any native-born resident of that time--92 years, 6 months, 29 days. Her death occurred May 29, 1927.

An interesting landmark torn down in February, 1914, was the homestead of Dr. Reuben Saunders, who discovered an efficacy in the treatment of cholera. It was a large two-story frame house surrounded by massive trees and lawns, and at the time of its construction was one of the most pretentious in the city. Dr. Saunders was the grandfather of Irvin S. Cobb, who, like Mr. Cobb's mother, was born in the house. The landmark stood at 321 South Third Street, where a brass marker in the sidewalk reads;

> This Tablet Marks the Birthplace of Irvin S. Cobb
> June 23, 1876

Fond memories are associated with the Judge L.D. Husbands place, a typically Southern homestead of the better class, which stood at the northeast corner of Tenth and Jefferson Streets. Originally a slabstone walk led from Broadway to the spacious residence which was ideally set in a grove of oak trees, said to be three centuries old; two of the huge oaks remained until 1919, when they were blown down in a severe windstorm. The home was built in 1849 by D.A. Given and bought by the Husbands' in 1867. It was torn down in 1943. The home had large rooms with 14-foot ceilings. The Queen of Sheba never wore a tiara as magnificient as the wreath of blossoms which crowned the apple tree in the old orchard nearby, and the peach tree arrayed in her robe of pink was the fairest, daintiest daughter nature ever let forth to greet an April day.

The Langstaff home which stood at 800 Broadway was in the olden days the home of William F. Norton, and Ekstein Norton, brothers, who operated a banking institution at the northwest corner of First and Broadway. The home of Victorian gothic style was built in 1850, ante-dating the Civil War. It was occupied by the George Langstaff family for many years. It was razed in 1949.

Adjoining the old Langstaff homestead was a bomb proof shelter eighteen feet deep and containing two stories. It was built by the Nortons during the Civil War (1860) as a refuge in event of shelling by gunboats. When the Federal vessels opened fire the heavy charges cleared the shelter, but a cannon ball struck the preserve closet above. Splashed perserve stains were still on the walls of the pantry when the Langstaffs moved into the house in 1872.

Richard S. Ratcliffe, prominent attorney and banker was attracted to Paducah by the "boom of 1840" along with scores of other pioneer residents. This era of prosperity loomed greatest during the decade from 1840 to 1850, when it seemed Paducah was destined within a few years to become a city of extraordinary size owing to its river facilities. The railroads, however, changed the aspect of rival communities, but having cast his lot in the city Mr. Ratcliffe remained, built a handsome house near the southwest corner of Fifth and Broadway, and showed his faith in Paducah by other liberal investments.

When the "boom of 1840" was still in its glory, N.G. Hammen established a wagon factory which was located on the east side of Second Street between Monroe and Jefferson. It proved an important spoke in the industrial wheel, doing an extensive business up and down the rivers and, later, by rail.

Having contended with the elements of many years, but still in good condition for those years, the venerable Brazelton home at 332 S. 6th, built in 1958 stood as a monument to the past, with which it was prominently identified. It was here that General Lew Wallace, celebrated soldier and later author of *Ben Hur*, had his headquarters while assigned to Paducah, and it was in this house that General U.S. Grant remained over night on his second visit to the city the latter part of October, 1861. The house, a two-story frame fronting Sixth was torn down July, 1946.

Honor of running the first locomotive operated in this country was bestowed upon a young engineer who later made his home in

CAPTAIN LAWSON'S LOCOMOTIVE PREPARING FOR THE FIRST TRIP IN THIS COUNTRY.

the city--Captain John ("Jack") Lawson, who lived at the northeast corner of Seventh and Broadway. He came to the United States from England with a locomotive called the "Stourbridge Lion", and was the first to operate it on the Carbondale & Honesdale Railroad in Pennsylvania. The railway was built of wooden rails capped with a thin surface of iron. The locomotive was a wood-burner. The line was begun in 1827 and opened a little later. The first locomotive in U.S. to run on rails was August 8, 1829.

Particular historical interest attaches a marker at the foot of Campbell Street, for it was this point that Captain John ("Jack") B. Sleeth ran his celebrated submarine cable[1] to the Illinois shore in 1847--the first successful under-water cable used by the Western Union Telegraph Company. Captain Sleeth was born at Pittsburgh in 1826 but later lived in Paducah at 438 South Sixth Street. He died at Paducah in 1895 and a 22-foot shaft marks his grave in Oak Grove Cemetery.

The wires of Captain Sleeth's submarine cable were carefully covered with gunny-bags and tar, and then taken aboard flatboats and lowered on the bed of the river, beginning on the Kentucky side. The experiment was successful. Unfortunately the tablet at the foot of Campbell Street sets the date of this experiment ten years later than it really occurred.

Captain Sleeth was visited by Cyrus W. Field, financier and projector of the Atlantic cable, and persuaded to go to Chicago, where several large concerns wished to buy the patent and manufacture the cable under Captain Sleeth's supervision. But he returned to the city of his love, spending his last days in the Paducah harbor as a steamboat pilot, for--

> He was made of unpurchasable stuff,
> He trod the ways when ways were rough.

Paducah's supremacy as a tobacco and whiskey center carried the community's fame throughout the country for more than half a century. The dawn of prohibition brought about the disappearance of its famous distilleries, while a diversification of crops is causing the tobacco market to wane. Yet the memory of these one-time leading industries will live for many years. Tobacco continues in an important role, but is no longer the chief source of return.

The distillery business first took ground here in 1852, when W.H. Slack entered the trade. Others soon opened distilleries and within a score of years the city took on the name of being the home of famous whiskey brands. By 1900 the wholesale liquor business had grown to huge proportions and such bottled brands as "Brook Hill", "Three Rivers", "Red Rock", "J.W. Palmer", "Early Times", "Old Terrell" and other famous distilled products were sought the country over.

John G. Fisher organized the Eureka Brewery during the middle of the nineteenth century and did a thriving business, both local and out of town. A later brewery of considerable size was the Paducah Brewery Company, which in 1900 built the large brick

THE STORY OF PADUCAH 109

structure later occupied by the City Consumers Company. "Belvedere" and, later, "Paducah" beer were favorites, not only in

OLD BRAZELTON HOME AT SIXTH AND CLARK STREETS AS IT APPEARED IN 1927. DURING THE CIVIL WAR THIS WAS HEADQUARTERS FOR GEN. LEW WALLACE AND ALSO THE PLACE WHERE GEN. U. S. GRANT STAYED OVER NIGHT.

the city but for many miles around. Like the wholesale bottle and jug liquor dealers, the breweries did an extensive business.

Gigantic tobacco cargoes were and still are a common sight here, the streets frequently offering a crowded picture with farmers bringing in the loose-leaf weed to warehouses. The same streets would be jammed with transfer wagons laden with hogsheads en route to shipping terminals--veritable streams of the dark weed headed for manufactories in other parts of the country and abroad, there to be converted into cigars, cigarettes, chewing tobacco and snuff.

Two large tobacco handlers and manufacturers antedating the Civil War were A.R. Lang and D.B. Sheerer. As tobacco became the king of the Purchase District, other dealers went into the business. The early growth of the industry is seen by the fact that in 1884 more than 12,000 hogsheads were sold, each weighing 1,600 pounds, making a total of more than 19,000,000 pounds. The crop that year netted $1,536,000. Three years later, in 1887, more than 18,000 hogsheads were sold. The old Western District

Warehouse at the northeast corner of Second and Jefferson Streets had the largest floor space of any warehouse in America. (1897)

Paducah-made cigars were well known, including such brands as "Irvin S. Cobb", "First National" and "Chancellor". A popular smoking tobacco labeled "Forked Deer" began manufacture here in 1889. The best known brands of chewing tobacco made in Paducah were "Pride of Dixie", "Silver Tip", "Turkey Twist" and "Forked Deer Twist".

Many years ago some of the most prominent sites were occupied by livery stables. Jim Long had a stable on the northeast corner of Third and Broadway, where long lines of vehicles, from buckboards to heavy farm wagons and an occasional hearse, lined the spaces one either side, their shafts propped high with notched boards. On the southwest corner was Ben Harris' popular stable, showing everything from quick-stepping horses to their accompaniment, whether a sulky or prim little gig with glass-sided square lamps at the sides of the seat in which candles were burned--enough to attract any gay Lochinvar bent on courtship back in--

Those days now gone, to come no more,
Except as flashed from memory's shore.

To residents of Paducah who lived in the early 1900's, the horses water fountain at 10th Street and Broadway was a

THE STORY OF PADUCAH 111

familiar sight. There were few automobiles in that day and many a horse was driven to the watering place for a refreshing drink.

There has been great danger of its destruction by cars if left at the location. Mr. Eugene Katterjohn sensed the need for removal from the street and with great love for Paducah and her history he financed the moving of the fountain to a grassy island nearby. Mr. Walter Beasley of Beasley Marble Company supervised the change of location.

It is made of granite and weighs six tons. It was given to the city by Hermon Lee Ensign who willed a large portion of his estate to the Humane Alliance to erect animal drinking fountains. It will remain as of now (1979) without water but as part of Paducah's history.

The inscription reads:

> '1907, presented by the National Humane Alliance,
> Hermon Lee Ensign, Founder.

---

[1] A second cable was laid across the Ohio just below Paducah in May, 1927, supplying Brookport with continuous electrical service from the Kentucky Utilities Company.

CHAPTER XI

SPORTS AND AMUSEMENTS

Entertainments in the early days were not as varied nor exciting as those of today, but the young folks thoroughly enjoyed themselves just the same. There were no moving picture shows, vaudeville houses and other modern diversions; yet time did not hang heavy, for parties were popular, with their quaint old games, and itinerant shows contributed to the gaiety of years gone by.

At a caucus of the Board of Trustees of the town, called June 3, 1834, the license fee for various kinds of traveling entertainments was listed as follows:

Resolved, that no transient theatrical companies, ventriloquists, or sleight of hand performers, or men exhibiting wax figures, or caravans of animals, or any other exhibition or show be permitted to exhibit or perform without paying $5 in advance to the supervisor, if the admittance be 25 cents per head; if admittance be over 25 cents they shall pay the sum of $10 per day or night.

Captain John Betts, an English actor, built the first theater here in 1834, locating it on the north side of Broadway between First and Second Streets. It was a two-story building, the upper story serving as living quarters for Captain Betts and Mrs. Betts, and sister-in-law, Miss Nancy Stanard, all of whom assisted in the show's offerings. The proprietor was popular with various troupes and induced many excellent companies to "make" the town. The bills ran from funny sketches to reproduction of lighter dramas. In April, 1836, Captain Betts and his company staged a benefit for the town, a sum of $27 being turned over to the Board of Trustees.

One of the early showboats touching the crude levee was R. Letton's "Floating Pavilion", which paid a license of $12.50 to exhibit in the harbor in January, 1837. The town collector demanded $10 from T.C. Combs for an "exhibition of human skulls and other apparatus together with a specimen of fine arts", as noted in the town records May 30, 1837. In August of the same year the sum

THE STORY OF PADUCAH 113

of $5 was deposited with the treasurer by an itinerant who "exhibited snakes". An especially well-liked organization of performers was the "Chapman Family", showing every night except Sundays for three weeks in December, 1840.

During the summer months outdoor performances were given by traveling showmen who came by river. Two to five persons generally composed these shows, part of whom served as ticket sellers or in other capacities until their parts were called. Blackfaced characters often paraded the streets preceding performances, drawing crowds to the show by their antics. Showboats were well patronized in the early days and continued popular as late as 1900, when their prestige began to wane until now they are a rarity.

Medicine shows followed in the wake of these early attractions, first on Broadway and then on vacant lots over town. The free performances drew large crowds. Each act closed at the most exciting point, giving the distinguished-looking medicine man an opportunity to sell various remedies without fear of the crowd dispersing. Large bottles of medicine displayed and described in such manner as to convince the most doubtful, offered panaceas for all ills.

Besides the shows, the old-time parties held a warm place in the hearts of young people. Games included chess, checkers and guessing contests. Somebody in the crowd could play a fiddle and everybody clapped hands. The favorite dances of those days were soon in full swing, and even grandparents sometimes joined in to the jollification of all present. Refreshments on such occasions were cider, apples and cake. The hilarity would proceed as the revelers shouted:

Happy is the miller that lives by the mill;
The mill turns round of its own free will.
Hand in the hopper and the other in the sack;
The wheel turns round and he cries out: Grab!

While the young folks participated in games and other diversions, their seniors did not forget the social side of life. In practically every respect a Southern town, this spirit in Paducah revealed itself in no way more strongly than in the hospitality of its people. And many were the gatherings and long will they be remembered.

Probably none of these stands out more prominently than the reception David Watts tendered when he moved into his new home at 710 Broadway. A sumptuous feast awaited the guests and much merriment followed. The guests were reluctant to leave and Mr. Watts who had enjoyed the occasion as much as anyone, sensed this regret. Whereupon he mounted the hall stairway and announced: "Friends and neighbors, we have had a most delightful evening, and I now wish to say, come back, every soul of you, tomorrow night and we will have the party all over again!!" An appreciative cheer greeted his words and the next evening the housewarming festivities eclipsed even those of the night before.

In the spring of 1860 St. Clair Hall, 112-114 South Second Street between Broadway and Kentucky Avenue, became Paducah's chief amusement center in the show line and continued in this role for a quarter century, or until Morton's Opera House was opened in 1885, on the east side of South Fourth Street near Broadway. This latter playhouse, which was destroyed by a spectacular fire, seated 1,100 patrons. The Kentucky Opera House, later the Orpheum Theater, was erected in 1900, on North Fifth Street between Broadway and Jefferson Streets. Its seating capacity was 1,600, which included the main floor or auditorium, balcony and gallery.

Adorned with an electric sign fifty feet high, the largest in the state, the Columbia Theater on Broadway near the southwest corner of Fifth Street swung open its doors to the public April 18, 1927. With the opening performance it introduced the vitaphone or talking pictures, then only three months old. The playhouse accomodates 2,000 people and is very nice. Five thousand dazzling lamps are used in the sign and the marquee is brilliantly illuminated with 1500 bulbs.

THE STORY OF PADUCAH 115

Attractions at the Kentucky Opera House which opened in the fall of 1901 included such road shows as "On the Bridge at Midnight", "Forty-five Minutes from Broadway", "Simple Simon Simple", "Busy Izzy", and "Rip Van Winkle", which was a benefit play for the San Francisco earthquake sufferers, several parts being taken by Paducah actors in conjunction with the traveling troupe. Richard Mansfield was featured that year as well as Paul Gilmore, and the Depew Stock Company paid two visits. Lillian Russell and Company showed here December 5, 1913 in "Wildfire".

HANDSOME NEW COLUMBIA THEATRE OPENED IN 1927, SHOWING LARGE ELECTRIC SIGN

Six years later in 1912, the playhouse offered "The Rose Maid", "Mutt and Jeff" and "Get-Rich-Quick Wallingford", while the Garside Stock Company proved popular over several weeks, summers of 1910-1911 with dramatic productions including "East Lynn" and "Under Two Flags." Al G. Field's Minstrels were presented during the season. Nearly all the great actors known to the Thespian art from 1901 to 1915 were billed at the Kentucky Opera House at one time or another. The large theater and the big road shows that played there have all the nostalgic charms of a family album.

Moving pictures made their advent in the winter of 1901, at the

Young Men's Christian Association building at 6th and Broadway. Public schools were dismissed to allow children to attend. General admission was five cents. There was no regular plot, the screen showing only fire engines tearing down the street, locomotives racing across country, prize fighters in action, horse races and other fast-moving objects. The daily picture show was established in 1904 at 516 Broadway. Screen attractions eventually brought about the doom of road shows in Paducah. By 1912 Paducah had five theaters, namely: Kentucky, Arcade, Kozy, Bijou and the Star.

The most enjoyable excursions for all from 1900 to 1910 were the Illinois Central Railroad trips each year; usually at Kuttawa or Eddyville. Other enjoyable trips were to Smithland, Golconda, Metropolis and Cairo by boat. The steamers *Dick Fowler, Rapids, Dorothy* and *George Cowling* ran Sunday excursions to these points, carrying hundreds of pleasure seekers for the day's outing.

The big circuses afforded Paducahans many a treat in past years and even now are looked forward to by young and old as a veritable Pandora's box. The pink lemonade, the shriek of the calliope, the laugh of the spangled jester, who was redolent with flavors of kerosene and sawdust, revive the memory of happy occasions. Paducah has known all the famous clowns, great riders, animal trainers and freaks that traveled with the white tops.

Smith's Great American Circus was one of the first to make the place, showing matinee and night on the Fourth of July, 1857. The circus could well afford to pay the $75 license fee charged by the city, for the whole populace virtually turned out to see the holiday attraction.

When Dan Rice (1822-1900) came through Paducah in April,1870 with his own circus he pitched his tent on the north side of Broadway between Seventh and Ninth Streets, long popular show-grounds. This site, ideal in every respect--size, location, and cleared, level area--was said to be the best suited of any on circus routes. It afforded easy access for traveling shows by river, and, later, by rail. Dan Rice, the lovable clown was a riot of color, fun and fancy. He was the owner of the fascinating showboat, *The Great Pavilion Circus*. He made a number of appearances in Paducah.

Besides Rice, who gave to Paducah its first steam fire-engine in recognition of kindnesses bestowed when he was without funds, these grounds held the glitter and tinsel of Van Amburg and Forepaugh. Hemmings & Coopers' big show and menagerie exhibited there in 1874.

William F. Cody, better known as "Buffalo Bill," appeared here three times--in 1895, 1900 and 1913, the last time with Pawnee Bill as partner.

As Paducah grew it became necessary to seek other locations farther removed from the heart of town. In 1895 the large commons between Eighth and Eleventh Streets, bordered by Ohio and Jones Streets proved a mecca for circus-goers, and was known as the Ninth and Tennessee grounds because the main entrance was at the corner.

Features at this time included a balloon ascension, a local aeronaut generally volunteering. One afternoon a certain daredevil reached a height of probably two hundred feet and suddenly started downward. Something had gone wrong and the balloon dropped on Seamon's grocery store at Fifth and Tennessee Streets, jarring the occupant out of the notion of ever going up again.

All of the larger circuses used the Ninth and Tennessee grounds, such as Barnum & Bailey, Ringling Brothers and the John Robinson Shows. Several years later William F. Cody, the original "Buffalo Bill's Wild West Show," the latter sponsored by A.S. Terrell (1862-1922) and Fletcher Terrell (1866-1944) of Paducah, commenced exhibiting here, usually pitching tents at Sixteenth and Harrison Streets. The Adam Forepaugh organization carried Louise Montague, "the $10,000 beauty" and Boliver, "the biggest elephant in the world".

One of the grandest spectacles ever seen on the Ninth and Tennessee grounds was the "Destruction of Rome", staged by Barnum

& Bailey. The gorgeous scenes and elaborate costumes, the incomparable electrical effects and the splendor of it all made it an event long remembered, well worth the liberal patronage Paducah gave.

In 1900, Buffalo Bill in person made his second appearance in Paducah. The show pitched tents at Sixteenth and Harrison, which was then a broad field. Cody himself was featured shooting glass spheres tossed in the air. The Boer War had just closed in South Africa and Cody had a large number of Holland Dutch Boers, veterans of the war, who demonstrated their prowess as soldiers.

Shortly after this performance street fakirs invaded the city and stood on street corners featuring phonographs. For ten cents the public could put tubes to the ears and hear the Boer War--a conglomeration of booms and such, with an occasional bugle call or cheer.

Dr. Don Gilberto (1836-1911) had the first "real" phonograph in these parts, with a horn and other improvements, which he played for the entertainment of scores of friends assembled in the evenings at his home, 606 South Fourth Street. The instrument was placed at the window so that the public could hear easily in summer, and people would bring chairs or sit on the curbing while listening to the records. Frequently the street was blocked with buggies.

One of the most unique attractions the city ever knew was "The Last Days of Pompeii", in 1904. This sat at Sixteenth and Harrison. A volcano of cardboard ran up some fifty feet behind a make-believe Roman city. The show carried a large troupe of actors but hired several hundred "extras" among city boys.

The play represented the iniquities and follies of the ancient city, until at last sin had gone its limit and the volcano took revenge. It was graphically portrayed--the sword fights, wild dances and boisterous parades, in which the cross was featured in derision with I. N. R.I. on it. Finally, Vesuvius rumbled and emitted an ominous puff of smoke. Then came the real eruption, done by powder and other explosives. It was hair-raising as the chariots dashed and people fled.

Another unusual show sat in the Wallace Park baseball grounds in 1908. It was Gregory's "Moscow", a representation of Moscow, Russia, in anarchistic reign of terror. A large number of "extras" were picked up from boys around the tent. Like "Pompeii", it showed the city pictured by scenery; then statues turning to life, dances and sword fights. At length the anarchists went wild and blew up houses, and Russian troops dashed here and there, until, amid the din and confusion, the "extras" actually became more afraid than the audience.

With the tented attraction was an "expert rifleman", a cowboy who shattered half a dozen objects amid air with as many shots. It was a headliner and particular stress was laid upon the rifleman's use of rifle balls. The crowd cheered lustily as the crack shot started to draw his weapon from the holster. Unfortunately the gun was accidentally discharged at an angle of 25 degrees. The accident was embarrassing, for while only one shot was fired, seven persons were struck with buckshot!

A side show with the Barnum & Bailey circus furnished an amusing incident at the grounds at Ninth and Tennessee when a farmer expressed doubt that the tall man P.T. Barnum exhibited was eight feet seven inches. At length the famous showman called upon his skeptical friend to come and measure. The farmer drew a tapeline from his pocket and checked the giant. "Seven feet four inches!" he bellowed, to the amazement of Mr. Barnum. "Well, that's strange," said the showman, grasping the situation. "Last night when we measured him he was eight feet seven inches. He seems to have lost fifteen inches over night!" And for the remainder of the afternoon and that night the giant was no longer referred to as the "tallest man in the world," but the "man who lost fifteen inches over night"!

Twelfth and Trimble streets, or rather the large expanse which began at that point, took on the air of circus grounds with the turn of the twentieth century. "Speedy" made his debut to

Paducah there by diving from a lofty ladder into a small tank and the Gibson Girls in fencing outfits shocked the populace by standing on the platform in front of a side show in knee dresses. Most of the old sites have been transformed into residential districts, crowding the white tops farther and farther out as the city takes on new growth.

Among the most favored grounds in 1927 were located at Twelfth and Pine Streets. Ringling Brothers and Barnum & Bailey, combined, the largest traveling amusement enterprise ever billed here, was scheduled to show at Twenty-Second and Jackson Streets in October, 1927, but heavy rains made the grounds too soggy for exhibition. Later the tented attractions chose the Terrell grounds off of North Eighth Street.

In 1906 the Elks Lodge had a street Fair that stretched from Seventh and Kentucky Avenue to Ninth Street. The entrance was at Seventh Street and the whole thoroughfare was lined with concessions, while shows stood on the vacant lot at Ninth Street where later was built the Carnegie Public Library, in 1902. The same year the Redmen's Lodge gave an Indian Pow-Wow at the West End Fair Grounds, 29th and Jefferson. All the actors were members of the lodge in the city, and presented frontier and wildwest acts. Following success of the Elks Street Fair, another was held the next year between Fifth and Sixth Streets on Kentucky Avenue, the concessions monopolizing the street while tented attractions availed themselves of vacant lots nearby.

No spot holds greater affection in the hearts of older citizens than the Fisher Gardens, in Fisherville, sometimes called the Belleview Gardens. This recreational center had its location south of Husbands Street and extended to Cross Creek, running from a point just east of Seventh Street almost to Tenth Street. There is nothing today that would indicate the existence of this amusement park, a ten-acre plat, save the large brick brewery cellar near Ninth and George Streets, by which parents of that section used to frighten their disobedient offspring into better behavior, telling them of the terrible "whilloper-wholloper" that lived in the dark holes.

THE STORY OF PADUCAH 121

Horse racing provided great sport for other generations. The first Fair Grounds opened in 1866 were located on the Old Mayfield Road nearly a mile beyond Guthrie Avenue. This old track sat on the east side of the road, stretching along the highway almost a half mile to where the road made a curve to the southwest on its way to Eden's Hill. Fast events staged there attracted wide attention in the days of horses. The track was a mile long. Special railroad excursions were run on gala occasions from Eleventh and Broadway to the grounds. The grandstand faced the east and was on the west side of the field. The structure was razed in 1899, and the broad expanse turned to agriculture.

Swift running later witnessed at the West End Fair Grounds drew many visitors to the city. This course was located at Twenty-ninth and Jefferson Streets, and was half a mile around. "Possibility," a fleet runner established the best record there, making the mile in 2:10 flat. This mark was hung up in 1918, two years before the West End track was abandoned. Racing was revived however and the oval renamed Carson Park owing to the generous impulses of Luther F. Carson, business executive and sports enthusiast.

Most of the pleasure seekers in those days (1869-1890) reached the Fisher Gardens on foot, the buggy proving a conveyance for the wealthier class. On special days a tallyho carrying forty passengers ran regular trips from First and Broadway. Bicycle riders jogged over the rough streets and furnished a quota of guests--and dust. The old-timer "bike" with its large front wheel and small one behind created wonder in the minds of children.

Sawdust spread over the floor of the pavilion beckoned dancers to try familiar steps, and young and old swayed to the weird waltz or did the difficult scottische. When the string band struck up "Life Is a Dream", "Arkansas Traveler" or "Oh Susannah", the sweet strains could be heard for blocks around.

A small lake at the foot of the hill answered for bathing purposes. Target shooting drew many marksmen. Ten-pins, horseshoe throwing, fastening a ring over a hook, and other games requiring skill and strength were among the pastimes.

While the Fisher Gardens seldom lacked a crowd in season, the Fourth of July was the signal for a generous outpouring, and as many as 6,000 people thronged the park to hear patriotic addresses in the afternoon and witness a show of pyrotechny at night. On these and other special occasions extra policemen were employed. It was the custom to select the city's most troublesome characters for this duty, since it was explained the usual disturbers were thus employed and others feared them--not so much through their authority, but reputations.

LaBelle Park became the chief amusement center with the passing of the Fisher Gardens (1890). This beautiful park, more than a mile west of the then city limits, was accessible by streetcar, vehicle or foot, and was the scene of many happy occasions.

It consisted of rolling hills and well-kept lawns, with a scattering of apple trees whose leafy branches afforded shade for picnickers. An artificial lake, 200 by 500 ft. was popular for both bathing and rowing. Long bathing suits were the order, garments that would appear ridiculous nowadays. The spacious dancing pavilion proved a mecca for hundreds who glided over its smooth floor. "After the Ball" and "Over the Waves" were popular dance pieces there. In the summer season, stellar attractions were offered at the casino.

The name was changed to Wallace Park in 1900 and in 1903 baseball diamonds were laid out, surrounded by a nine-foot fence with a grandstand at the northeast end, seating 2,500 people. Two stands of bleachers accommodated 500 additional spectators. A first-class brand of minor league baseball was staged by Kitty League players. "Chief" Harry Lloyd's Indians won a pennant in 1905.

Paducah held membership intermittently in the Kitty (K. I. T.) League, and for a season previous to the Kitty League, had a berth in the Central League (1897), using the Rowlandtown baseball field. The Kitty League's best years were from 1904 through 1906. George Harper, George Block and Doris (Dixie)

THE STORY OF PADUCAH 123

Carroll may be mentioned among those who received their training on lots around town before donning the uniform at Wallace Park and then moving upward.

Hook's Field at Eighth and Terrell Streets was opened as baseball grounds May 29, 1927. B.B. Hook acquired the grounds in September 1934 and made extensive improvements for revival

SCENE AT WALLACE PARK, SHOWING LAKE AND PAVILION.

of professional baseball the following year. The grandstand seated 1,500 fans. The playing field was 400 feet square. Semi-professional baseball was featured.

Colonel Ben Weille (1858-1932) was the first Paducahan to ride over the city in an airplane. He made an ascent with Tony Janus when the daring airman dropped from the clouds for Home-Coming Week, in May, 1913 and gave an expedition. Charles R. Iseman was the first Paducah man to own an airplane, which he brought here in August, 1927, and kept at a flying field on the Smithland Road just beyond the reaches of town.

Radio had its earliest devotee in Roy Katterjohn, whose statement, in 1920, that he was "getting music out of the air", aroused much interest. Henry Rudy was the second to have this form of entertainment transmitted into his home by wireless. Others who pioneered included Paul Barnes, Richard Rudy, Roy Petter, Ed Sears, Harold R. Hummel, P.L. Rapier, Ernest Grant and Charles Bichon.

THE STORY OF PADUCAH

Installation of broadcasting equipment by the Evening Sun afforded radio fans a treat from Station WIAR. This station had a 360-meter wave length, and began operating November 27, 1922. It remained in service a year during which time various programs were sent out and the city widely advertised. E.J. Paxton, Sr. suggested the salutation "Howdy Folks", which preceded each number, giving it a warmth and cordiality of the old South. WPAD was founded in 1930 by Pierce E. Lackey and Houston McNutt. The station WKYB started November 27, 1946.

The radio broadcasting station WKYX was opened in 1946 by the Paxton family. They sold out in the fifties. There were actually two stations WKYQ fm and WKYX am in 1946. Eight years ago a man from the Bristol Broadcasting Co. of Bristol, Virginia bought the stations and began the broadcasting under Mr. Gary Morse, as general manager.

WKYX has the largest daylight coverage of any radio station in Western Kentucky. The two stations WKYQ fm and WKYX am combined have the largest radio department in this section. Thirty persons are employed, ten of them annoucners and eight salespeople.

WPAD am radio station began operation in the Ritz Hotel on August 23, 1930. Mr. Pierce Lackey and partner Mr. Fred Olcott were owners until a year later, Mr. Olcott sold his interest to Mr. Houston McNutt. A few years later Mr. Lackey became operator, buying out his partner. Mr. Edward B. Fritts bought out the station in 1967 upon the death of Mr. Lackey. WPAD fm went on the air in 1946.

The station is located on 1700 N. 8th Street. Twenty-two persons are employed.

Television was introduced earlier to Paducah through other channels but WPSD, the city's channel 6 began operation in 1957.

It is owned and operated by Paducah Newspapers, Inc. with Mr. Fred Paxton as president.

The station is located off Lone Oak Road in Forest Hills on 100 Television Lane. It has brought much enjoyment with programs throughout the day and evening over approximately 40,000 TV sets in Paducah. It gives employment to about 75 persons.

Sunset Beach, a natural sandbar on the Illinois shore opposite the city, furnishes an opportunity for natatorial sport and is widely popular. While the sandbar had been in process of forming nearly a score of years, it was not until 1921 that suitable lockers and other conveniences were provided.

Formal opening of the Lake View Country Club, two miles beyond the city on the Lone Oak Road, occurred September 1, 1926. Four leading civic clubs--the Lions, Rotary, Exchange and Shrine--were guests the first week. The club house and grounds represent an investment of more than $150,000. Like the Paducah Country Club, built in 1913, and still popular, the Lake View Country Club maintains a modern club house, golf links, bathing pool and other features for the diversion of its members. The Club was called Rolling Hills Country Club in later years.

The Paducah Country Club skirts the city on the western boundary and took the place of a still older pleasure resort which stood in Wallace Park.

Complying with a bill passed by the State Legislature authorizing appointment of a park commission for second class cities, Mayor David A. Yeiser, Sr., in 1906, named the following citizens: Dr. D.G. Murrell, George W. Walters (1872-1911), Charles Reed, Colonel H.C. Rhodes and E.J. Paxton, Sr. The city had legitimate license to be park proud. This body, called the Board of Park Commissioners, held its first meeting May 7, 1906, when Dr. Murrell was chosen president and Mr. Walters secretary. Colonel Rhodes remained with the Board continuously from its beginning and since 1911 served as president.

Kolb Park, an especially attractive recreation spot at the northeast corner of Sixth and Broad Streets was bought by the city in 1912. The park is triangular in shape, fronting 475 feet on Broad Street and 450 feet on South Sixth Street. It was deeded to the city by Louis C. Kolb at an unusually low figure and in token of his considerate spirit the park was named in his honor. Mr. Kolb was born in 1842 and died September 11, 1928.

Wallace Park was named for George C. Wallace son of Captain Phil H. Wallace who lived in brick house at the top of the area, at the southwest corner of Forest Circle and Cedar Lane. The home still stands and is in good condition. Realizing that Wallace Park was destined to the same fate as former recreational spots, due to the city spreading westward, the park commissioners bought 105 8/10 acres on the Hinkleville Road, February 4, 1915. Eleven years later all structures in Wallace Park were razed, with the exception of the antebellum residence of the late Captain Philip Wallace and his wife. In the 1830's the Wallace house was purchased by H.D. Nichol, Sr. Miss Jane Nichol and her brother Julian Nichol, are now residents of the beautiful old house.

The lake was filled and the whole converted into a residential site, proving the park board's foresight in purchasing the new playground. The sum paid was $25,000.

The large wooded area lay unimproved for a decade when Captain Robert H. Noble (1855-1937) donated $10,000 toward its improvement with the understanding that the city match the gift. Prompt acceptance of Captain Noble's generous gift was followed by the Board of Park Commissioners renaming the grounds "Bob Noble Park". A concrete wall was constructed in front along with an ornamental entrance, and a heavy wire fence placed entirely around the grounds.

Beckoning visitors at all times is the large and inviting entrance, giving access to the main driveway which circles the park. A dam near the rear makes possible the large lake stocked with fish. The attractive bandstand overlooking this body of water is brilliantly illuminated and lights scattered through the park add to the beauty of the night scene. The site is especially popular as picnic grounds. A concrete swimming pool, 100 x 200, was built in 1936, and opened in 1937; it measures $3\frac{1}{2}$ feet deep at shallow end, and 12 feet at diving point.

Tablets on either side of the archway were placed there in 1926 at the instance of the Board of Park Commissioners. The board's

THE STORY OF PADUCAH 127

personnel, included Colonel H.C. Rhodes, Richard Rudy, Dr. H.P. Sights, F.E Lack and H.S. Wells, all of whom were active in forwarding work tending to beautify the city. D. Harry Jamieson is mentioned as the architect. The year when the park was given its present name and improved for use is also recorded--1926.

The inscription on the dedicatory tablet was written by Irvin S. Cobb as an expression of Paducah's appreciation of Captain Noble's magnanimous gift. It reads:

ENTRANCE TO BOB NOBLE PARK

CAPTAIN "BOB" NOBLE
Native of Paducah, life-long resident, patriotic Kentuckian, Southern gentleman, whose generosity made possible the beautifying of this playground for the people of his home town, this tablet is gratefully and affectionately dedicated, 1926.
--Irvin S. Cobb.

The Park Board announced December 13, 1930 that woodlands adjoining the Leo F. Keiler home on West Broadway had been given to the city by the Keiler family, in token of which it was called Keiler Park.

CHAPTER XII

ALONG THE RIVER FRONT

Nothing contributed more to the early growth of Paducah than its river facilities. Located at the mouth of the Tennessee where that stream empties into the Ohio and just twelve miles below the Cumberland and fifty miles above the broad Mississippi, Paducah is rightfully called the "River City". It enjoys more miles of navigable water than any inland city in the country and boasts an open harbor the whole year round--two factors that gave impetus to early growth and prosperity.

While the red man's canoe first breasted the waters at this point, then known as Pekin, an occasional flatboat drifted by with the turn of the nineteenth century. Hunters and adventurers gazed at the site where wigwams stood on the hill, the Indians looking down at the palefaces with equal concern and even greater curiosity.

But the red men suffered their greatest anxiety December 7, 1811, when the steamer *New Orleans*, the first steam vessel to ply the Ohio River, came noisily into view. She left Pittsburgh in October on her maiden trip bound for New Orleans, and as she hove into sight at Pekin she looked like an animated water mill. She eased into port here at the foot of what is now Broadway. She remained throughout the morning, the crew obtaining fuel from the Indians whose wood pile stood at this point. Reaching her destination December 24, 1811, the steamer remained in the lower Mississippi trade until she ran afoul a snag July 13, 1814.

The steamer *New Orleans* had a 138-foot keel and a 20-foot beam. Her hull was painted a vivid sky-blue and this compartment was used for freight storage, the deck affording little protection from the weather. Her burden was 300 tons. Passenger cabins were small and comfortless. Owners of the steamer valued her at $40,000.

Next came the *Comet*, in 1812, a small steamer of 25 tons, followed two years later by the *Vesuvius*, a much larger craft, the third steam vessel to land at Pekin. The *Enterprise* was launched the same year and marked a new era in steamboating, proving the first to stem the current to any considerable distance; she ran from New Orleans to Louisville in twenty-five days. In 1817 the steamer made the round trip in forty-one days. Thirty-six years later, when steamboating was in its glory, a speedy craft made the round trip in 105 hours, illustrating the development of steam power.

Realizing Paducah was destined to become a great river port, the Board of Town Trustees had the hill at the foot of Broadway graded to afford greater ease in handling cargoes. The town appropriated a sum of $1,000 on March 20, 1842, toward "further improvement of the levee," which included graveling. But the greatest improvement occurred in 1895 when a block stone wharf costing $30,000 was laid from Kentucky Avenue to Jefferson Street and from near the top of the levee to the low water mark, which was 0.7 below zero in the fall of that year. Contract for this work was awarded to Pat Halloran (1842-1922).

The first wharfboat was brought here in 1850. Captain Joseph H. Fowler (1833-1904) served as clerk.

As Paducah grew, Valentine Owen (1803-1872) realized the value of ferry service to the Illinois shore and in 1830 established a ferry consisting of two flatboats, each capable of carrying a horse and wagon and several passengers. The convenience proved profitable. Twenty years later he built the *Transport*, a sidewheel steam craft 140 feet in length. This was the beginning of steam ferry service. The *Blue Bird* with a tonnage of 72 tons was completed April 1, 1861 and entered the ferry trade that year. Ferried A.A. Herdy during Forrest's raid. The stern-wheel broadhipped *Bettie Owen*, 137 x 40, waddled back and forth in this trade for years.

Meanwhile the harbor became the mecca for steamboats of

every description and famed, too, as a place for their construction. A system of marine ways, patented by Captain Elijah Murray (1795-1855), a master mechanic of St. Louis, brought Paducah into prominence as a boat-building and repair center, the city engaging Captain Murray to introduce his plan. Contract for the project was awarded in October, 1843, whereby the town was to pay the patentee $1,000 in addition to $500 for superintending construction. A disagreement ensued and the plan was dropped. Ten years later interest was revived and actual work begun, the town trustees on May 15, 1853, granting E. Murray & Company the second contract, calling for marine ways of eight sections capable of holding boats 350 feet in length. The ways were completed in March, 1854, only a few months before the inventor's death July 11, 1855. An 8-foot shaft in Oak Grove stands at his grave, erected by friends.

Dry docks and other places for building and repairing boats sprang up along the river front as river transportation increased. Approximately a third of Paducah's population was dependent upon the rivers for a livelihood from 1870 to 1900, for aside from those engaged in shipbuilding a large number were employed in various capacities on packets and towboats.

TYPICAL SCENE AT THE MARINE WAYS, ONE OF THE CITY'S OLDEST INDUSTRIES.

THE STORY OF PADUCAH						131

Steamboats of the larger side-wheel variety built at Paducah included the *Falls City* and *Rosa Lee*. The first *Kate Adams*, reminiscent of the old days when side-wheels were so much in vogue, was built on blocks at the foot of Clark Street, by Thomas Murray. Other side-wheel craft constructed here were the *Eastport, Chickasaw* and *Huntsville*.

One of the later Paducah-built boats was the *Tom C. Powell*, christened 1915, which struck an ice gorge near Smithland in January, 1924, and sank in the "River of Many White Caps", as the early missionaries called the Ohio. Miss Jane Rhea Massengale christened the *Tom C. Powell*.

The Enders brothers controlled the first Paducah-owned steamboat, the *Walk on the Water*.

Larger craft redolent of the old romantic steamboat days tied up for the winter in Duck's Nest or what is more commonly known as the "chute", at Paducah, a haven still lending protection from the season's ills.

Records show the Tennessee River has frozen over only twice in the last century for a distance of 165 miles from the mouth--1876 and 1918. The latter freeze resulted in great havoc at Paducah, particularly in the chute, which is situated just above the mouth of the Tennessee.

Steady snowfall in early December 1917, heralded the coldest winter in years and by the 8th of that month blanketed the city with sixteen inches of snow. It now fell intermittently and the thermometer continued dropping until the middle of January, 1918, when 20 inches of snow covered the ground and the mercury indicated eleven degrees below zero. This was the heaviest snowfall since 1864.

On the night of January 14, 1918, the Tennessee River harbor reaching down to the lower end of Owen's Island froze over eight inches thick. The next morning, Saturday, a stream of visitors promenaded the surface, most of them stepping from the shore at Washington Street and walking to steamboats and barges packed solidly in ice on the other side. The novelty of "walking on the river" drew an even larger number Sunday, the majority going over afoot while others rode in sleighs or glided on skates. Monday the ice began to melt and Tuesday the chute and harbor cleared, leaving craft intact.

But much concern was felt over ice flows farther up, particularly at the Gilbertsville bridge, twenty-two miles away, which impeded passage. At length the gorge broke there, sweeping down the Tennessee River with great force. Shortly before 4 o'clock on the morning of January 29, Paducah was awakened by a roar and resounding crash, and the people knew the expected had happened. Lodging here, the main flow piled fifteen feet high and offered a sad spectacle to river men.

Preceding the white mountain came an avalanche which swept from the chute of the steamers *Grey Eagle* (250 x 40), *Black Hawk*, *Rapids* (135 x 28), and the towboat *Josh Cook*. A minute later lines holding the dry docks snapped like threads and the downstream procession was joined along with the towboats *Rescue, Pavonia, Klondike* and *Margaret*. From almost every mooring point some vessel or barge yielded to the swift march.

THE GUNBOAT PADUCAH.

The *Spread Eagle* (225 x 35), packet *Peoria, Rapids* (135 x 28), *Josh Cook* and *Pavonia* and numerous barges were sent to the river bed below the city. Total harbor damage ran to $1,000,000.

Efforts to dislodge the second or main floe by dynamiting proved futile and the Tennessee River remained choked two days for a mile at its mouth, when the gorge broke loose of its own accord and passed from sight without further damage.

Enjoying an elevation of 326.33 feet above sea level, reckoned from and by Sandy Hook, New Jersey, the city of Paducah has suffered inconveniences from high water on only rare occasions, and then in no proportion to that of other Ohio and Mississippi valley communities. Lives were rarely lost nor outside aid needed, although the gauge registered 53 feet or more at six periods in the city's history--1832, 1867, 1884, 1913 and 1937. The official government flood stage is 43 feet, but five or six feet more can be anticipated without thought of discomfort.

One of the highest stages ever recorded was on February 23, 1884. Numbering about ten thousand souls, the entire city stood aghast at the rising waters which inundated lower sections and then crept upon the business district and choice residential spots. The crest reached 54.2. Those witnessing the memorable flood never tired of telling others about it.

Some of the younger generation scouted the possibility of such an unusual stage, when water flowed several feet deep through the streets and scores of residents took to second floors to avoid the raging currents. Yet many of them lived to see the sight thirty-one years later.

In the spring of 1913, the Mississippi River reached an enormous height. Heavy upstream rains poured into the Ohio, which already was swollen. River men prophesied a high stage, but the steady rise passed even their predictions. With the Mississippi 47 miles below Paducah unable to carry its burden to the Gulf, and the Ohio taxed to its capacity, the latter soon again overran its channel. the gauge registered 54.3 feet April 7, 1913. The water covered part of the city and rendered a hundred homes inaccessible.

Making the best of the situation, young and old hurriedly built johnboats and paddled through the streets on missions of business and pleasure. Lumber mills supplied patrons with material for building the boats, carrying lumber on large flatboats to various parts of the city and unloading it at high places.

Remaining above 50 feet from April 1 through April 10, people became accustomed to conditions and soon made merry of them. Before a week passed the flood took on the appearance of a festival and became known as the "Water Carnival". It was springtime.

Many humorous incidents occurred during the Water Carnival. Frolicking crowds paddling through streets in boats of every conceivable size and description, collided with one another or jostled with "gum boot brigades".

The holiday spirit was even manifested in the curious names and legends improvised boats bore. Policemen sauntered through shallow places in boots and assisted in turning boats around or giving them a "shove".

The current at Second and Broadway was so swift that row boats were unmanageable, dashing them against telephone poles and buildings. Three feet of water flowed there. Scores of other streets resembled those of Venice.

LOOKING WEST FROM FOURTH AND BROADWAY DURING THE FLOOD OF 1913, WHEN ROWBOATS WERE THE PRINCIPAL MEANS OF TRAVEL.

THE STORY OF PADUCAH 135

Erection of a temporary refuge camp at Colonial Heights met requirements of many whose homes were inaccessible. Supplies were also given the needy at the courthouse by the Relief Committee. No outside assistance was permitted, the city and county appropriating $6,000 for the purpose, and government rations sent in were sold and the proceeds remitted to federal authorities. Electrical current was cut off during the water rampage and newspapers, curtailed in size to four pages of three columns each, were run off by hand power on job presses.

Health experts commented on the admirable manner in which the situation was met. No typhoid resulted and three weeks after the flood health conditions were not only equal, but actually above normal.

While houses floated past the city during the 1913 flood and other communities suffered severe loss, Paducah emerged without physical damage or mental distress.

When the Tennessee River overflowed in the spring of 1927, and the Mississippi at the same time inundated thousands of square miles, Paducah rested secure. In fact, a relief fund totaling $6,262 was forwarded from here to the flooded districts.

The 1913 flood, however, was only a dress rehearsal for the super-flood of 1937, when seven-eighths of the city was inundated. For nearly a month, from January 21 through February 15, Paducah suffered more than 50 feet of water. The all-time high mark of 60.8 was registered February 2. The record flood struck the community at a time when it was least prepared. With the temperature below freezing, more than 32,000 of its 40,000 odd inhabitants made a hurried exit in motor craft, johnboats and canoes. The river was seven miles wide at Paducah.

In the face of the catastrophe, Paducahans at moments forgot their cares and joked about the situation. Most of the refugees were brought out Broadway and Jefferson Streets. A concrete monument stands at 29th and Jefferson marking the place where the waters receded.

The base of the monument is 10 feet six inches by 4 feet 8 in-

FLOOD MARKER OF 1937

ches with a height of six feet. A beautifully carved eagle of stone preserved from the old postoffice at 5th and Broadway was placed on the top giving it a height of 12 feet. The total weight of the stone is 41,000 pounds. It was erected through the efforts of the Junior Chamber of Commerce in June 1938. The inscription reads:

AN EXPRESSION
OF GRATITUDE TO ALL
WHO GAVE AID
DURING THE FLOOD OF
1937

After the flood, two questions were uppermost in the minds of residents--what caused the flood and will it ever happen again? The January rainfall in Paducah was 17.52 inches, half as much as ordinarily falls in a whole year. It rained continuously for sixteen days. Meteorologists attributed the flood to the excessive rainfall during the wettest month in the nation's history.

Peculiar meteorological conditions between January 28 and February 5, 1902 resulted in a series of horrors and delights known in local annals as "White Week". Coming in the midst of

THE STORY OF PADUCAH 137

winter, rain and sleet fused with snow caused $200,000 damage. Street cars remained motionless on the streets, newspapers were printed on foot-power presses, and telephone and electrical service was paralyzed. Telephone service suffered $60,000 damage and finding its wires in a hopeless tangle, the Company employed a small army of 250 linemen to restore order out of the icy chaos. Out of 1,200 telephones only 38 were in working order.

Strangely enough, no lives were lost during this period, when, as Irvin S. Cobb wrote "the city was as a mailed knight, clad in shining armor of hard and steely glazed white two inches thick, and the wicked and just stood in slippery places". Mr Cobb, then managing editor of the News-Democrat, was engaged to write a pen picture to accompany an illustrated souvenir booklet of "White Week". The vivid description reads in part:

When the city, combing the accumulated snow and sleet and ice of a fortnight from its brow, opened it eyes, so to speak, it found everywhere traces of the ravages of the elements. Mighty oaks splintered and split, lay prostrate on the ground or exposed their naked fibers to the winds. Fruit trees had become mere stumps, while their boughs, fit now for nothing save school ma'ams' switches, littered the half-thawed, half frozen earth.

TWO THOUSAND WIRES FELL AT FIFTH AND BROADWAY
DURING THE SLEET STORM OF 1902.

Telegraph and telephone wires, electric light wires, trolley wires and fire alarm wires, were mingled together in vast metallic webs. In these tangles overthrown poles, broken cross-arms, twisted cables and glass insulators were interwoven in picturesque but perplexing confusion. Roofs were leaking and house tops in some instances were already collapsed or threatening to tumble in at sightest provocation. The avalanches of melting sleet and snow coasted constantly down the sloping walls of mansards. The gutters overflowed with rivers of murky ice water.

There was scarcely a structure in Paducah, from cottage to office block, but had leaks in it. Merchants came down town through the slush to find torrents of water pouring in upon their stocks of goods. In numerous cases, hundreds of gallons entered the stores. Meanwhile the rain descended pitilessly, steadily and wetly. This last word may not appear in Webster's or the Century, but it describes the kind of downpour that occurred in this locality that day. From leakage alone the damage was close to $40,000.

This, however, was only the beginning. Some news came from outlying sections that trees and telephone poles were beginning to fall. All the rain had not found a way through the sieve-like roofs of shops and factories. Some of it had fallen on wires and tree limbs, and much of it remaining there, began to freeze as the weather grew colder. Great cedar masts laden with miles of finely-drawn wires and branching cross-arms were snapping off like so much stick candy, all over town.

Soon telephones grew silent and telegraph tickers went dumb, while fire alarm boxes no longer useful, became mere ornaments on convenient street corners. Live wires began to sputter and spit, as they dropped across other wires. There was enough unchained electricity at the top of every towering pole to kill fifty men. The situation called for quick action.

The fire chief saw the mayor, and the mayor sent men hurrying posthaste to the power houses. Every bit of current was shut off in every dynamo. Street cars stopped in their tracks. With a despairing hum and sizzle the motors came to a sudden standstill in factories and newspaper offices. For the first time in any week day since the Civil War no daily paper was printed in Paducah on Wednesday afternoon, January 29. Electric lights blinked, winked and went out, people hurried off the streets, theaters went dark, business was practically suspended, everything came to a standstill--everything except the rain, which by now was mixed with snow. It kept falling. And it kept freezing.

That night Paducah, to quote Mark Twain, was "as dark as the inside of a cow". The streets between the rows of business houses were like tunnels. No electric lights burned, and merchants and citizens who had no gas connections fell back on coal oil lamps and tallow candles. Occasionally a spark would gleam in the inky night as some bold spirit struggled home through the storm, lantern in hand, dodging fallen tree limbs and dangling wire-ends as he went.

But the beauty of it!. Every object, overhead and under foot was clothed in glittering, glistening white. It was as if nature had sought to cover its ravages with a spotless mantle. Each twig was a fairy wand, with a diamond tip. Every wire was a glittering necklace of jewels, festooning the street. Ice covered all things, beautifying the commonplace and almost causing one to forget the ruin that had been wrought in admiration of the beauty of the scene.

The staidest and dullest of streets became a vista of magic loveliness. Each succeeding view of the panorama seemed more entrancing than its predecessor. When

THE STORY OF PADUCAH

the sun shone the landscape was almost blinding in its shining coat of mail. At night the lights from windows lit it up until the effect of lights and the shades of the scene, with the blue of the ice and white of the snow meeting in contrasting colors was indescribable.

Trees and shrubbery were burdened with a thick covering of ice Christmas Day, 1926, resulting from a sudden drop in temperature during a rainstorm. Giant limbs were torn off and shrubbery bent and broken in a sleet storm occurring January 23, 1927, when the heaviest sleet of a quarter century encumbered the city.

The most disastrous hail storm on record was that of March 19, 1920, the pelting doing greatest damage to greenhouses. The hail was driven by a strong wind from the northwest and caused a loss of approximately $50,000. Hail measuring two inches in diameter, the largest known here, fell May 1, 1893.

Few river men experiencing the town's first recorded tornado on August 9, 1851, ever forgot the destruction of the *Dover* and *Caledonia*, or damage done the *Cherokee, America, Nashville, Globe, Elk*, and *John Simpson*, all moderately large craft. it swept from the west, carrying many streamers in helter-skelter fashion to the Illinois shore. Another storm April 2, 1862, and still another in August, 1890, caused excitement on the river. The pounding winds wrecked several steamboats. One man was killed on the river front during a gale in July, 1897. No serious consequences resulted from a tornado which visited the city March 26, 1913. Towboat *J.N. Pharr* overturned in a sudden squall sweeping up the Ohio at 11:30 A.M. June 30, 1936, near Towhead Island. Pilot and four negro deckhands drowned.

Through naming of a gunboat after Paducah in 1904, the city's name was carried to distant parts of the world. The *U.S.S. Paducah* was so named at the instance of the Honorable Charles K. Wheeler, (1863-1933) congressman from the First District of Kentucky. The vessel is 174 feet long and has a displacement of 1,085 tons. Her personnel in regular service was nine officers and 152 men. She was christened by Anna May Yeiser October 11, 1904. Since the World War I she has been used in training naval

140   THE STORY OF PADUCAH

reserves. The vessel cost $392,698.

In 1907 the city council authorized a special committee to select a $1,500 silver service set for the namesake. The silver pieces were placed in a handsome chest made by F.W. Neuman (1860-1936), cabinet maker, and the gift was then taken to New Orleans by the committee, official delegates and several visitors. The gunboat Paducah was met in the New Orleans harbor. Presentation took place aboard January 17, 1908. Miss Anna May Yeiser sponsored the vessel and Congressman Wheeler made the presentation address.

STEAMER PADUCAH, BEAUTIFUL TENNESSEE RIVER PACKET
NAMED AFTER THE CITY.

The steamer *Paducah*, a moderately large craft plying the picturesque Tennessee, is symbolic of the city whose name it bore as proudly as a crack cruiser floats its admiral's ensign. Miss Elizabeth Smith, now Mrs. Russell Shelton christened the beautiful steamer January 6, 1917. The steamer *Paducah* made weekly round trips to Florence, Alabama, three hundred miles upstream. She boasted a sonorous whistle which could be heard ten miles up and down the river. Until 1928 paid respects each week-end to the town from which she received her name.

For more than half a century daily packet service was kept up between Paducah and Cairo. The *Emma Brown* began service bet-

THE STORY OF PADUCAH   141

ween the two cities in 1856, paying the city fifty cents a day for use of the wharf. Two years later the *St. Thomas Scott* went into the field and at the same time the *Silver Star* entered the Evansville-Paducah trade, making the round trip every other day.

The Evansville and Cairo routes eventually fell into the hands of Gus Fowler, Joe Fowler and Dick Fowler, Paducah brothers whose three boats bore their names. Paducah's harbor never boasted a faster steamboat then the *Dick Fowler*, which threaded the Ohio twice daily between Paducah and Cairo, a distance of 45 miles. In May, 1893, she established a memorable record by running from Cairo to Evansville, a distance of 200 miles, in 14 hours and 47 minutes. The *Idlewind* had previously in 1871, made the run in 15 hours and 29 minutes. One of the best known packets and excursion steamers was the *George Cowling*, between Paducah and Metropolis.

The service of the Fowler boats is a fragrant memory along the river. Theirs was an honored name.

While most of the larger steamers have disappeared from the inland waters, the harbor is visited each summer by mammoth excursion steamers, such as the *Washington, Majestic* and *Island Queen*. The latter, a huge side-wheeler, has glass-enclosed decks and a capacity of 5,500 persons.

The *Sprague*, the largest towboat afloat at the time, carried 60 loaded barges of coal downstream. Some idea of the tremendous dimensions of these cargoes may be had when it is known that a freight train eleven miles long could not carry the coal the *Sprague* has had in tow on a single trip while passing here. An opportunity was afforded Paducahans to inspect the sternwheeler at close range in 1909, when she tied at Owen's Island for several months. The *Sprague* did heroic rescue work at Vicksburg and other points in the flood of 1927. She retired at Vicksburg in 1948 and is on display there.

CHAPTER XIII

WAR AND THE WARRIORS

Great and noble in elemental grandeur is that people whose sturdy sons are ready for battle when a righteous principle is involved; but greater still are they whose daughters stand beneath the weight of conflict, succoring the fallen on the battle field or engaged at home in support of those in sanguine struggle.

On four occasions Paducah women left their homes to become followers of Florence Nightingale's example, giving aid to all who needed care or comfort. They did as much as the men in winning battles. They made a proud record in the Mexican War, the Civil War, the Spanish-American War and the World War.

THE MEXICAN WAR

The Mexican War in 1847 afforded another opportunity for Paducah's daughters to show their loyalty, and it is to their credit that some served as nurses in hospitals and others made handmade clothing at home and sent it to the scene of hostilities. Deft and nimble fingers plied the wool back home, and a steady stream of garments went forward to the boys on the firing line.

When the Mexican War began, Lieutenant Harry Easton, of the regular army, formed a company of ninety men, who lodged at the old Fisher Hotel during the period of recruiting. This company, organized at a time when Paducah's population was about 2,000, joined volunteers from sister counties in the Purchase District. Several members of the Paducah group became teamsters under Captain Gholson, of Ballard County.

During the Battle of Buena Vista, February 23, 1847, the Second Regiment of Indianians gave way acting under a mistaken order, and the army for a while was in peril; but the troops from Kentucky and other states rallied to the breach and the onset of Mexicans was hurled back amid volleys of grapeshot. The enemy

THE STORY OF PADUCAH 143

capitulated by dusk. A count revealed 750 Americans killed and wounded, among whom were three soldiers from Paducah.

Upon cessation of hostilities the greater number of Paducahans in service returned to the town and again took up the pursuits of civilian life. Among those who returned was M.M Connor, proprietor of the American Hotel of olden days.

THE CIVIL WAR

With the beginning of the Civil War, Kentucky assumed an anomalous position of "armed neutrality", seeking in this way to save the commonwealth from the conflict of arms and its consequences. But this psuedo-neutrality was soon abandoned, for by the early part of September, 1861, the Federals invaded the southwestern part of the State at Columbus and Paducah.

Citizens then discussed the situation with great fervor and asked one another: "Are you for the South, or are you for the North?" Sentiment in Paducah was somewhat divided, though most of the citizens obviously leaned toward the South. Owing to this pronounced feeling the city in some parts wore the title of "Little Charleston."[15] Meanwhile many young men were borne into the ranks, the Federal reverse in the Battle of Bull Run increasing enthusiasm of Southern symphathizers and augmenting enlistment.

The air was vibrant with the sound of drum and fife, of clanging accoutrement and martial command. Raw and ungainly troops mingled with trim State Guards. There were tender partings and long good-bys, so long to some that not yet has word of home greeting come. It seemed a great thing to be a soldier in the Civil War when pretty Paducah girls decked the parting ones with flowers and sang to them "The Girl I Left Behind Me", "Maryland, My Maryland", and that Marseillaise of the South--

Den I wish I was in Dixie,
Hooray, hooray,
In Dixie land I'll take my stand
To lib an' die in Dixie,
Away, away, away down South in Dixie,

Away, away, away down South in Dixie.

Due to Kentucky's invasion by Northern troops the Legislature ordered the United States flag hoisted upon the capitol to proclaim the State's Union attitude, and thus it became necessary for men to make decisions. But before this, on July 15, 1861, Captain Lloyd Tilghman, a civil engineer and veteran of the Mexican War, entered the Confederate service, taking with him a large number of fellow Paducahans, including George W. Jarrett, (1807-1885) D.A. Given, W.A. Grief, Joseph Ullman, (1838-1912) Dr. John G.

PONTOON BRIDGE AT PADUCAH OVER WHICH FIVE THOUSAND FEDERAL SOLDIERS CROSSED IN 1861.

Brooks, Thomas J. Flourney and Charles Reed. He was placed in charge of the Third Kentucky Regiment which went into training near Clarksville, Tennessee, where, three months later, the Paducah officer was made a brigadier-general.

At a later period, after the state became involved in the war, Paducah furnished recruits by the score for both sides. Many of the Southern volunteers were given to General Nathan Bedford Forrest's command. The Union ranks bore a lesser number of Paducahans away in organization of the Sixteenth Kentucky Calvary. Of this battalion, Company A was headed by Captain Charles Bachman and Lieutenants M.M. Pierce and Henry Bunting, and was made up largely of McCracken County men. Company B was in charge of Captain John E. Williamson and also had other Paducahans' names on its roster.

Coming up from Cairo, Illinois, with 5,000 men, General U.S. Grant reached Paducah environs aboard a gunboat in the early

THE STORY OF PADUCAH 145

morning of September 6, 1861. His army, however, marched on the Illinois side to a point opposite Campbell Street, where a pontoon bridge was constructed and the men passed over to the Kentucky shore. General Grant's gunboat was accompanied by several other vessels of similar type.

While passage of General Grant's soldiers acros the Ohio River at Paducah does not occupy the place in history of Caesar's crossing the Rubicon, Washington's struggle across the Delaware, or Napoleon's breasting the Beresina, the successful crossing of a hurried span by so many men is not without interest. An insufficient number of flatboats or barges were brought here from Cairo and other points, and the Government commandeered such craft in the local harbor to finish the span.

Military engineers in charge of construction used Towhead Island, a small strip of land half a mile below Owen's Island to advantage by bridging the river after reaching it with nine 40-foot barges. The river proper, 3,600 feet wide, was spanned with 114 barges held in position with joists on which boards were placed crosswise. Upon completion of the structure a steady stream of humanity poured across, the men marching four abreast and all crossing without mishap before noon.

Meal tents were then set up at the foot of Burnett Street. At 3:30 o'clock that afternoon the troops, headed by mounted officers and four bands of music marched to Seventh and Broadway, and then proceeded down the main thoroughfare four abreast to the river, to the tune of "Union Forever". An awestricken populace turned out to witness the procession.

Paducah's novel bridge remained in position till October 8. Since the swaying structure was of a temporary nature and easily dismantled, it was soon removed and river traffic was permitted to pass up and down the river again.

As the gunboats neared Paducah in September 6, 1861, a large Confederate flag was seen waving from a pole near the southwest corner of Third and Broadway. Two of the gunboats started firing at the banner, hung there by Southern sympathizers.

Just as soon as word reached Mrs. Emily Gant Jarrett (1820-1889) that "Grant's coming up the river", her first thought was rescue of the flag which her son, Charles F. Jarrett (1829-1923) was defending. Motioning for the nine-year-old black boy in her employ, she pushed him into a rockaway and dashed

MRS. EMILY JARRETT'S DARING RESCUE OF THE CONFEDERATE FLAG NEAR THIRD AND BROADWAY.

from her home at 166 Farley Place, holding the reins herself. The horse sped to the scene at breakneck speed.

When "Aunt Em", as she was familiarly known by everyone in this community, neared the flag, the gunboats intensified their firing. Jumping from her carriage, she forced the quivering boy up the pole against his loud protests, which could be heard for blocks around. Shrapnel, cannon balls and rifle shots were piercing the tattered banner, but the brave matron insisted it should not be captured. In a moment the terror-stricken boy released the treasured emblem and "Aunt Em" hastened with it to her home, she and the boy hurrying from the scene.

Coming ashore, General Grant[16] ordered the flag captured, and a squad of soldiers learning Mrs. Jarrett's name and address, was detailed to bring it to headquarters. She refused their request, whereupon they searched the little cottage. After much questioning and intimidation the soldiers reported a fruitless assignment. It is thought she was wearing it as a petticoat.

Throughout the leaden-footed years of the Civil War, the emblem lay hidden in Mrs. Jarrett's home. When she died nearly twenty years later, the faded cloth was laid in her casket, given to rest with the brave matron who imperiled her life in its rescue. She was a fearless daughter of the South--a real Barbara Freitchie whose intrepidity surpassed even that of the imaginary heroine of Whittier's famous poem. A bronze marker on Broadway near the southwest corner of Third Street indicates the spot where the endangered flag waved. It reads:

> Fifteen Feet South of This Point Was Raised the First
> Confederate Flag in Paducah, Ky.

Great excitement prevailed when the gunboats came in sight, part of the populace fleeing panic-stricken to sections south and west of the city. They feared General Grant's men would harm them. To allay this feeling, Grant issued a proclamation of good will which he read at the southeast corner of First and Broadway. A marker at that place says:

> At This Point Gen. U.S. Grant
> Stood and Read His Proclamation to the South,
> September 6, 1861

Realizing that only a small portion of citizens heard the message, the officer sent for Mayor John S. Sauner and gave it to him for publication. It was printed on white paper seven by ten inches, the text being set in three faces of type. The proclamation read as follows:

General Grant's appearance as he came up the levee was recalled by Louis C. Kolb, aged Paducah resident in 1927, a year before the latter died. Mr. Kolb says the officer "smoked a big cigar and was dressed in regulation military uniform, with epaulets as the only distinguishing mark".

Paducah, Ky., September 6, 1861
To the Citizens of Paducah:
I have come among you not as an enemy, but as your fellow citizen; not to maltreat or annoy you, but to respect and enforce the rights of all loyal citizens. An enemy, in rebellion against our common government, has taken possession of and planted his guns on the soil of Kentucky, and fired upon you. Columbus and

148 THE STORY OF PADUCAH

Hickman are in his hands. He is moving upon your city. I am here to defend you against the enemy, to assist the authority and sovereignty of your government. I have nothing to do with opinions, and shall deal only with armed rebellion and its aiders and abettors. You can pursue your usual avocations without fear. The strong arm of the government is here to protect its friends and punish its enemies. Whenever it is manifest that you are able to defend yourself and maintain the authority of the government and protect the rights of citizens, I shall withdraw the forces under my command.

U.S. GRANT, Brigadier General Commanding.

Before returning to Cairo that day, General Grant posted an order giving Brigadier-General E.A. Paine command of the troops, which he said should number no more than necessary to have "possession and control of the city". It was stated part of the troops could be quartered in the Marine Hospital, which was soon converted into a military stronghold and called Fort Anderson. He further declared no harm should be done inoffensive citizens, cautioning his successor to "exercise the strictest discipline against any soldier insulting citizens or engaging in plundering private property".

From Cairo, General Grant sent the following dispatch, descriptive of conditions at Paducah, to Major General John C. Fremont at St. Louis:

Cairo, Ill., September 6, 1861.
Major General John C. Fremont, St. Louis, Mo.
Have just returned from Paducah; found secession flags in different parts of the city, in expectation of greeting the arrival of Southern army, said to be sixteen miles off, 3,800 strong; took possession of telegraph office, railroad depot and Marine Hospital; found a large quantity of complete rations and leather for the Southern army.

U.S. GRANT, Brigadier General.

General Charles F. Smith followed General Paine on September 14 in command of the Union forces at Paducah, assuming control September 14, 1861. This change met with approval among the people, who were dissatisfied with Paine's ruthless manner. The city was still threatened by the Confederates stationed near Columbus, so that it had been found advisable to retain the 5,000 men brought here the week before.

Conditions now seemed to take on a more serious aspect and it was deemed wise to bring General Lew Wallace here to assist in

THE STORY OF PADUCAH 149

studying the situation. Wallace reported to General Smith whom he found to be "the handsomest, stateliest commanding officer I had ever seen." The two went over military maps together and visited Fort Anderson, then in process of construction. The fort was built around the Marine Hospital, which was destroyed by fire in 1861. Nothing serious happened, however, and while General Wallace remained for several months, the greater part of the military contingent was sent elsewhere.

General Grant, who had already rendered valuable service to the Union cause in seizing Paducah, came back in October on a tour of inspection. The officer remained overnight at General Wallace's headquarters, the two-story frame house at the northeast corner of Sixth and Clark Streets. It was torn down in July 1946. In *Lew Wallace: An Autobiography* (Vol. 1, pp. 351-352), the celebrated soldier-author remarks:

> In the latter part of October, 1861, General Ulysses S. Grant visited Paducah accompanied by his staff. Not having rooms in his house for the entertainment of the entire staff, General Smith requested me to take some of them; and, with his usual courtesy, he allowed me to choose whom I preferred. General Grant and Major John A. Rawlins, his adjutant general, were assigned to me.
>
> The afternoon was dark and chilly. A good fire burned in the parlor. My servant took the belongings of the strangers, hats and overcoats; after which General Grant drew his chair towards the grate, and said, spreading his hands before the blaze and looking around: "Well, this is cheerful!"
>
> I opened a box of cigars, and he smoked incessantly. After dinner, which was chiefly of commissary stores, General Smith called and took my guest walking. They were gone two hours.

Next day General Grant inspected the camps and returned to Cairo.

Once the Federals occupied the city, a war cloud hung like a gathering storm over Paducah like the sword above the head of Damocles. Military rule prevailed and Union soldiers variously under Generals E.A. Paine, Charles F. Smith, Sol Meredith and Colonel Stephen G. Hicks patrolled the streets.

Despite the strict rules laid down by Federal officers, several Southern sympathizers annoyed the equanimity of the troops. On one occasion the men were marching past the home of Robert Owen Woolfolk at 631 Kentucky Avenue, formerly occupied by

150 THE STORY OF PADUCAH

FORT ANDERSON, IMPREGNABLE STRONGHOLD ABOUT WHICH
THE BATTLE OF PADUCAH CENTERED.

General Lloyd Tilghman who was then with the Confederacy. As the soldiers passed, Mr. Woolfolk hoisted a Confederate banner and shouted "Hurrah for Jefferson Davis!" The men were marching under General Wallace, who was next in command to General Smith.

At the instance of General Wallace, an aide was sent into the house with the request that the occupant remove the flag. Mr. Woolfolk refused. Whereupon several Union soldiers climbed the back steps and brought the flag down by force, tearing it in pieces and substituting a United Stated flag. Meanwhile Mr. Woolfolk appealed to Smith, the senior officer, who sent an aide ordering the United States flag lowered. A controversy arose and a physical encounter ensued, one of the aides going down for the count, the United States flag continuing to fly.

Places of military advantage and usefulness were practically commandeered, such as George M. Oehlschlaeger's bakery at 825 South Third Street, and Ferd Hummel, Sr.'s gunshop, then on Broadway near Second Street. Bread for the troops was supplied by the former while the gunshop proved a handy place for repair

THE STORY OF PADUCAH

of firearms. Leading residences were taken by commanding officers as headquarters. Churches, schools, factory buildings and warehouses were taken over and converted into makeshift hospitals.

Throughout the war Confederate troops threatened the Federal intrenchments. False reports that the "Rebels are Coming" were frequent, but nearly three suspensive years passed before an attack really occurred.

BATTLE OF PADUCAH

No event in Paducah's history ever gave the people as great a thrill as General Nathan Bedford Forrest's raid, more commonly known in West Kentucky annals as the Battle of Paducah. Coming here from Mayfield over the Old Mayfield Road, 1,800 calvarymen under General Forrest reached the picket lines at Eden's Hill at 2:10 o'clock on a melancholy Good Friday, March 25, 1864. Their course to the city is determined by a marker in the sidewalk where the Old Mayfield road and Guthrie Avenue now join. It reads:

> This Tablet Marks the Road on Which Gen. N.B. Forrest
> Entered in the Capture of Paducah, Ky.
> March 25, 1864.

The invading troops now cut crosswise and halted at a point near Fifteenth and Broadway, where the men dismounted to await further orders. From there a number of them could see the homes they left to join the Confederate ranks, and knowing their interest, a detail of six Paducahans was chosen to carry a message to Colonel Stephen B. Hicks, commanding the Federals. They delivered the message to Fort Anderson, which was garrisoned by 665 men who had filed into the walled enclosure like Noah's host into the Ark. The dispatch read:

Colonel:

> Having a force amply sufficient to carry your works and reduce the place, and in order to avoid the unnecessary effusion of blood, I demand the surrender of the fort and troops, with all public property. If you surrender, you shall be treated as prisoners of war; but if I have to storm your works, you may expect no quarter.
> N.B. FORREST,
> Major-General, Commanding Confederate Troops.

As the demand was being borne to Colonel Hicks and pending a reply, the Third and Kentucky regiments of 105 and 75 men respectively, took positions near Ninth and Broadway.

Eager for an attack, the men sat in their saddles ready for the word to advance. The Eighth regiment was in the heart of the city ransacking commissary stores and raiding Government stables for horses, mules and wagons.

Now came Colonel Hicks' answer, reading:

Sir:

I have this moment received yours of this instant, in which you demand the unconditional surrender of the forces under my command. I can answer that I have been placed here by the Government to defend this post, and in this, as well as all other orders from my superiors, I feel it to be my duty as an honorable officer to obey. I must, therefore, respectfully decline surrendering as you may require.

S.G. HICKS
Colonel, Commanding Post.

It was 4:30 o'clock. At last, came the order to charge, General Forrest issuing his unique command, "Forward men, and mix with 'em!" Led by Colonel Albert P. Thompson, of Paducah, the gallant calvarymen swooped down on the stronghold. The structure itself was 400 feet long and ran 160 feet toward the river, surrounded on the west, north and south by 50-foot ditches filled with water. Dismounting, the men ran toward the citadel in the face of bitter fire from within and a barrage of grapeshot and canister from the newly-converted gunboats, the sidewheel tinclad Peosta and Paw-Paw, the latter piloted by Captain William L. Ballowe (1831-1885) of Paducah.

Unable to ford the watery trenches, they drew back, renewing the charge a second time only to be met with equally determined resistance. Withdrawing momentarily, half of the Confederates surged forward once again, many of them entering residences nearby and firing down into the fort from second-story windows, effecting good aim. The fusillade increased until General Forrest rode up. Seeing the futility of capturing the breastworks without heavy artillery, he ordered a cessation of the firing.

At this instant a cannonball from a gunboat struck Colonel

TRAGIC DEATH OF COL. A. P. THOMPSON IN THE BATTLE OF
PADUCAH, MARCH 25, 1864.

Thompson, killing him instantly. The officer was seated on his charger at 516 Park Avenue. The horse fell close by. A tablet in the sidewalk now denotes the spot where the brave officer met death. He was succeeded by Colonel Ed Crossland, who a few minutes later was wounded in the right thigh and carried off the field.[17]

Lingering around the fort until 8 o'clock, the troops slowly siphoned from the city, clearing before midnight by the same route they came. Official reports showed 14 killed and 46 wounded on the Federal side, while the Confederate loss was 11 killed and 39 wounded.

Anticipating another attack, Colonel Hicks issued an order early Saturday morning for all houses within firing range destroyed. Sixty homes from which the Confederates fired were thus leveled. This action was later explained as a military necessity, and Paducahans who tried to have the government reimburse them for their loss were told that usages of war made burning the property a means of defense, and restoration would set a bad precedent. The action was dictated by the urgency of the situation, a

154	THE STORY OF PADUCAH

sense of duty. Colonel Hicks' order read as follows:

Paducah, Ky., March 26, 1864
Major George F. Barnes, Sixteenth Kentucky Calvary, will take a portion of his command and burn all houses in musket range of the fort from which the sharpshooters of the enemy fired upon us yesterday.
By the order of Col. S.G. Hicks.

A.F. TAYLOR, Post Adjutant.

Scores of civilians left the city posthaste when they learned the Confederates were coming, most of them departing for the Illinois shore. Louis C. Kolb (1842-1928) who crossed in a rowboat, said the smoke and fire of battle was visible from Brookport, four miles below.

George M. Oehlschlaeger ran coatless from his bakery at 825 South Third to the river, where he crossed for the night. Mr. Oehlschlaeger had just received a large cash payment for supplies furnished the Federals, and was counting the money when the warning came. In haste he threw a newspaper over the table containing the money--$2,628 in silver, a fortune in those days. The next morning a rumor was afloat that the bakery had been burned, but upon returning he found not only the store but the money as well. The store was ransacked, but none of the plunderers thought to look under the carelessly tossed newspaper which covered the mound of silver.

A mournful interest attaches Colonel A. P. Thompson. Leaving a profitable law practice here to cast his lot with the Southern colors, he entered the conflict to see it through. Steadfast till his tragic death, he upheld the waning fortunes of the Confederacy as did Hector those of Troy. He was a tall, stalwart man, with dark hair and mild countenance. He was commonwealth attorney here at time of enlistment, his term expiring in August, 1862. At the time he was killed Colonel Thompson was 35 years old. His grave in Bowman cemetery, a private burial ground two miles north of Murray, Ky. is marked by a ten-foot square base monument.

While viewing effects of the Battle of Paducah on the following day, a squad of Federal soldiers found a dead Confederate trooper near Ninth and Madison Streets. The dead man was seated on the ground, with his back to a tree. His eyes were riveted on some object tightly clasped in his hands.

As the soldiers drew nearer they saw that the man was holding an ambro-type likeness of two children. Hardened soldiers though they were, the sight of that man who looked on his children's photograph for the last time in this world, brought tears to their eyes which they could not restrain. Great lumps gathered in their throats. They stood looking at him for some time.

Then they dug a grave at the spot and laid the poor fellow to rest with his children's picture clasped over his heart. Over his grave, on the maple tree against which he had sat, they inscribed these words:

"Somebody's Father. March 25, 1864."

THE SPANISH AMERICAN WAR

Three days after Congress declared war against Spain in April, 1898, Captain Brinton B. Davis of Paducah organized a large group of volunteers here, known as Company K. This unit was mustered into service May 28, at Lexington, Ky., and June 1, proceeded to Chickamauga Park, Georgia, going into camp the following day.

On July 27, orders were received to break camp and proceed to Puerto Rico by way of Newport News, Virginia, but upon reaching port orders to continue were countermanded with signing of the protocol. The company then returned to Lexington and pitched camp at the Weil farm, later marching to Camp Hamilton. Upon orders to proceed to Columbus, Georgia, and then to Savannah where the Minnewaska was boarded for Mantanza, Cuba, the outfit remained six days, departing January 28, 1899, for Union de Regas.

Company K then returned to Mantanza and boarded the transport Florida for the United States, docking at Danfuskee Island on April 13. Orders were then received to return to Savannah, which was reached on the date of sailing, April 18. The company was mustered out Savannah, May 16, 1899, and the greater part of the personnel returned immediately to Paducah.

THE STORY OF PADUCAH

Besides Captain Davis, the commissioned officers included First Lieutenant Alfred D. Stewart, and Second Lieutenant Lewis L. Bebout. First and second sergeants, respectively, were Ernest Karnes and M. G. Caldwell. Among those who served were Jack Nelson and George A. Hannin, Sr.

Noted for the efficiency and soldierly qualities of its members, Company K was frequently commended by Gen. Fred Grant at Newport News, and other high ranking officers.

Dr. Frank Boyd, prominent in surgical work at the Illinois Central Railroad Hospital, served as chief surgeon of the Third Regiment in Puerto Rico. His service elicited high commendation from all quarters of the Medical Department.

THE WORLD WAR

An enviable record was achieved by Paducah in the World War. Not only did her sons fight and die in the Meuse-Argonne and Somme sectors, at Chateau-Thierry and on the Aisne, succored by her noble daughters as Red Cross nurses and in other capacities, but in every call made by the Government for financial aid or war necessities, those remaining at home responded with promptness and overflowing plenty.

More than 1,250 men were in the service from the city. Four hundred of these were volunteers and 850 came within the selective drafts. Of the latter, 250 were colored. Most of them entered training at Camp Zachary Taylor, located on the outskirts of Louisville, Ky.

The first draft contingent left September 19, 1917, and during the remainder of that month and October, 143 men departed for the Louisville barracks. The largest single draft quota was 178, which left June 23, 1918. On July 21 following, 151 recruits departed. Fifty-three men left April 28, 1918, and sixty more were called in August. There were fifty-one general and special calls, of which more than forty were special, although five of these were canceled.

Assembling at the courthouse, the draft contingents formed in line and marched to Union Station, where special trains conveyed

THE STORY OF PADUCAH 157

them to the State's chief training quarters. Large crowds of relatives and friends met the conscripts at the depot, and departure of each contingent was a signal for touching farewells and renewed faith in the coming victory.

Scores of young men entered the Officers' Training Schools. In recognition of their military ability three Paducahans received the rank of major--James G. Wheeler, J.T. Stites and C.H. Ellsworth. Among those killed was First Lieutenant Sam T. Adams, who fell in the Argonne forest September 29, 1918.

Dr. P.H. Stewart, a prominent surgeon, attained the highest rank of any West Kentuckian in the Medical Corps, receiving the title of lieutenant-colonel. Dr. Warren Sights came back as a major. Drs. C. E. Harkey, E. B. Willingham, Vernon Blythe, B.A. Washburn, S. B. Pulliam, R. E. Hearne and others of the medical fraternity performed creditable service in their calling, both in this country and on foreign battle fields.

The first Paducah soldier's body returned from the battlefield was that of Robert C. McCune, killed at Chateau-Thierry on July 18, 1918. Reaching Paducah after the armistice, it was laid to rest in Oak Grove cemetery on Sunday afternoon, May 15, 1921. With memories of the war still fresh on their minds, five thousand people turned out to honor the dead hero. Dr. John Weber, chaplain of Chief Paduke Post of the American Legion officiated at the services, which were very impressive.

Next to Louisville, Paducah led all Kentucky cities in Thrift Stamp sales. In the Red Cross drive in the middle of 1918, the city was asked for $25,000 and gave $40,000. Subscription to the Third Liberty Loan was 210 per cent, and in every other call for funds the appeal was met with unrivaled generosity. Commendation from high sources was received by various women's organizations which gave unstintedly of time and means that the nation's ideals might be upheld.

The American Legion was founded in Paducah in September, 1919, by members of the Soldiers' and Sailors' club, which was formed December 25, 1918. John P. Campbell was the organiza-

THE STORY OF PADUCAH

tion's first presiding officer. The legion is known as Chief Paduke Post No. 31.

[15]See - Harlow, "Weep No More My Lady." P. 156. Cobb, "Exit Laughing" P. 41. Cobb, brochure, "Kentucky". p. 41

[16]General Grant's appearance as he came up the levee was recalled by Louis C. Kolb, aged Paducah resident in 1927, a year before the latter died. Mr. Kolb says the officer "smoked a big cigar and was dressed in regulation military uniform, with epaulets as the only distinguishing mark."

[17]See Crossland's Book, library.

CHAPTER XIV

MEANS OF TRANSPORTATION

RAILROADS

One of the earliest bond issues submitted to the town's voters called for $200,000 worth of bonds, which would insure a railroad for Paducah. The proposition was submitted to the people June 29, 1852, and results indicated the community approved the bonds without the slightest opposition. Tabulation showed 306 in favor and none against. Balloting was at the courthouse.

The Board of Town Trustees adopted an ordinance March 1, 1853, authorizing subscription of $200,000 worth of stock in the New Orleans and Ohio Railroad. Fifteen months later the town's first railroad was ready for operation, marking a new era in Paducah's history.

Train service on this pioneer line, extended from Paducah to Florence Station, now Fremont, a distance of seven miles, and was inaugurated July 4, 1854. It was the occasion for a mammoth celebration and barbecue at Florence, people coming from many miles around to see their first locomotive.

The engine had two drive wheels on each side and a grotesque "diamond" smokestack, common in the old days. Consuming cordwood and belching forth smoke, the "iron horse" followed by two flat cars rolled into Florence at the rate of twenty miles an hour.

The locomotive and cars had been brought to Paducah by boat and many residents had assisted in unloading with the promise of "a free ride", which was realized when the engine and several cars moved out Kentucky Avenue to the terminal.

When the New Orleans and Ohio Railroad laid its tracks at Paducah the roadbed came in Kentucky Avenue at Eleventh and ran all the way down the street to the river. Objection was raised to having the railroad run through the heart of town. The company then removed the rails on Kentucky Avenue and made connection by crossing to the north.

In those days the depot was a combination passenger-freight terminal located at Twelfth and Washington Streets. It was a small wooden building. Later, another depot, passenger and

SECTION OF ILLINOIS CENTRAL RAILROAD SHOPS UNDER CONSTRUCTION IN 1926, SHOWING STEEL FRAMEWORK.

freight, was built at Eleventh and Broadway and, in time, still another at Sixth and Campbell Streets. The last called Union Station at Union and Caldwell Streets, an attractive brick structure, was opened for use in the summer of 1900.

Extension of the line Hickory in the fall of 1854, and to Mayfield the next year, marked further progress, while in 1857 it was completed to Gibbs, Tenn., giving Paducah a railroad outlet toward the south. Other extensions followed and lent added prestige to the earlier carrier, which was Paducah's only railroad for eighteen years.

Rail service northward was established in September, 1872, by the newly organized Paducah-Elizabethtown Railroad, which connected with the Louisville and Nashville Railroad at a junction, thus affording an avenue to northern markets. Construction of the road, 183 miles long, began in 1869. Moving equipment in

THE STORY OF PADUCAH 161

1873 consisted of twelve locomotives, eleven passenger cars, and 163 freight cars.

By various maneuvers the New Orleans and Ohio Railroad and the Paducah-Elizabethtown Railroad were consolidated in 1882 as the Chesapeake and Ohio Southwestern Railroad. Two years later shops were completed near the present Illinois Central roundhouse site. It was largely through the tireless efforts of Q. Q. Quigley that the company decided to locate its industrial units in Paducah. Buildings included a machine shop, a car shop, a blacksmith shop, a boiler shop and a brass foundry, the whole layout with yard trackage representing an investment of $107,000. Only six small engine stalls were required in the roundhouse built in 1884.

Following a period of receivership, the Chesapeake and Ohio Southwestern Railroad was acquired by the Illinois Central Railroad on August 1, 1896. Construction of a new roundhouse with fifteen stalls was undertaken in 1897, and the shops enlarged in 1898. The shops were again extended in 1902, and still later in 1918 the roundhouse was enlarged to thirty-six stalls, at a cost of $250,000. The railroad company built a fire-proof hospital at Fifteenth and Broadway in 1919, at an expense of $165,00.

In the years 1901-02 the Paducah-Cairo line was built by the Illinois Central. The Edgewood cut-off which passes through West Paducah was opened for operation between West Paducah and Fulton on April 4, 1927.

The city subscribed $100,000 toward the Paducah, Tennessee and Alabama Railroad, issuing bonds in January, 1889. Work was begun immediately and carried to early completion. Eventually this line became known as the Nashville, Chattanooga and St. Louis Railway. A new and modern brick freight terminal at Third and Washington Streets was opened in January, 1925.

The Chicago, Burlington and Quincy Railroad, which built a $4,000,000 bridge across the river twelve miles below the city, entered Paducah over the Nashville, Chattanooga and St. Louis Railway lines in 1918. The Gulf, Mobile and Northern Railroad also came in over this line, the road's first train coming to this city August 1, 1926.

Official announcement that the Illinois Central Railroad would expand its Paducah shops was made January 15, 1925. Ground was broken and construction started March 12, that year. The $8,000,000 project embraced twenty-three buildings and covered eighty-eight and a half acres. This large addition gave the shops plant an area of 110 acres. It is one of the four largest industrial plants in the state.

While work was progressing on units at the north end, such as driving piles for the foundation, laying concrete bases and erecting steel framework, a forlorn hollow extending from Washington to Jones Street was raised to the level of the yards. This stupendous undertaking was started in March, 1926, and completed in 190 working days. It made a remarkable change in the appearance of the place.

Mahomet, the Arabian prophet, called a mountain to him and when it failed to come he went to the hill. The Illinois Central was more successful; it called and the mountain came. A total of 625,000 cubic yards of dirt were needed to fill the large ravine, and nothing short of a near-mountain would answer the purpose. Engineers immediately set about removing Coleman's Hill, sixteen miles away and long famed as the highest point in McCracken County, and brought it to the basin at the rate of 235 cars a day. Altogether 44,560 carloads of dirt were hauled to the hollow.

All buildings in the new shops area are set on concrete foundations pillowed with red cedar pilings. In constructing the locomotive shop, which measures 682 feet in length and 245 feet in width, 3,760 piles were driven into the ground, or 89,770 lineal feet. Twenty-six carloads of creosoted wooden blocks were used in laying the floor. The steel alone in this mammoth structure weighed 2,865 tons, while a total 1,659,000 brick was used.

The locomotive erecting shop has a floor area of 3.9 acres and houses a veritable forest of machinery. There are 181 machines of various dimensions, including a device for slotting locomotive frames, which cost $42,000. This unit also contains twenty-seven engine pits and five cranes, the largest having a capacity of 250 tons and costing $57,750. This monster crane spans 95 feet and is

VIEW OF BOILER SHOP UNIT AS SEEN FROM ROOF OF LOCOMOTIVE ERECTING SHOP.

capable of carrying the largest locomotives. The clearing limit is 22 feet and six inches.

Other buildings in the layout also make an interesting study in colossal structural work. The boiler shop, harboring four cranes and divers machines, including a hydraulic flanging machine weighing 280 tons and costing $44,900, required the driving of 1,369 piles and laying of 1,055,000 brick. Measurements of the storehouse are 622 by 67 feet, the blacksmith shop 460 by 84, and the paint and tank unit 624 by 100 feet. Two chimneys at the powerhouse measured 44 feet in diameter at the base, and rose to a great height. Outside craneways extend from Kentucky Avenue to Tennessee Street, bearing two 20-ton cranes which, like the others, are electrically operated. Total cost of the buildings when completed in 1927 was $27,000,000.

Credit for bringing the massive shops to Paducah belongs in no small degree to Charles H. Markham, former president of the Illinois Central Railroad, and who, as head of that line, furthered the project. To show its appreciation the city and Paducah employees of the railroad erected a bronze bust at the shops to the distinguished executive. The unveiling took place June 15, 1927, in the presence of a thousand people.

Brief but impressive exercises marked the occasion. Besides the guest of honor, other noted railroad commanders were in attendance. The Paducah Illinois Central Shops Band accompanied George M. Rock as he sang Herbert B. Collier's special tribute song, "We Love You, Mr. Markham".

Following the song, James C. Utterback, Paducah banker in charge of the program, made a brief address setting forth virtues of the community and its pride in Mr. Markham's distinct contribution. An enthusiastic ovation greeted the railroad executive who rose to speak as Mr. Utterback presented him with a leather-bound memorial volume containing names of 2,400 donors to the statue. Dainty little Mary Pat Ryan pulled aside a curtain from the bust at this instant. The former railroad general was deeply moved as he expressed appreciation of the friendship evidenced, and renewed his faith in Paducah's future.

Moving pictures were made of the unveiling ceremonies and also of the railroad shops. "Markham Day" closed with a dinner and dance at the Lake View Country Club, attended by several hundred visitors and members of the entertainment committee.

The Illinois Central Railroad employs (1979) 1100 persons. It changed from steam engines to diesel in the spring of 1956--from coal to oil burning.

Two large smoke stacks standing 265 feet were torn down in 1973.

STREETCARS

Until the mule-drawn streetcar made its advent here in 1872, no real effort had been made to solve the transportation problem. Before that time riding was limited to private vehicles or cabs, which were beyond reach of the ordinary citizen.

THE STORY OF PADUCAH 165

James W. Magnor helped build the first streetcar. When completed it was placed in a newly-constructed car barn at the southwest corner of Third and Clark Streets to await completion of the track. The first line extended from Broadway along Third to Broad Street.

When the light-weight track was finally laid in the fall of 1872, the small car was rolled out of the barn by hand and loaded to capacity with boys. Then a mule was led out and hitched to the end of the car. Unable to budge the load, several men gave a push and Paducah's first streetcar proceeded toward Island Creek. The mule soon got into a trot and within two blocks of the starting place was galloping to the delight of a score of young passengers and a hundred eager onlookers.

Initial success greeted the initial route and new lines were added. There were two routes in 1878, known as the Locust Street and Railroad Depot, the latter running from First and Broadway to the depot, then at Eleventh and Broadway. The fare was ten cents for adults and five cents for children. Bells were put on the cars in 1881.

The People's Railway Company took over in 1887 and maintained service on Broadway between First and Fountain Avenue; on South Sixth to Willie Street; on South Third to Broad Street, and the Cemetery Line which ran north on Sixth to Trimble and then west to Oak Grove Cemetery. Liberal patronage was extended these lines.

Eventually came the electric streetcar with the overhead trolley as conceived by Frank J. Sprague, first operated with practical results in 1887. In less than three years an electric streetcar made its advent in Paducah, the tryout occurring July 4, 1890. This was the second electric streetcar in the state, and was much swifter and a great improvement over the mule-drawn car. The Green Street Line of Louisville was the first.

New routes were projected from time to time. Stone & Webster, Incorporated, acquired the street railway system in 1905; and continued improvements in routes and service, maintaining a

166 THE STORY OF PADUCAH

high standard of efficiency. Eighteen miles of street railway laced the city and environs by 1920, including lines to the Paducah Country Club, Oak Grove Cemetery, Rowlandtown, Union Station, the end of Guthrie Avenue, and across Island Creek on Bridge street to where it intersects with Mill.

The Kentucky Utilities Company obtained the properties in the latter part of 1925. This company introduced single-deck motor busses as conveyances June 20, 1926, using the Third Street and Oak Grove Cemetery routes for the experiment. The idea met with public approval on these two routes. Within a few months the company decided to abandon trolley service for the busses on the South Street route which extended into Tyler, and there upon began removal of rails on the streets affected. In the summer of 1927 busses were substituted for electric cars on the Broadway route running west to Avondale Heights. Quicker service resulted. With the Broadway busses the company's flotilla was increased to seven.

Prior to the busses, thirteen electric cars were used to handle daily traffic on all routes. In 1927, with busses in operation on several routes, the number of trolley cars was cut to seven.

Passengers carried by streetcars and busses in the year 1926 totaled 1,490,005.

An up-to-date terminal at Fourteenth and Broadway housed both streetcars and busses.

AUTOMOBILES

No little curiosity was aroused by appearance of a "horseless wagon" on the streets in the spring of 1901. It was sent here for advertising purposes by an eastern medicine concern and attracted wide attention as it paraded Broadway during its week's stay. In some respects it resembled a modern laundry truck, except that the wheels were much larger and of lighter construction, typical of automobiles in the early days of the industry. Instead of a horn, this pioneer motor vehicle sounded a gong to keep pedestrians out of its path. Horses scared and plunged; cattle ran in terror as the machine flung itself along the gravel streets.

THE STORY OF PADUCAH 167

Arrival of Dr. J. D. Robertson's (1862-1914) automobile in the fall of that year really ushered in the so-called mechanical age as it affects Paducah. He bought an Oldsmobile, which made its debut on the streets November 2, 1901. The Evening Sun of that date described its introduction as follows:

Dr. J. D. Robertson has received his new automobile and this afternoon had it out on the streets. It is of medium size. The trial trip was made this afternoon about 1 o'clock and the horseless carriage worked admirably. Dr. Robertson will use it in his practice.

It is the first automobile to be used in this end of the State for such a purpose and is also the first machine of its kind owned by a Paducah man.

Possessing only "one-lungers" cylinder, the speed of the car was limited to less than thirty miles. It had no steering wheel, a lever

DR. J. D. ROBERTSON'S OLDSMOBILE. THE FIRST AUTOMOBILE OWNED BY A PADUCAHAN.

answering for this purpose. The car was painted a bright red and quickly gained the name "red devil". Like all other automobiles of that day, Dr. Robertson's car gave a great deal of trouble and was frequently stalled, at which time the owner would have it pulled to the machine shop by a team of horses. The owner often endured the jibes of friends and pedestrians often cried out "Get a horse." These early cars on the streets of Paducah stimulated others to try the motors, and within a few years several hundred were seen.

Growth of the automobile industry in these parts is indicated by the sale of license tags since 1920, when 2,100 license plates were purchased in McCracken county. In 1921, the county clerk issued 2,920; 1922, 3,659; 1923, 4,492; 1924, 5,350; 1925, 6,135; 1926, 6,597; 1978, 38,300 cars and 12,756 truck licenses. There were 13 cars in Paducah in 1902. O.M. Seitz had the first closed car (1920), a Cleveland sedan costing $3,000.

Business transacted by the principal motor concerns in 1926 was $1,845,110. There were 1,499 new cars sold in the city that year, and 1,260 used cars. Total expenses of automobile dealers during the same period amounted to $324, 254. The industry's payroll here was $209,190, and 363 persons were dependent upon it for their livelihood.

So numerous had automobiles and trucks become in 1927 that the horse in Paducah gave currency to a witticism that at once became nation-wide. "There's only one thing that frightens a horse nowadays," says the first person. "What's that?" comes the natural query. And the reply is, "Another horse!"

Advent of the automobile and its subsequent popularity increased traffic hazards, but traffic signals and other precautions have minimized accidents. Occasionally a disastrous wreck occurs and tragic deaths result. But even during the old "horse days" these happened, for runaways were frequent. At such times a team of horses came down the street at breakneck speed, followed by a bouncing carriage, after which there was a cloud of dust and a day's excitement. The last notable runaway to date was witnessed on Jackson Street in December, 1926.

Garages, filling stations and automobile repair shops are as numerous nowadays as livery stables and watering troughs twenty years ago. Hacks and carriages have disappeared, all firefighting equipment has been motorized, and horse-drawn ambulances and hearses which once went lazily over the city streets have given way to the modern motor vehicle.

CHAPTER XV

EDUCATIONAL FACTORS

Interested in proper training and education of the young, Paducah's pioneer residents soon sought schools in which their children might be educated. The demand was at first met in 1829 by Prof. Robert Ball's private school at the southeast corner of First and Kentucky Avenue, where he and his talented daughter, Miss Susan Ball, conducted classes. Another school was established in 1831 at the southwest corner of Third and Broadway. Ministers soon accepted pupils at their homes for private tuition between Sundays, the Reverend John Speer and the Reverend A. Wheeler Campbell performing particularly meritorious service.

Donation of four acres to the town by John W. Jones in 1836 marked a distinct forward step in educational circles. This land, at the northwest corner of Ninth and Broadway, was given as the site for the Paducah Male University, which was erected jointly with the Female Academy, a smaller institution planted at the northeast corner of Fifth and Kentucky Avenue on ground donated by General Wiliam Clark. Funds for the erection of the two schools came by way of a lottery, which the State Legislature permitted for the purpose. The sum of $60,000 was raised. The Paducah Female Academy, Reverend J.R. Ash, A.M., principal, opened February 13, 1854. Charles T. Bronson also had private school which closed when General Grant came to Paducah in September 1861. Prof. Lyon's school for boys opened in early 70's at 121 North 5th.

Public schools opened in 1864. Two schools were established. Four teachers were on hand the opening day and 350 pupils.

There were four schools in 1881, including the Jefferson School, Prof. John T. Ross, principal; the High School at Fifth and Kentucky Avenue, Prof. D.C. Culley, principal; the Fourth District School, a two-room brick, near Third and Elizabeth streets, Miss Dora Nunn, principal and the Lee School, Prof. James E. Willis, principal. In 1886 the Third District School was opened with Miss Elizabeth Singleton, principal. In 1893 the total enrollment reached 2,187.

Expanding with the city's growth, the public school system made a creditable record.

Teachers in all public schools numbered 151 for the year 1926. This number mounted to 180 at the opening in September, 1927. The Arcadia School became city property when the boundaries were extended, and with the pupils there the total white and colored enrollment for October, 1927, reached 5,390.

Graduates from the Paducah High School made a long and formidable list. The first graduates came from its doors in 1874, when four received diplomas. There were eleven graduates the next year and seventeen in 1876. Washington Junior High was built in 1897.

The Augusta Tilghman High School was erected at a cost of $164,000 on a $20,000 site donated by Frederick Tilghman and Sidell Tilghman, after whose mother it is named. The cornerstone was laid March 18, 1921, and the handsome structure thrown open to classes September 19 of that year. In 1922, there were 69 graduates; 1923, 68; 1924, 79; 1925, 62; and 1926, 81. Ninety-eight graduates, the largest number since the public school system began, received their diplomas at the June, 1927, exercise.

Through the liberality of John W. Keiler (1862-1929), a sum of $5,000 was donated in 1923 toward improvement of the hollow back of the Augusta Tilghman High School and preparing it for suitable athletic grounds where school children might indulge in sports and other entertainments. The grounds were properly drained and fenced, and seats erected for the comfort of 1,000 spectators. In token of the donor's gift, the stadium was given the name "Keiler Field". The stadium cost $15,387, while the whole field with all improvements represents an investment of $30,661.

For many years Washington Junior High School which stood at

THE STORY OF PADUCAH 171

Twelfth and Broadway, held first rank among the city's educational institutions. Previously, the Paducah University, erected in 1871 at the cost of $28,000, occupied the site.

The Robert E. Lee School at the northwest corner of Fourth and Ohio Streets, is the oldest schoolhouse, having been built in 1874. Prof. John T. Ross held the principalship at Lee School for more than a decade, a position also honored by Miss Elizabeth

ANDREW JACKSON SCHOOL ON PARK AVENUE.

Singleton. Professor Ross, a familiar figure in educational realms for forty years, died April 14, 1918 at age 84. Noted for her mental attainments and tact, Miss Singleton, who died July 24, 1916, at age 55, left her impress upon all with whom she came in contact; she taught thirty-five years. Miss Emma Morgan, former principal, who died in 1927, had been identified with Paducah's schools for forty-six years. This was the longest period that any teacher ever served the city public schools.

Opened with 103 pupils on January 31, 1927, the Andrew Jackson School at Twenty-first and Park Avenue represents an expenditure of $90,000. The Franklin Junior High School, immediately east of the Franklin School on South Sixth Street, was built at a cost of $50,000, and opened February 9, 1927. A two-story addition and basement were added to the McKinley School in 1927.

As early as 1858 the Catholic Sisters of Charity established St. Mary's Academy at Fifth and Monroe Streets, with Sister Martha Drury as superioress. The school then consisted of a small cottage, but more pretentious buildings soon graced the corner, while in 1908 these were razed and a handsome two-story brick structure erected. It consisted of twelve large rooms. The largest graduating class left the academy in 1922--sixteen girls and four boys. Eighteen sisters were in attendance as instructors. The enrollment averaged well above five hundred.

Few women in the state have dedicated more years to teaching than Mrs. Katie M. Dorian, principal of the Dorian Private School at 420 Washington Street. Joining the public school staff in 1881, as a grade teacher, Mrs. Dorian became principal of the Paducah High School four years later, the first woman to hold such a position. In 1900 she opened the Dorian Private School. A dinner honoring her was given in 1937 on the roof of the Irvin Cobb Hotel. There were three hundred in attendance.

CARNEGIE PUBLIC LIBRARY

Contributing to the educational life of the community, The Paducah Public Library at Ninth and Broadway furthers happiness, efficiency and capacity for learning. The Rev. J.B. Perryman of the First Baptist Church, procured a $35,000 donation from the Scotch financier and philantropist, making possible the handsome book home. Plans for the structure were drawn by A. L. Lassiter. The city purchased the lot for $15,000 and the cornerstone was laid October 8, 1902. Two years later, on October 4, 1904, the library opened its doors to the public with 2,000 volumes.

An annual appropriation of $3,500 was set aside by the city for maintenance and purchase of new books. This sum was increased to $5,000 in 1910, and raised to $10,000 in May, 1927, when the county also began giving $250 a month and nearby residents were accorded library privileges. The library has grown steadily, its shelves in 1906 holding 4,322 volumes; in 1920, 10,080; in 1920, 19,079, and in 1927, 19,120. Five librarians served the

THE STORY OF PADUCAH   173

institution--Miss Mayme Baynham, Miss Jessica Hopkins, Miss Mary Goode English, Miss Parmelee Cheves and Miss Harriet Boswell.

Miss Boswell, who died this year, 1979, at age 84, served as librarian at Carnegie Public Library from 1924 until her retirement in 1959. Her grandparents were pioneer families of the area and the Boswell estate is the present site of the Paducah Country Club and Heather Hills.

No one evidenced greater interest in the library than Judge E.W Bagby, who served for many years as president of the Board of Trustees. He was a charter member of the Board. Incidentally Judge Bagby owned the first typewriter in Paducah, a big and cumbersome affair, and unwieldly.

Fire destroyed the building in 1969 thus ending its 66-year history in Paducah. Damage was so great that it was razed and grounds sold to the Grace Episcopal Church, adjoining it. Temporary headquarters were set up in the old Paducah Jr. College building in the 700 block on Broadway. This was used until a new and spacious building was constructed at 555 Washington Street, in 1970. As of May 31, 1979 the library contained 92, 978 volumes.

Mr. Thomas Sutherland serves as Director and head librarian. Mrs. Arthur G. Simon has held the post as reference librarian since 1950.

NEWSPAPERS

Potent factors in the development and progress of Paducah, the newspapers have worked zealously toward the advancement of its commercial and social life. While the town was yet in its infancy, in April, 1834, R.R. Willis established a weekly called The Express, and advocated Whig principles. This journal lasted only two years but pressed the town's interest during its lifetime.

John M. Lambdin (1834-1885) next established the West Kentuckian, in 1844, but disposed of it shortly afterward (1847) to William Greif who in turn sold it to H. M. McCarty and R. W. Perry. The weekly, published on Wednesdays, then changed its title to the The Paducah Journal. It relinquished the field in 1856. Later, in 1870, the Daily Kentuckian was launched by John Martin, Jr., this paper lending its editorial support to the Democratic cause.

Declaring Whig policies, The Pennant, under management of Samuel Pike, began publication in 1853. It was superseded by the Paducah American whose chief rival was the Paducah Daily Democrat published by R.B.J. Twyman & Co. on Main and Water Streets, between Broadway and Jefferson every morning except Sundays; four pages of four columns each at ten cents per week. Meanwhile, John D. Goodwin purchased the defunct Journal plant, from whose ashes now appeared The Sentinel flying Whig colors, though for only a year. William Rollston published The Commercial from 1859 to 1861.

Col. John C. Noble (1815-1901), long esteemed Nestor of the West Kentucky press, began espousing Democracy's cause in The Paducah Herald in 1857, at the Northeast corner of First and Kentucky Avenue. A tri-weekly, it ceased publication in 1861, when the editor joined the Confederate ranks. Col. John C. Noble lived at "Villa Calhoun", hillsite occupied later by Ed D. Hannan. Returning in 1865, Colonel Noble revived The Herald as a daily in January 1866 and operated it in this field until 1870, when the name ws changed to The Daily Kentuckian, operated by John Martin, Jr. It faded from the picture a few months later.

Publication of The News was begun in 1871, by Thaddeus C. Ballard (1834-1895) and James P. Thompson, continuing until 1901, when it was merged with the Democrat. Henry E. Thompson became managing editor and tutored Irvin S. Cobb when the latter began there as a cub reporter in 1893. Within two months the young reporter was "covering" major events. When Colonel Thompson engaged in other pursuits, 1896, Mr. Cobb was promoted to the "desk". Owing to his youthful age, nineteen, he was widely known in West Kentucky as the "boy editor". He was the youngest editor of a daily newspaper in the United States. Mr. Cobb remained in this capacity until the latter part of 1898, when

THE STORY OF PADUCAH 175

he went to Louisville.

In 1884 the four Leigh brothers--Robert W., Edward O., Oliver P., and Clinton B.--established The Standard. This daily, one of the most important of that period, was published first at "9 Broadway" and then later at 108 Broadway. It was an 8-column 4-page handset, with ads on all pages. Noble J. D. Dilday bought it May, 1889 and three years laters erected a four-story building at 115 North 4th Street.

The Register, under supervision of James E. Wilhelm, was the first Paducah newspaper to equip its office with linotype machines. Two machines were installed. The Register, pioneering as a morning daily, abandoned the field in 1908. It had its office at 523 Broadway.

It was Paducah's good fortune that Col. Urey Woodson, (1859-1939), owner of the Owensboro Messenger, was here on a visit March 4, 1901, when President William McKinley was inaugurated for the second time. Three daily newspapers were published, but none of them carried a full account of the event at Washington. This attracted Colonel Woodson to Paducah and two months later he established the Democrat, equipping it with a Scott perfecting press, stereo-typing outfit and linotypes. The Associated Press and a special State news wire by way of Louisville were featured.

In addition to the special wire service, Colonel Woodson brought Harry Hurst here as a cartoonist, his drawning enlivening local news stories. He succeeded in bringing Irvin S. Cobb back from Louisville Evening Post where he had gone in the meantime, paying him a handsomer salary than he received on the Falls City Daily. As managing editor, Mr. Cobb displayed the resourcefulness of a field general. Besides assigning reporters on good leads and editing their copy, he wrote three or four columns himself and handled the editorials and headlines.

Colonel Woodson bought The Daily News in September, 1901, and consolidated it with The Democrat. The News-Democrat under his management resulted from the merger.

176   THE STORY OF PADUCAH

John J. Berry (1873-1945) and Noel A. Berry soon acquired The News-Democrat, which changed from the afternoon to morning field in 1909. Previously the Register was in the daily morning field. The Berry brothers disposed of the News-Democrat January 5, 1922, to George H. Goodman who immediately put in a Cox tubular press, new linotypes, a monotype machine and other equipment, and improved the news service. Its office was moved in 1910 from 118 to 124 North Fourth Street. Lloyd P. Robertson was managing editor. On September 29, 1927, a special 68-page "Illinois Central Shops" edition was issued, the largest single edition ever published in West Kentucky.

The Evening Sun was established in September, 1896, by Frank M. Fisher. The daily had the old Scripps-McRae telegraph service, supplemented by a State service. Later the United Press became the chief source of out-of-town news and still later the Associated Press.

Edwin J. Paxton, publisher of The Evening Sun, came to the paper June 10, 1900, and in 1911 assumed control. In 1919 the plant at 113-115 South Third Street was remodeled and $30,000 spent on new equipment, including a Cox tubular press. Three new typesetting machines were installed in February, 1924. The news service was greatly extended and many new features added.

For a number of years Guy Rollston held the "desk" or managing editor's position on The Evening Sun, relinquishing it to join the editorial staff of the New York Evening World where he was engaged for more than a score of years. L. Vance Armentrout, chief editorial writer on the Louisville Courier-Journal, was managing editor at a later period. He left Paducah in 1911. Elliot C. Mitchell became managing editor in 1914.

The Evening Sun installed a radio broadcasting station--WIAR-- the latter part of 1922. It remained in operation a year and gave the city considerable publicity. The programs included market reports, weather forecasts and other news features aside from musical selections by local artists.

The Evening Sun and the News-Democrat consolidated May 1,

1929 and was known as the Paducah Sun-Democrat and moved into a new building on Kentucky Avenue, July, 1934. The name was again changed in 1978 to The Paducah Sun. Mr. Fred Paxton is President and publisher and Mr. Jack Paxton, editor. The daily subscribers number 30,212 and on Sunday 33,011.

CHAPTER XVI

CEMETERIES, FIRE DEPARTMENTS; TELEPHONES

CEMETERIES

Every community has one or more places where the proud has at last surrendered his dignity, the politician his honors, the worldling his pleasures, and the laborer rests from unrequited toil; for in the democracy of the dead, all men are at last equal and Dives relinquishes his millions and Lazarus his rags. The mightiest captain succumbs to the invincible adversary which disarms alike the victor and the vanquished. Paducah has several "silent cities" for those who have stepped from the walks of life.

Before Oak Grove Cemetery of forty three acres became Paducah's chief City of the Dead, the town had a burial ground on the west side of Fourth Street between Washington and Clark. This plot lay on the outskirts of the early town limits and was used as a cemetery for several years.

Upon the murder of Pierce Jones early in 1837, his body was buried at a site which now includes Oak Grove Cemetery. Other burials followed and the town trustees counseled as to advisability of purchasing the ground. Thirty-six acres were bought April 19, 1847, for $3 an acre. Adolph Miller surveyed the cemetery and divided it into lots. At a called meeting of the Board of Town Trustees held May 21, 1847, it was ordered that "each of the lots for sale be valued at $10". In 1906 much smaller lots ranged in price from $50 to $125 and since then the price has gradually gone up.

The original cemetery embraced only what is now known as the "old part", an addition having been added January 22, 1902 near the entrance. For a long time the burial ground was in a way neglected, the Board of Town Trustees finding it impossible to appropriate any large sum for improvement.

In 1854 a number of influential women circulated a "memorial"

THE STORY OF PADUCAH 179

addressed to the Board of Trustees of Paducah, asking that body to "take some steps to have the cemetery put into a condition that will enable the friends of the deceased buried there, to find their graves, in order that they may beautify and adorn them."[1]

In 1880 means were provided and the grounds beautified with plants and shrubbery, making the "silent city" one of the most attractive in the state.

Funeral services for the Reverend George E. Flower (1847-1884) were widely attended. Having served the First Christian Church as pastor for twelve years, Dr. Flower had also endeared himself to a large number of people outside his congregation. Approximately seven thousand persons were present when the body was lowered into its last resting place at Oak Grove Cemetery.

Services for Robert C. McCune, killed in France, July 18, 1918, whose remains were brought back to Paducah after the World War and interred May 15, 1921, were held in the presence of approximately five thousand people.

Will E. Covington's death March 15, 1927, occasioned the greatest number and most elaborate floral tributes known in Oak Grove Cemetery previously.

While Oak Grove Cemetery is the oldest and largest burial ground, the home of more than approximately 45,000 (1943) who have gone the way of the unreturning, Maplelawn Cemetery which adjoins it, and several private cemeteries in the county contain countless graves. Maplelawn, which comprises thirty acres, is cared for perpetually. The first grave was made May 19, 1918, that of J.W. Watson. Mt. Carmel (Catholic) Cemetery is located on the Mayfield Road, Mt. Kenton and Temple Israel on the Lone Oak Road and Woodlawn Memorial Gardens on the Mayfield Highway.

The first burial in Temple Israel Cemetery took place September 26, 1864. Funeral services there for Joseph L. Freidman who died in 1913 were attended by thousands of people and the floral offerings covered nearly an acre of ground.

180   THE STORY OF PADUCAH

The city's death rate in 1912 was 15.1 per thousand while the birth rate was 18.2; there were 453 deaths and 546 births.

The heaviest death rate was in the year 1918, when an epidemic of influenza swept the country. It was 22.1 that year in Paducah. Including that abnormal year, the average death rate for the city over a decade was 17.2.

FIRE DEPARTMENTS

Four fire hooks and two ladders constituted the entire equipment of Paducah's first fire department. This equipment, which, according to the early town records was bought in December, 1835, responded to fire calls of those days, being carried to the scene by volunteer firefighters.

At a meeting of the Board of Town Trustees held July 23, 1839, it was resolved to have the citizens "meet at the courthouse on Saturday morning next at 8 o'clock for the purpose of organizing a fire company". This was the first attempt to organize anything like a systematic volunteer unit. It failed to materialize, and following a fire the next year the Board of Town Trustees counseled as to best methods to pursue in organizing a company. At length it was decided to draft ninety-four men for the purpose. They were named September 4, 1840.

Previously, the town bought a 24-manpower pumping engine. In operating the pump, twelve men were required at either end while others concentrated the contents of a well upon the blaze with the hose at hand. The pumping engine cost $900 and was kept in the pioneer fire shed standing on the west side of Second Street opposite the market house. The fire shed was built in 1841 at a cost of $135. Minutes of the Board of Town Trustees for February 19, 1842, reveal the finding of a stove in the street which no one claimed, and it was placed in the primitive fire station.

For many years Paducah's fire protection lay in the "24-manpower pump", but in November, 1851, new apparatus was bought in the form of an engine costing $1,070 and representing the lastest improvement in fire-fighting equipment. It was sent to the town by a Philadelphia firm. Further progress was evidenced by construction of a two-story brick fire station at No. 726 South Third Street, the lot calling for an investment of $160

CENTRAL FIRE STATION ON NORTH FOURTH STREET IN 1906.

and the structure $450. The building was ready for occupancy in August, 1854, and bore the name "Mechanics Fire Company No. 1".

Another volunteer unit was being organized at this time, known as "Relief Fire Company No. 2". Its headquarters at No. 124 North Fourth Street were completed in 1855; the building measured 22 feet by 75 feet. A large well was sunk at the rear of the building, for it frequently occurred that water was out of reach of the blazes and the engine thus came supplied. The town fathers provided this unit with a $150 bell which could be heard all over the community as it called the volunteers to duty.

Speaking of wells there were ten public cisterns scattered over the residential area of Paducah in 1872. These were constructed of brick and the walls were nine inches thick. Each of the cisterns contained from 500 to 700 barrels of water, which was used for drinking purposes and, in case of neighborhood fire, to quench the flames. Volunteer firemen of that day often formed bucket brigades from the cisterns to the blaze.

The public cisterns were located at or near the following intersections; Third and Monroe Streets; Third and Washington; Fourth and Broad, or Jersey City as that section was then called; Fourth and Tennessee; Fourth and Harrison; Sixth and Monroe; Sixth and Jackson; Sixth and Washington; Seventh and Harrison, and Seventh and Broadway. A fire cistern on Sixth Street at Jackson (1945) six by sixteen feet deep was found when that thoroughfare was repaired.

A few years later the Hook and Ladder Truck Company No. 1 was established at 211 South Second Street. This truck, like other apparatus then in service, was drawn by a team of horses. Fires in those days were not of every day occurrence, and the horses were kept busy hauling gravel for the streets until a fire alarm sounded according to Ferd A. Hummel, Jr. (1853-1931) a member of the volunteer crew. Then they raced to the station, hitched to the waiting truck, and started to the fire.

Shortly before these fire stations were completed Dan Rice, the great pantomimist, arrived at Paducah with his show boat (1852). He had experienced a hard season and was stranded. Seeing his plight the town trustees granted him permission to exhibit without paying the customary license fee, and he made enough from the performance to tide him over the sea of distress. Rice so appreciated the courtesy that in the latter part of 1855, when he had recovered his finances, he made Paducah the gift of a steam fire-engine.

During Mayor John W. Sauner's administration the city bought another steam fire-engine, a somewhat heavier machine than any in use and far in advance of the hand pumps. The name "John W. Sauner" was painted on the sides in token of the chief executive at whose instance it was purchased. A third steam engine was added to the equipment under Mayor Meyer Weil's tenure of office, and his name was painted on it. These steam devices were acquired by the city while the departments were still manned by volunteers.

Due to the city's growth, need of a systematic fire fighting force

THE STORY OF PADUCAH 183

was becoming more and more evident. A paid corps of workers was therefore employed for this service, the paid fire-fighters taking up their duties in 1882. Tobe Etter was appointed chief of the fire-fighters, a post which he held for two years, being succeeded by W. E. (Billy) Augustus who served four years followed by James J. Wood (1861-1913).

Chief Wood served only one year at that time, when Augustus took the reins again for two years, the former then assuming the post for the second time and serving a couple years. Charley Voight now followed Chief Wood, but two years later Chief Wood became head of the department for the third time and remained in that capacity until his death. John M. Slaughter (1872-1937) then served the remainder of that year and through 1914, at the end of which time Joe Collins assumed leadership. The next year (1916) Chief Slaughter was again appointed and served until fall, when Thomas B. Glynn took charge. He headed the department until 1920, since which time Chief Slaughter guided its destinies.

Steady progress was made by the department under the paid system, which introduced more orderly methods of fighting fires and a greater dependency. Sweeping changes have been effected since the department was reorganized in 1882. The period has witnessed the evolution of the fire-fighting organization from an imperfect horse-drawn unit to the modern system with its large pumpers, ladder truck, and other improvements.

Previous to November 1, 1912, when the city purchased a four-cylinder automobile for the fire chief, the entire department was horse drawn. Seventeen horses were in service. The horse-shoeing and blacksmithing bill alone amounted to $800 during 1912, while the feed bill exceeded $2,300. Gradual motorization of the entire department set aside the horses and eliminated this expense. The department was completely motorized by the close of 1916.

Efficient work of the department is shown in low fire losses despite the valuable property at risk. In 1906 the men answered 144 alarms with a total damage to building and stock of only

$42,198. The damage in 1912 was $48,333, with 258 alarms registered. At this time the city had 458 fire plugs.

Property valued at over two million dollars was at risk in 1926, yet by prompt action the firemen succeeded in holding the actual damage to $115,371, of which nearly half was on contents.

TELEPHONES

Telephone service in Paducah dates from 1880, when the Paducah Furniture Manufacturing Company had a private wire installed in its factory at Third and Jones Streets connecting with its salesrooms on 114-116 South Third. Though telephony was in its infancy, the pioneer telephone gave reasonably good service.

The same year a system of telephones was placed in residences and business houses. R. G. Terrell Sr. (1850-1937), had the first residence phone and Captain Ed Farley the second, while Henry Burnett had the first professional "speaking and hearing device" installed in his law office. The Johnson Foundry and Machine Company was the first concern to have an instrument set up in its plant by the company.

Headquarters of the telephone company's exchange were located on lower Broadway, with Miss Anna Haney in charge of the switchboard. There were twelve subscribers. Patronage grew steadily and the next switchboard contained spaces for fifty connections. A supplementary board was soon added with eighteen connections.

Becoming increasingly popular with the years, the telephone found entrance into hundreds of homes and business establishments. The 5,000th telephone was installed November 28th, 1927. In 1949 there were 11,615 in use. In 1979 there were 27,192 telephones in the city.

The switchboards have frequently been supplemented and numerous other improvements tending to expedite service have been realized. Long distance communication was opened simultaneously with that at other points.

In former years all the wires were strung on telephones poles, but more recently these have been eliminated in the downtown

THE STORY OF PADUCAH

district by use of underground cables.

The Southern Bell Telephone and Telegraph Company which owns the properties in Paducah, employs sixty-five operators. The total working force numbers 103.

The introduction of the dial system has proven to be very helpful, saving time and giving faster service. Long distance as well as local calls are made by the individual patron from his or her home.

¹See Paducah Daily Democrat, March 31, 1854

CHAPTER XVII

SPHERE OF RELIGION

Spiritually inclined, the early residents of Paducah virtually worshipped as did believers of old--in forests and groves. They found a cathedral among the trees. Conditions in the youthful village of Paducah offered little encouragement for church extension, owing to absence of suitable places for public gatherings and the distance circuit riders had to come. But these hardy messengers persevered.

The faithful soon assembled in private homes for prayer service, or regular worship upon arrival of a circuit rider. Members of the few religious sects then in the community generally gathered at the home of a more zealous worker when the visiting minister came.

Methodists blazed the way toward organization by meeting for that purpose in a small schoolhouse which stood at the southwest corner of Third and Broadway. That was in 1834. Eight years later they built the town's pioneer church building.

Stirred by the passionate appeals of primitive divines of Baptist tenets, members of that faith banded into a unit in 1840 and erected a place of worship before the close of 1842. The Presbyterians followed by organizing in 1842 and building a church house four years later. Members of the Protestant Episcopal faith formed a congregation in 1846, and the Roman Catholic in 1848. The Christian communion dates from 1849, the Lutheran 1868, the Jewish 1868, the Evangelical 1874, the Christian Scientist 1900, and the Church of Christ 1908.

From these obscure beginnings has come a multiplication of churches, until in 1927 there were thirty-one for the white population alone. Eight of these were Methodist, seven Baptist, four Presbyterian, two Christian, two Lutheran, and two Churches of Christ.

The early clergymen were notably of a high order. Their splendid gifts were devoted to the elevation of society, the banishment of wrong, and the salvation of the world. Steadfastly contending for righteousness, they shook the bulwarks of entrenched wrong and made names for themselves that are heard to this day.

BROADWAY METHODIST*

Methodism is Paducah had its origin when a small group of worshippers assembled in a schoolhouse at Third and Broadway, in 1834. They met there regularly for a time at the instance of the Reverend George W. Martin and the Reverend George W. Cayce, who organized the congregation. The schoolhouse soon proved too small and the services were transferred to the courthouse, then at Second and Kentucky Avenue.

OLD BROADWAY METHODIST CHURCH AT SOUTHEAST CORNER SEVENTH AND BROADWAY.

In 1841 the members voted to construct a church home and the same year the Reverend James Young came as the first stationed preacher to what had now become an independent charge. Plans were drawn for a suitable place of worship and the building erected in 1842 at the northwest corner of Fourth and Broadway. It was a quaint structure, with the seats facing the entrance. This feature was evidently designed to spare the congregation the pangs of ungratified curiosity. It was the first church in the community for several months.

For thirty-three years this pioneer structure served as a place of worship, but under the leadership of the Reverend R. H. Mahon a larger church home was built in 1875 at the southeast corner of Seventh and Broadway. This was abandoned June 28, 1896, when the congregation moved into its commodious stone structure diagonally across the street, which represented an outlay of $80,000.

The first Board of Trustees consisted of Joseph G. Cole, S. S. Givens, James Brown, Henry L. Jones, James B. Husbands, M. Markland and David C. Peters. The Ladies Aid Society was organized in 1876, the Ramsey Society in 1885, and the Woman's Missionary Society in 1887. Under pastorate of the Reverend G. W. Wilson, the Epworth League became a reality in 1891.

Dr. E. C. Slater held the charge from 1863 to 1867, one of the most trying periods in the congregation's history. Strong partisans of either side of the Civil War constituted the Board of Trustees, and it was only with great tact that Dr. Slater united the scattered units during the dark days.

More than forty resident ministers have occupied the pulpit at the Broadway Methodist Church. These included Dr. Smith W. Moore, whose discourses were a train of iridescence. The Reverend E. B. Ramsey, who came to the charge in 1893, was a power in building up the church. Modest and unassuming, Dr. G.T. Sullivan, who occupied the pulpit at a later period, was yet a man of great popularity.

Dr. John L. Weber who assumed the pulpit November, 1919, was at once a ripe scholar, a superior orator, alike on the platform and in the pulpit, an exemplary citizen, and a distinguished patriot. His death in 1923 occasioned widespread sorrow. Following Dr. Weber came Dr. George B. Winton and Dr. T. W. Lewis, the latter in 1925.

A total of 203 new members were added to the church roll in 1926, bringing the membership up to 880. Extensive repairs were made to the handsome building in 1926, including redecoration of the interior.

Lighting struck the church on June 1, 1929, and it burned to the ground. Work began immediately for construction of a new building. The present sanctuary which stands at Seventh and Broadway was opened October 19, 1930. The cornerstone for the

Ford Annex was laid on November 16, 1969. Still another addition was added in 1970 called the Igert Fellowship Hall in memory of Mr. and Mrs. Louis Igert, Sr. through the generosity of their family.

The Reverend Nowell Bingham, pastor, came to Paducah from Grace Church, Memphis, Tennessee. The church has a large recreactional facility which includes a swimming pool. Mike Bostrom is the director.

Alben W. Barkley was a former member of the church.

FIRST BAPTIST

Organization of the First Baptist Church took place in the old county courthouse November 14, 1840, under direction of the Rev. James P. Edwards. In the latter part of 1842 the members built a brick structure costing $8,000 at No. 322 Broadway. There were twenty-one charter members.

Use of the church on Broadway was continued until the latter part of 1861, when it was seized by the Federal forces and used as a hospital. Services were then discontinued until after the Civil War, except in private homes.

At the close of the war the membership was brought together again and immediate steps taken to erect a new brick structure. To this end, the Norton family gave a site at the southwest corner of Fifth and Jefferson Streets with the understanding that it was to revert to the donors should the grounds be used for any other purposes. The congregation built a red brick edifice facing Fifth Street, from which rose a lofty spire. The tower contained a large bell and above this a huge clock.

Construction of a larger and more modern church plant was undertaken in May, 1914, and dedicated in June, 1916. The handsome building cost $125,000. When the old building was torn down the congregation was given a deed to the site. In 1920 the membership had grown to 1,229 while in 1927 it was approximately 2,000.

Dr. George C. Lorimer served the congregation as pastor for two years beginning in 1859. He was the father of George Horace

THE STORY OF PADUCAH

OLD FIRST BAPTIST CHURCH.

Lorimer, editor of the Saturday Evening Post. It was largely through efforts of another pastor of this church, the Reverend G. W. Perryman, that the city in 1902 received a $35,000 donation from Andrew Carnegie for establishment of a public library.

Among the most successful ministers at the church was Dr. M. E. Dodd, whose prodigious force, comprehensive sweep of thought, unquestioned piety, and often ornate expression made him an orator of great popularity. Another was Dr. S. E. Tull whose chief ability lay in his genius to unravel to simplicity, the most difficult and abstruse subjects. Dr. D. B. Clapp came to the congregation in February, 1922, and won favor for his fearless denunciation of sin of every character.

In protracted meetings and other campaigns the First Baptist Church has brought distinguished pulpiteers to its place of worship, the most prominent including Drs. T. T. Shields, J. Frank Norris and W. B. Riley. Dr. Riley conducted a ten days'revival in October, 1925.

A new church building of contemporary design was constructed at 2890 Broadway. Dedication services were held May 9, 1965. Under the leadership of Dr. John A. Wood and associate pastor, Mr. Robert Kersey, the congregation has grown to be one of the largest in Paducah.

A special feature of the church is the service under the stars. In the three months of summer the congregation moves to the out of doors for worship in the evening. Members and friends may attend and remain seated in cars if they so desire. Special programs are arranged for the Sunday evening services.

FIRST PRESBYTERIAN

Organization of the First Presbyterian Church dates from October 29, 1842, when the Reverend A. Wheeler Campbell called a meeting of those interested in that faith at the home of Judge James Campbell on Broadway. The charter members were: William Allen, Mrs. E. B. Allen, Nehemiah Woodbury, Mrs. E. B. Calhoun, Judge James Campbell, Mrs. Mary Campbell, George A. Flournoy and Mrs. Margaret Flournoy.

With only a handful of members, the Reverend Mr. Campbell held services in homes until the summer of 1843. The courthouse was then used and as interest grew the congregation voted to build a church home. A brick structure was raised in 1845 near the southwest corner of Third and Kentucky Avenue, under which the first pastor was buried following his death on January 9, 1848, at age 45. Services were held on South Third Street until 1888, when the property was sold. The next year (1889) the congregation moved into its ornamental brick home at the northeast corner of Seventh and Jefferson Streets.

Although it is one of the oldest congregations in the city, only ten ministers served as pastor to the year 1927. These were the Reverend A. W. Campbell, Dr. J. D. Matthews, the Reverend F. Senior, the Reverend L. H. Van Doren, Dr. J. T. Hendricks, Dr. W. E. Cave, Dr. H. W. Burrell, the Reverend Peter H. Pleune, the Reverend Cary R. Blain and the Reverend Armand L. Curry. Two of its ministers served more than twenty-five years each, Dr. Hendricks and Dr. Cave occupying the pulpit from 1859 to 1909.

Few churches have known such a galaxy of able preachers. Dr. Hendricks was of intense earnestness and wielded a great influence in the community. His successor, Dr. Cave, was equally sincere and moved great auditories by his persuasive power and striking personality. The Reverend Mr. Pleune, who assumed the ministry in March, 1916, and continued until October, 1920, was popular as a speaker both in and out of the pulpit, and bore the sobriquet "Everybody's Preacher". The Reverend Mr. Blain, who came in June, 1921, won favor with all who heard him. Arrival of the Reverend Mr. Curry in May, 1926, added another name to the list of those who successfully prosecuted ministerial duties at the church.

OLD FIRST PRESBYTERIAN CHURCH ON SOUTH THIRD STREET.

Revival meetings conducted within the walls of the First Presbyterian Church have attracted wide notice. One of the most successful was that of the Reverend W. P. Fife. In the winter of 1920, Dr. J. M. Vander Mulen reached hundreds during a two weeks campaign, and in January, 1923, Dr. J. E. Thacker aroused much interest.

The church was destroyed by fire in 1932 and the present building of Oxford Gothic styling, was erected during the ministry of Reverend Frederick Olert. In construction five kinds of rubble stone were used. Dedication services were held in December, 1933. The present pastor, (1979) is Dr. F. Harry Daniel who accepted the charge in October, 1978.

GRACE EPISCOPAL

Full of the romance of missionary effort and tears of self-sacrifice on the part of the faithful few, the Grace Episcopal Church stands as a monument to that small band of workers who met in the parlor at the home of Adam Rankin in 1846 and formed the congregation. The Reverend William M. Cowgill organized

THE STORY OF PADUCAH   193

the parish. Services were held in the courthouse until a frame church was constructed on the west side of South Second Street between Washington and Clark.

This building, which was built in Louisville and sent down the river by boat, was 30 by 60 feet. The windows were diamond-shaped and beautifully colored by General Lloyd Tilghman, who was a member. It served as a place of worship for twenty-six years, the Reverend William M. Pettis holding final services there June 14, 1874. The first vestry was composed of Adam Rankin, P. Marouse, F. M. Flournoy, A. Slee, Jacob Baker, O. G. Bullitt and J. Wyatt Jones.

During the Civil War the Federal troops used the church as a hospital, the rector, the Reverend Thomas J. Pickett, meanwhile having cast his lot with the south. To make room for hospital cots it was necessary to put the plain little wooden benches in the yard, where army mules "sharpened their teeth" upon their crude backs. The rectory adjoining the church became quarters for doctors and nurses.

At the close of the war the dilapidated building was returned to the congregation, now a scattered remnant. The benches were brought in and the congregation prepared for the first Easter service in three years. Consecrated women were decorating the neglected interior with a profusion of apple and cherry blossoms when the clatter of hoofs and the arrival of soldiers stopped them. They were told that President Abraham Lincoln had been assassinated and black draperies would have to be substituted. Whereupon trembling hands laid crepe over the gay colors.

The church was fortunate in securing the Reverend Mr. Pettis in 1869. He was a man of vision, faith and consecrated devotion. Plans for a new church were drawn and the project undertaken in 1873. The present edifice on the south side of Broadway near Ninth Street soon took form. The cornerstone was laid April 26, 1873. First services were held June 14, 1874, although the walls were not plastered and the window spaces remained open or partly covered with boards at that time. The members, far in debt for the noble undertaking were obliged to bring the old benches from the abandoned church overlooking the river.

By yielding their own interests and sacrificing at every turn, the faithful members cleared the debt. Stained glass was then placed in the windows, new seats procured, and a noble spire erected, giving the structure an ecclesiastical appearance comparable to any of its type in the South. The church seats 600 people.

The rectory was built in 1890 and the parish in 1904. An addition was made to the parish house in 1915.

The first rector was the Reverend Caleb Dow. Besides the Reverend Mr. Pettis, who was renowned for his deep spiritual insight and who was rector from 1869 to 1876, the church shared the labors of the Reverend David C. Wright from 1904 to 1910, and the gifted Clinton S. Quin from 1911 to 1916. Dr. Quin later became bishop coadjutor of the State of Texas. The Reverend Custis Fletcher came to the charge in February, 1918.

The Grace Episcopal Church remains one of the oldest and one of the most stately in the city. A new pipe organ has been added in recent years. The Rector Perry C. Burton serves the church at the present time. (1979) A Parish missioner, the same as a missionary in other churches, is a delegated place filled by the Reverend Tim Taylor, and he does it well.

ST. FRANCIS DE SALES ROMAN CATHOLIC

Formed in 1848 through the missionary efforts of the Reverend Father Elisha J. Durbin, the congregation of the St. Francis de Sales Roman Catholic Church is numbered among the oldest charges in the city. Assisting Father Durbin in organizing the church were Benjamin Austin, Mark Lydon, John Grief, Sebastian Glauber, Mrs. Mary E. Fisher, and Mr. and Mrs. Adrian Grief and their three sons, Frank, John and William. This small group and others who joined in the services met for a year at the home of John Grief.

Under guidance of the Reverend Father Durbin, the congregation purchased ground at the southeast corner of Sixth and

Broadway and built a small brick building there in 1849. Prospering with the years, the congregation outgrew its first quarters in twenty years and razing the old structure in 1869 began work on a more commodious house of worship. It was completed the following year.

Through the ministrations of able priests the congregation found need for larger quarters again. The old building, with its consecrated memories, was torn down to make room for an imposing structure suited to the requirements of the parish. The cornerstone was laid June 5, 1899, and an appropriate sermon delivered by the Reverend P. M. J. Rock of the Cathedral, at Louisville. Formal dedication occurred May 13, 1900. An impressive ceremony marked the occasion, which was widely attended.

OLD ST. FRANCIS DE SALES ROMAN CATHOLIC CHURCH.

Built of pitched face buff brick with Bedford stone trimmings and surmounted by two artistic domes gleaming in the sunlight, the St. Francis de Sales Roman Catholic Church suggests the Italian renaissance in its style of architecture. The windows are set with beautiful stained glass, and the elegant altars, attractive pulpit and handsome pews add dignity to the interior. The structure was erected during the pastorate of the Reverend Father H. W. Jansen, beloved priest who served the congregation from 1882 to 1909. He died in 1924.

Remaining with the congregation more than twenty-five years, the Reverend Father Jansen became one of the best known clergyman in West Kentucky. He was a prodigious influence in the community and was held in high esteem by members of all denominations. His successor was the Reverend Father Henry A.

Connolly, a scholar ripe and comprehensive, who resigned January 1, 1927, after seventeen years of faithful service. He retired to St. Joseph's Infirmary, Louisville, where he died in 1936 at age 87. In those years the Reverend Father Connolly had come to know and love Paducah, and departing in February, he responded to his poetic nature and wrote the following verses:

> Paducah dear, farewell, farewell.
> My love for thee no tongue can tell,
> Nor brain, nor mind, its depth can sound;
> It's e'er so strong, sincere, profound--
> Paducah dear, farewell, farewell.
>
> For years I've dwelt beneath thy dome
> And with thee always felt at home;
> Thou'st been so kind and true to me,
> While life shall last I'll think of thee--
> Paducah dear, farewell, farewell.
>
> May Heaven its smiles to thee e'er throw
> And naught but happiness may thou know;
> To heights sublime move ever on
> And thy dear God e'er lean upon--
> Paducah dear, farewell, farewell.

The Reverend Father John D. Fallon took up the ministerial duties in the early part of 1927. A new priests' home, corresponding in design to the church, was built immediately back of the church in the summer of 1927. The present pastor (1979) is the Reverend Paul P. Powell.

FIRST CHRISTIAN

Formation of the First Christian Church dates from the spring of 1849, when Elder Robert Rice organized the congregation with twenty-six members. For the first year services were held in the Enders building on the river front, awaiting completion of a frame church costing $600, at 405 South Second Street. The lot was donated by the Woolfolk family.

Enjoying a steady growth under the ministry of the Reverend J. C. Walden, the first minister, and his successors, the congregation in 1867 elected to build a larger and more substantial place of worship. Brick was chosen for the structure. The church was built at 212 North Fourth Street.

THE STORY OF PADUCAH   197

In less than twenty years more commodious quarters were required. A plan was set on foot in 1895 to erect a handsome church edifice suited to the needs of the expanding congregation, and on September 24 of that year the cornerstone was laid for the $30,000 structure on the southeast corner of Seventh and Jefferson Streets. A handsome annex was built on the Seventh Street side in 1923, meeting the necessity for increased space for educational purposes. The annex cost $35,000 with equipment. Dedicatory exercises were in charge of the Reverend U. R. Bell, pastor, and Dr. E. E. Violette of Kansas City, Mo.

In its sphere of activity the First Christian Church has been particularly fortunate in having men of more than ordinary ability as pastors. These included Dr. George E. Flower (1847-1884), whose preaching was distinguished by superb rhetoric, vigor of thought and dramatic power. Dr. L. H. Stine, a graduate of Harvard University, was a scholarly divine whose thought was fresh and rare, well out of the ordinary paths. During the eleven years of his pastorate, the Reverend W. H. Pinkerton became known as a sound reasoner.

FIRST CHRISTIAN CHURCH ON NORTH FOURTH STREET.

From 1915 to 1920 the pulpit was occupied by the Reverend Roy Rutherford, except for the year of the war when the popular young minister served as Y.M.C.A. worker in the camps. He was succeeded by the Reverend E. W. Elliot, who resigned shortly on account of illness. The Reverend U. R. Bell took the charge in October, 1922, and became noted for his grace of manner and fluency of speech.

In bringing Dr. E. E. Violette to the church in 1920 for an

evangelistic effort, the congregation made a distinct contribution to the city's revival history. His addresses were a train of brilliance, soaring, careening, coruscating, and yet so in keeping with the speaker that it seemed nothing was more befitting the occasion.

The First Christian Church--Disciples, built a sanctuary at 415 Audubon Drive and the congregation dedicated the new building in 1965, under the leadership of the pastor Reverend Herbert J. Simpson, B. D. It is beautifully located in a new area. Reverend Simpson has served the church since 1961.

ST. PAUL'S EVANGELICAL LUTHERAN

At the instance of the Reverend Bernard Sickel, a group of Lutherans met in the old Cumberland Presbyterian Church at 311 South Third Street May 24, 1868, and organized the St. Paul's Evangelical Lutheran Church. Among those prominent in organizing the congregation were Henry Diehl, Sr., Ferd Hummel, Sr., Henry Mammen, Sr., and Louis C. Kolb.

For five months the newly-formed congregation worshipped in the Cumberland Presbyterian Church through courtesy of that body, after which services were held in a small frame building just completed for that purpose at 416 South Fourth Street. With the church home a reality and a degree of permanency assured, the congregation filed incorporation papers January 26, 1869.

Two years later a resolution was passed calling for a more pretentious structure equal to the needs of the growing congregation. This undertaking meant real sacrifice--an heroic effort destined to stand more than fifty years as testimony to the self-denial, consecration and abounding faith of Lutheran pioneers in West Kentucky. The brick structure was formally dedicated January 7, 1872. A tower with belfry was added at a later period and, in 1909, the church was enlarged, the interior redecorated and handsome pews provided.

While the charge was served variously from 1868 to 1873 by the Reverend Mr. Sickel and other missionaries, the congregation secured its first regular pastor in the Reverend B. J.

THE STORY OF PADUCAH 199

Ansorge.After eight years he was succeeded by the Rev. Emil Knappe, whose ease of utterance received the advantage of learning. The Reverend Mr. Knappe remained with the congregation from 1881 to 1893. Sermons by the Reverend J. H. Hartenberger were published in book form; he occupied the puplit from 1898 to 1901.

Nine clergyman administered to the regular duties of the communion. The Reverend A. C. Ilten was a fluent speaker and performed meritorious service during his three-year stay. He was followed in 1907 by the Reverend William Grother, a young divine who spent more than a decade in building up the congregation. Majestic in build, stentorian in voice, and highly gifted in oratory, the Reverend Mr. Grother enjoyed great popularity.

Ferd Hummel, Jr., rendered faithful service for many years as the congregation's president.

Celebration of the golden anniversary of St. Paul's Evangelical Lutheran Church on September 18, 1921, occurred during the ministry of the Reverend Gerhard Groerich and was an event that attracted much notice. A young man imbued with energy and enthusiam, the Reverend Mr. Groerich began his ministrations in 1921 and won instant favor.

In the year 1929, St. Paul'sLutheran congregation built a nursery and kindergarten school at 211 South 21st Street. It was very successful and has operated for a number of years. Later in 1939 a sanctuary was constructed. A new pipe organ was installed in 1964. The Reverend Paul Donner has served the church as pastor for thirteen years(1979).

TEMPLE ISRAEL (JEWISH)*

Incorporated May 24, 1893, Temple Israel (Jewish) succeeded Kelo Kodesh Bene Yeshurum, which in turn succeeded Paducah Chevra Yeshurum Burial Society, chartered February 20, 1864. Plans were set in motion for Jewish worship in the fall of 1868, and the first services of New Year and the Day of Atonement were held on the third floor over a dry goods store at Second and Broadway. The services were continued there until a place of worship was built.

Organization of the B'nai B'rith Lodge in 1870 marked a step toward building a house of worship. M. Livingston was named chairman of a committee to purchase a lot and construct a modest synagogue. A two-story frame building went up on the east side of South Fifth Street between Clark and Adams. It was built at a cost of $2,500 and dedicated in September, 1871. Meyer Lieber served as the first president and Henry Burgauer secretary, and Rabbi Leon Leopold took charge of the flock.

Confirmation exercises held in connection with the "Feast of Shevouth", in 1872 packed the little building with an audience that witnessed the impressive occasion. There were six confirmants. The choir, which has always formed an important part of the services as well as in Paducah musical circles, rendered especially appropriate numbers for the event.

When the congregation built its handsome synagogue at the southwest corner of Seventh and Broadway in 1893, the name was changed from Kelo Kodesh Bene Yeshurum. This change occurred while Rabbi M. Ungerleider was in charge, one of the outstanding rabbis in the history of Paducah Jewry.

Other prominent men among the serving rabbis the congregation has know include Dr. Morris Fluegal, author of several volumes on religious subjects, who served from 1888 through 1889. Rabbi Meyer Lovitch took charge in 1912, and enjoyed a wide reputation as an orator and earnest worker.

Taking the pulpit in 1918, Rabbi Pizer H. Jacobs gained wide favor as a speaker. His voice was sonorous, rolling and rich; it rose gradually and the audience was not aware that the thunder was going to roar until it found itself in the center of the storm.

Rabbi H. R. Richmond assumed the pulpit in 1926 and at once became active in all phases of religious and civic life.

In 1963 Temple Israel moved to 330 Joe Clifton Drive where the congregation had erected a house of worship.

Rabbi Anthony Holz occupies the pulpit at the present time (1979).

UNITY EVANGELICAL AND REFORMED

Called together by Reverend D. Eschenbrenner on August 16, 1874, a small band of men and women organized the Unity Evangelical and Reformed Church on that date and rented an old schoolhouse at 431 South Third Street for religious services. Two years later the building was bought and converted into a church house, formal dedication taking place the next year, 1877.

Combining a tale of self-sacrifice and rugged determination, the early years of the congregation were marked with hardships but eventual victory. The first officers were Jacob Karch, president; Henry Heube, secretary; Paul Mattil, treasurer, and William Nagel and Charles Smith, elders.

Through constant effort on the part of faithful ministers and the congregation as a whole, an attractive new church home was built in the spring and summer of 1894 at 423 South Fifth Street. A large pipe organ was installed in 1896. Further improvements followed with the years, including erection of a modern Sunday school room in 1915 and conversion of the old quarters and church proper into a spacious auditorium for regular worship. Frank L. Rinkleff served as Sunday school superintendent from July, 1907 for many years.

OLD UNITY EVANGELICAL CHURCH ON SOUTH THIRD STREET.

In its long and successful period of activity the congregation has known fine pastors as leaders. The Reverend J. H. Digel, the third to have the charge, was pastor thirteen years and enrolled many new members. During the six-year pastorate of the Reverend B. Wulfman, the church debt was liquidated. The Reverend William Bourquin who succeeded the Reverend Mr. Wulfman in 1914 and who also served six years, did especially fine work in the Sunday School department. The congregation also was strengthened in various ways.

Due to the abounding personality and restless zeal of the Reverend H. C. Toelle, the congregation enjoyed both spiritual and numerical growth during his ministry. He assumed the pastorial duties in 1914 and remained until 1922. Deeply consecrated and of unquestioned piety, the Reverend E. C. Klutey took charge the latter part of 1922 and departed in August 1926.

The congregation observed a double anniversary in 1919--the forty-fifth anniversary of its founding and the silver jubilee year since erection of the church on South Fifth Street.

The last services at the church on South 5th Street were held on May 21, 1961 and on June 4, 1961 the new sanctuary at 4600 Buckner Lane was dedicated. It has since united with the United Churches of Christ and bears the name "The Unity Church--The United Church of Christ."

[2] For facts connected with the Broadway Methodist Church, the author has drawn largely upon "The Old and the New," a charming sketch written in 1869 by Miss Susan Morton and included in the booklet "Methodist Memories."

[1] Most of the facts relating to Temple Israel were taken from Isaac W. Bernheim's illuminating "History of the Settlement of Jews in Paducah and the Lower Ohio Valley", published in 1912.

CHAPTER XVIII

SPHERE OF RELIGION (Continued)

FOUNTAIN AVENUE METHODIST

Twenty-seven members composed the membership of the Fountain Avenue Methodist Church when that congregation met in an old store building at 511 North Tenth Street in 1892. It was organized by the Reverend G. W. Wilson, then the pastor of the Broadway Methodist Church following a revival conducted by the Reverend James Bigham in the downtown church.

Before the year 1892 closed a building committee was appointed to purchase a church site and erect a suitable frame structure not to cost more than $1,500. This committee was made up of C. W. Morrison, W. M. Karnes and J. M. Byrd. A lot was bought at 1051 Trimble Street and the building erected, known as the Trimble Street Methodist Church. The first pastor, the Reverend W. E. Sewell, served four years.

FIRST HOME OF FOUNTAIN AVENUE METHODIST CHURCH.

During the pastorate of the Reverend W. W. Armstrong the congregation voted to buy new church grounds and drew plans for a more pretentious home. It was deemed wise to continue the church in the western part of the city and accordingly a large lot was bought at the northeast corner of Fountain Avenue and Monroe Street, on which a handsome brick structure soon took form.

The edifice cost $25,000 and was dedicated as the Fountain Avenue Methodist Church on September 24, 1916. Members of the building committee were C. W. Morrison, B. T. Davis, B. J.

Billings and T. H. Bridges. A modern brick parsonage costing $7,200 was built immediately north of the church in 1921. The whole church plant in 1927 was valued at approximately $65,000. The sanctuary was remodeled and a pipe organ installed in 1945.

Strong men in the pulpit have been largely responsible for the growth in membership. Among the pastors were the Reverends J. W. Irion, E. R. Overby and R. A. Wood. The latter was succeeded in November, 1927, by the Reverend A. N. Goforth.

A. R. Steele served as Sunday school superintendent with unusual success, a position he held for many years.

Influential evangelists at the church in later years include the Reverend Burke Culpepper, who came in 1926, and the Reverend W. A. Swift in October, 1927.

Membership grew steadily through the years and now stands at 610 members. Additional floors have been added to the educational building and air conditioning throughout.

Dr. J. Allen Broyles is the present pastor. (1979)

MURRELL BOULEVARD CHRISTIAN

Resulting from a Sunday school organized in 1890 by L. M. Stein upstairs over a store at the southeast corner of Twelfth and Jackson Streets, the Murrell Boulevard Christian Church stood as a testimonial to the faith and perseverence of a handful of people who believed the time ripe for extension of religious activities.

Two years later, in 1892, P. B. Chalk and J. K. Bondurant advanced funds for the purchase of a building site at the northeast corner of Tenth and Ohio Streets, where the church was organized. A frame building was built on the site and served as a place of worship until it was outgrown. The first minister was the Reverend Mr. Egoff.

Prominent charter members included Miss Florence McCarty, C. E. Jennings, T. E. Judd and J. K. Bondurant. The latter served as Sunday school superintendent more than fifteen years.

The congregation was organized as the Tenth Street Christian Church but was changed to the Murrell Boulevard Christian Church when the old building was razed and the cornerstone of a

$47,500 structure laid October 1, 1922, the wide thoroughfare meanwhile gaining the name Murrell Boulevard. The handsome building, which seated 750, was dedicated March 18, 1923.

The Reverend Floyd A. Decker assumed the pastorate in October, 1925, and awakened much interest with a unique but persuasive combination of speech--a blend of exhortation, denunciation, pathos, humor and zeal that two years later gave the church a total membership of 450.

One of the best speakers to occupy the pulpit was the Reverend J. P. Bornwasser. Though young at the time he was pastor, the Reverend H. L. Calhoun is remembered among the best-informed ministers to hold the charge.

The flood of 1937 brought much damage to the church and it was in great need of renovation. At this time the congregation voted to join the membership of the First Christian at Seventh and Jefferson Streets whose shepherd was the Reverend L.K. Bishop.

THIRD STREET METHODIST

Forty charter members constituted the organization membership of the Third Street Methodist Church when that congregation was formed October 11, 1883. The Reverend W. H. Leigh, under whose direction organization took place, was called as the first pastor.

By constant effort a place of worship was built in 1885, but this was partially destroyed by a storm in August 1890. A new building was needed and within a short time the frame church at 1121 South Third Street was completed and ready for occupancy.

The congregation has enjoyed a substantial growth. This has been due to the activities of earnest workers in the pulpit and dependable efforts on the part of the membership, which numbered 240 in 1927. Leading ministers have included the Reverends G. W. Banks, Ocie Marrs, James Jenkins, Jr., and C. A. Coleman. Among the outstanding evangels at the church was the Reverend George Tucker, who carried on protracted meetings in 1919 and 1923.

A new church building was constructed at the southwest corner of Fourth and Norton Streets and cornerstone laid October 24, 1937. The name was changed from Third Street Methodist to Aldersgate Methodist at this time.

Reverend Fred S. French is the present pastor (1979).

TRINITY METHODIST

While the Trinity Methodist Church was first organized November 9, 1881 in a building on South Fifth Street, the services were subsequently discontinued and the congregation in a sense disbanded. However, reorganization took place July 12, 1893, when fifteen persons signed the charter for a new church in the section known as Mechanicsburg. The Reverend J. A. Barnett was instrumental in reorganizing the congregation.

Choosing a lot on Short Street, the small band of worshippers erected a frame building which was used for more than three decades. It was known as the Mechanicsburg Methodist Church.

The cornerstone of a new brick structure was laid July 12, 1925. Rather than incur a heavy debt, only one unit was built which consisted of the basement, where all the services were held pending completion of the auditorium. The basement costing $10,000, was free of all indebtedness in 1927, and a fund started for further improvements.

Under the pastorate of the Reverend C. H. Rayl the building was completed. He served as leader, architect and builder. With all the members as helpers and having a willingness to work, a beautiful and spacious church was erected. Stones were secured when the old post office at Fifth and Broadway was razed and a new one one built there. These were used in the building of the Trinity United Methodist Church at 227 Farley Place formerly known as Short Street because of its length.

The Reverend James Calhoun is the present pastor.

IMMANUEL BAPTIST

Formed by twenty members of the First Baptist Church who procured letters and met January 21, 1894, the Immanuel Baptist Church thirty years later took rank with the largest congregations in the city and pointed to a record of worthy achievement. It was organized as the Second Baptist Church, but changed to its present name shortly before leaving the old building for more commodious quarters, which were completed in 1922 on the east side of Murrell Boulevard between Clark and Adams Street.

Despite its small membership at the time of organization, the congregation immediately set out to build a place of worship. A frame church was built at the southeast corner of Ninth and Ohio Streets and with the arrival of Lloyd T. Wilson regular services were begun July 1, 1894. The first deacons were J. F. Hawkins, N. J. Bowland and James M. Fuller.

By steady and consistent effort the congregation outgrew its church home and appointed a building committee to direct construction of a modern church plant. Completion of a dark mat brick structure with stone trimmings marked the occasion for a memorable service February 12, 1922, when it was formally opened for worship. It contained forty rooms in addition to the main auditorium, which with balcony seated approximately 1,000. The edifice was 64 by 122 feet and cost $65,000.

Since its beginning the church has been known for its missionary endeavors. Many young men have entered the ministry from its membership.

IMMANUEL BAPTIST
CONGREGATION'S
FIRST HOME.

Assuming the pastorate in January, 1917, the Reverend H. W. Ellis met with phenomenal success. Modest and unassuming, his delivery quiet and unostentatious, while his ability to organize is reflected in the handsome church home planned and built during his ministrations.

Prominent evangels have conducted meetings at the new church. Dr. M. E. Dodd visited the congregation upon its entering the spacious building and in addition to increasing the membership by fifty-two, raised $16,000 in cash pledges for the building fund. The Reverend E. Frank Adams, who left the congregation in 1909 to study for the ministry, returned for a notable revival in 1925. His animated discourses were reinforced by his commanding person, and he exerted a wide influence before capacity audiences. A revival of much interest was carried on the latter part of November, 1927, by Dr. J. B. DeGarmo.

Reverend Frank Norfleet, pastor in 1952, led the church to purchase a site on Buckner Lane for erection of a new church plant. Construction began on educational plant and interim sanctuary in 1958 and the congregation moved from Murrell Boulevard to the present location in 1959.

Reverend T. L. McSwain became pastor in 1963 and he set about to complete a sanctuary and additional facilities. This was completed and dedicated on November 6, 1966.

A lighted steeple rising 140 feet above building can be seen for miles around. Carillon bells were a gift of Mr. and Mrs. James Biggs, in memory of their son, Roger.

Dr. Earl Cubine is the present pastor with the Reverend Phil Tallent, as educational director. Mr. Evans Gremillion, leads and directs five choirs ranging in ages from four years through adults. He also has Jr. and Sr. youths who play the handbells.

EAST BAPTIST

Organized in 1891 as the Island Creek Baptist Church, the congregation shortly afterward changed its name to the East Baptist Church. There were fourteen charter members.

The year 1911 saw construction of a handsome brick church at the southwest corner of Clements Street and Powell Avenue, under the pastorate of the Reverend J. P. Riley.

Among the ministers who have held the charge was the Reverend H. C. Hopewell, well known as a reasoner and convincing speaker. He was pastor during 1917 and 1918. The Reverend A. W. Leigh assumed the pulpit in October, 1923, and won consideration by his courageous and devout character.

THE STORY OF PADUCAH 209

At the close of 1927 the church reported a membership of 337. In the year 1928 the church was remodeled with the addition of a basement. An educational plant behind the sanctuary was begun in 1944 and completed in 1949. An educational annex was completed in 1961 giving adequate space for Sunday school. The Reverend Thomas M. Atwood has pastored the church the past few years.

KENTUCKY AVENUE PRESBYTERIAN

Built at the southwest corner of Sixth and Kentucky Avenue, the congregation known as the Kentucky Avenue Presbyterian Church occupied an attractive brick structure which compared favorably with that of other downtown churches. The cornerstone was laid March 29, 1894.

Prominent in its ministerial history was Dr. J. R. Crawford, whose discourses were characterized by profundity of thought, classical diction and convincing logic. He was followed by Dr. W. F. Padgett in October, 1925, whose messages were marked by a deep spiritual note and scholarly presentation. Revival meetings held at the church have been fruitful in results and have drawn much notice. Mrs. Grace Ludwig swayed capacity audiences in 1917, and Dr. Richard W. Lewis addressed large numbers three years later.

The Reverend Charles Bunce who served the church twelve years had a vision of another church in another location and with vim and vigor a building site was secured and a brick Gothic structure at 28th and Broadway became Westminster Presbyterian Church. It was completed in 1951.

FIRST CHURCH OF CHRIST, SCIENTIST

Services among members of the Christian Science faith resulted in an organized society in Paducah in 1900. Growth in membership brought about church organization in 1912, known as the First Church of Christ, Scientist.

The church was incorporated under the laws of the State of Kentucky, having a charter to transact business, hold property and conduct services.

In 1922, the church purchased property at 1331 Broadway on the northeast corner of Fourteenth and Broadway, remodeling the house thereon for purposes of worship. The auditorium seated 200 persons.

A new sanctuary was constructed at 500 Joe Clifton Drive in 1972. It is of modern architecture and very inviting.

Mrs. Edwin Owen serves as first reader and Mrs. Prudence Mayer as second reader.

BROADWAY CHURCH OF CHRIST

New church homes in the city include the Broadway Church of Christ on the north side of Broadway at Nineteenth Street, a fancy red brick and concrete structure completed in September, 1923. Work was begun in March, 1923. It represents an expenditure of $25,000.

Sixty-five members constituted the board of organization which met in June 1908, under a large oak tree which stood opposite the Goebel Avenue Church of Christ, the congregation's first home. This building, a frame church completed in August, 1908, was located on Goebel Avenue, a thoroughfare just off the eastern end of Guthrie Avenue. While the frame church was under construction, services were held each Sunday morning under the oak tree nearby.

The Reverend G. Dallas Smith assisted in organizing the congregation. The deacons were M. L. Akers, Robert Farthing, J. M. Wordly and Wheeler Houser. The elders were Charlie Houser, Sr., W. H. Thompson, H. M. Cookie and J. W. Jones.

Among the ministers who served the congregation were Reverends W. T. Boaz, J. S. Haskins, C. M. Stubblefield, H. M. Phillips, Charles Taylor and Tipton C. Wilcox, the latter taking charge in 1927.

The Reverend Mr. Taylor, under whose leadership the modern church plant was obtained, took charge in 1920. Besides proving an excellent organizer, he was well known for his Biblical research, every scene and incident in the Bible seeming ready to respond to his bidding.

THE STORY OF PADUCAH   211

When the congregation abandoned its Goebel Avenue property the name was changed to the Broadway Church of Christ. The auditorium in the new church seats 750, including the balcony. A membership of 350 was recorded in 1927.

The Broadway Church of Christ located at 2855 Broadway will observe this year their 20th anniversary since moving into the new sanctuary.

Danny F. Cottrell is the present minister (1979).

NORTH TWELFTH STREET BAPTIST

The North Twelfth Street Baptist Church was organized November 8, 1907, with sixty-five members. Twenty years later the membership had advanced to 360, and the congregation had replaced its original frame building with a modern type structure.

Coming to the church as its first pastor, the Reverend John R. Clark served in that capacity nearly five years when he was succeeded by the Reverend E. T. Chapman, who held the charge three years. The Reverend A. C. Abney followed and remained two years, doing splendid work.

Marked growth came with the ministry of the Reverend Jesse Neal, a devout leader who took charge July 1, 1918. Through his efforts the congregation erected its new $30,000 brick home, completed in 1920. The institution had seventeen rooms, including the auditorium, which seated more than 500 persons.

In 1966 ground was purchased adjoining and a new sanctuary was built. The former sanctuary was converted into an educational building and fellowship hall. The church is located at 1249 North Twelfth Street.

Last year (1978) the church observed its seventy-fifth anniversary with a home-coming. It was truly a happy occasion. Reverend S. M. Maddox is the present pastor.

PARK AVENUE CUMBERLAND PRESBYTERIAN

Largely the story of faithful effort, the Park Avenue Cumberland Presbyterian Church at 1051 Park Avenue, stood as a voucher for the zeal and earnest endeavor of a small group of Christian workers who in March, 1907, met in the First Christian

Church and elected elders and deacons. Services were held in the courthouse through 1907, and then for several months in a hall at Twelfth and Broadway.

Long before this, however, the Cumberland Presbyterians built a church at 311 South Third Street, the Reverend R. Searcy taking charge upon its completion in 1849. Twelve years later the Civil War came on and services were discontinued. Occasional services were resumed in the church after the war, but in 1888 the members began meeting in a hall at the southwest corner of Seventh and Kentucky Avenue, having disposed of the church five years before. In 1907 the Cumberland Presbyterians reorganized anew and the congregation as it is now known resulted from that action.

Church property on the present site was acquired in 1908 from the Methodists (was old Fountain Avenue Methodist home) and the congregation took the name Trimble Street Cumberland Presbyterian Church. The name was changed in 1927 when Trimble Street was designated Park Avenue. Meanwhile extensive alterations were made and the church, of timber construction made more attractive.

The Reverend Joe McLesky held services in the courthouse. The Reverend D. W. Fooks came to the church as pastor in 1908 and served with success two years. Admired for his superior preaching the Reverend W. W. Rudolph, pastor from 1920 to 1927, brought many hearers to an understanding of Christianity and was eminently successful in building up the church.

The Park Avenue Cumberland Presbyterian Church burned and a new location on which to build was given by Mr. Gus Hank, Sr. To honor his wife, the church name was changed to Margaret Hank Memorial Cumberland Presbyterian Church. This was the year 1938. The Church stands at 1526 Park Avenue (formerly Trimble Street).

Dr. Tommy Thompson serves the congregation as minister. (1979)

THE STORY OF PADUCAH 213

ST. MATTHEW'S EVANGELICAL LUTHERAN

Organized in the county courthouse April 1, 1921, St. Matthew's Evangelical Lutheran Church adopted its constitution July 17 of that year, and affiliated with the national body known as the United Lutheran Church in America. The Reverend John B. Gardner assisted in organizing the congregation, which numbered fifty-eight members. These chose Ferd Hummel, Jr., president, and Fred Woelpert, treasurer.

Pending construction of a $3,100 wooden church at the southeast corner of Fifth and Jackson Streets, the congregation worshipped in the Kentucky Avenue Presbyterian Church. Completed in September, 1921, the church was formally dedicated October 16 following, at which time the Reverend William J. Boatman, the first regular pastor, took charge. Under his ministry the church debt was partly liquidated.

The Reverend J. W. Paetznick assumed the pastorate in November, 1924, remaining until March, 1926. The Reverend T. W. Brosche became pastor in June, 1926.

The cornerstone was laid at 2701 Broadway in 1937, which marked the beginning of construction of a new sanctuary for the congregation of St. Matthew's Lutheran Church. Dedication services were held in 1938. The pastor of the church at this printing is the Reverend Ronald Schoo who has served the church the last ten years. Assistant pastor is the Reverend Will Peugeot.

WEST END BAPTIST

Twenty-seven members constituted the board of organization of the West End Baptist Church, when that congregation was formed in July, 1923. A small building at the northeast corner of Twenty-eighth and Clark Streets served as the first place of worship.

Work on a $15,000 wooden church on the site was begun late in 1925 and completed early the next year, affording improved quarters for extensive development. The membership had grown to 208 in 1927.

The Reverend Charles S. Gregston was the congregation's first pastor, serving until October, 1926. He was succeeded in December of that year by the Reverend T. G. Shelton.

Plans were begun in 1956 to build at 324 South Twenty-eighth Street. West End Baptist Church was dedicated and occupied February 1, 1959. The Reverend Terry Sills is the present pastor (1979).

MIZPAH PRESBYTERIAN

Although organized as a mission in 1888, the Mizpah Presbyterian Church at 423 Elizabeth Street, did not become an independent congregation until 1924. The mission and Sunday school were organized as an adjunct to the First Presbyterian Church, during the ministry of Dr. W. E. Cave. A hall at Third and Broad Streets was first used and then a schoolhouse on Third Street, the present frame church taking form later.

Calling the Reverend O. W. Wardlaw as its pastor shortly after assuming an independent status, the congregation took new life under his ministry. Reverend Wardlaw's service continued until March, 1926. The Reverend Hugh E. Bradshaw took charge in the early fall of that year and through constant effort brought the membership up to eighty-eight in 1927.

NORTHSIDE METHODIST

Organized in November, 1925, as a neighborhood Sunday school, the Northside Methodist Church at Eleventh and Palm Streets is the result of an idea conceived by Mrs. T. Neil Jones, a prominent member of the Broadway Methodist Church who served as superintendent of the new Sunday school.

Mrs. Jones mailed out invitations to Methodists in the community and urged them to form a congregation. The idea met with an enthusiastic response and following a revival meeting in that vicinity the Northside Methodist Church was formed May 16, 1926, with twelve charter members. The Reverend H. J. DeShazo became the first pastor in November, 1926, serving until July of the next year when he resigned because of ill health. In November, 1927, the Reverend W. M. Tidwell became pastor.

Construction of a church home was begun within a year after

THE STORY OF PADUCAH   215

the congregation was formally organized. The attractive building of wood construction with a large assembly room and five Sunday school rooms patterned after larger and standard schools, was dedicated July 17, 1927. The church roll then numbered twenty-six active members.

The church now known as the Northside United Methodist Church moved to their new location at 1731 North 11th Street in 1952. The present pastor (1979) is Dr. Rufus Moore.

SEVENTH DAY ADVENTIST

With a membership of fifteen persons the Seventh Day Adventist Church was organized in 1906. Itinerant ministers held the services until a regular pastor was procured. From that time the congregation has grown steadily in number and spirit.

An attractive stucco church was built in 1919 of sufficient proportions to care for the needs of the congregation, which in 1927 numbered fifty-three members. It is located at 1901 Bridge Street.

The Reverend A. A. Davis, who served the church in its new home, was prominently identified with the growth and activities of the congregation.

UNION EVANGELISTIC CAMPAIGNS

It would be an inconsistency to speak of the religious life of Paducah and omit mention of the union evangelistic campaigns the city has known. In several instances a great spiritual renaissance resulted and the effects extended over a wide period of time.

Dixie Williams visited Paducah in 1891, pitching a large tent on the site once occupied by the Kentucky Avenue Presbyterian Church. Audiences numbering two thousand persons gathered for the seven o'clock or sunrise services, and an even greater crowd was present in the afternoon and evenings.

In the spring of 1893 the inimitable Sam P. Jones (1847-1906) conducted a three-weeks meeting at Tenth and Monroe Streets, in a tobacco warehouse. He ws accompanied by the Reverend George L. Stuart. The famous evangelist returned for another engagement in 1902. He was then at the height of his fame and thousands flocked to a huge tobacco barn then at the southwest corner of Murrell Boulevard and Broadway.

Rules of custom, routine and conventionality were thrown aside by the Reverend Mr. Jones in the second campaign, and the curious were drawn by the score. His kind heart and unbridled, witty tongue softened the hardest hearts and brought strong men to tears, many of whom, like those in Goldsmith's familiar poem, "remained to pray".

Dr. W. E. Biederwolf led a union movement in 1901 at the Broadway Methodist Church that attracted considerable attention. While not of a city-wide nature, the visit of Dr. E. E. Violette to the First Christian Church in 1920 was an outstanding event.

HUGE PINE TABERNACLE ERECTED AT TENTH AND BROADWAY FOR THE HAM-RAMSAY REVIVAL, 1927.

An evangelistic campaign of considerable proportions was that of Brown and Curry, conducted in a tobacco warehouse at the southwest corner of Murrell Boulevard and Broadway--a mammoth pine structure which replaced the old barn destroyed by fire. These meetings were in September, 1909. The Reverend John E. Brown was the speaker.

Much interest was aroused by the coming of Dr. R. A. Torrey in October, 1910. The union services were held in the warehouse at Murrell Boulevard and Broadway, with capacity audiences in attendance. He was perhaps the most colorful evangelist ever to appear in Paducah.

Dr. Torrey, internationally known as a Bible scholar and evangelist, was a fearless speaker, pursuing his convictions with earnest zeal and urging them upon vast auditories with the resources of an oratory that was hardly more impressive than it was many-sided. The crowds joined heartily in singing such hymns as "Just When I Need Him Most" and "O That Will Be Glory".

Thousands attended the revival conducted by Dr. E.J. Bulgin in October, 1923, in the warehouse at Murrell Boulevard and Broadway, shortly before that large building was razed. His graphic word pictures and dramatic appeals had wide effect and brought hundreds to repentance. Dr. Bulgin's party included the Reverend Al Carter as song leader, and Alvin Roper as pianist. Hymns featured were "He Keeps Me Singing" and "I Was There When It Happened", while "The Gospel Train" was immensely popular with the railroad element.

Approximately one thousand coversions resulted from the eight-weeks campaign staged under a tent 100 by 190 feet at the southeast corner of Murrell Boulevard and Broadway by Howard S. Williams in September and October, 1924. It was a notable event in connection with the city's religious life and shook the community from center to circumference.

Mr. Williams, a layman evangelist of magnetic personality and boundless energy, launched a campaign designed to quell vice and create new spiritual life. The brilliancy of his discourses was fascinating and each evening he threw a spell over great audiences that was irresistible. His equipment included a radio broadcasting unit. The tent seated 4,500 persons.

In the Williams party was M. E. Perry, song leader, who afterwards joined the Immanuel Baptist Church as musical director. While the campaign hymn "Somebody Else Needs a Blessing" was sung each evening as Mr. Williams mounted the platform, other numbers included "He's a Wonderful Savior to Me" and "My Anchor Holds".

The Reverend Walt Holcomb held a potent meeting under two

tents at the same site in September, 1925. New songs characterized the services, such as "The Call of Christ", "A New Name in Glory" and "I Have Heaven Here".

An independent campaign of wide influence was the Ham-Ramsay revival beginning January 17, 1927, and lasting through March 22. Despite inclement weather immense crowds attended and more than 600 conversions resulted.

Preceding the meeting, a pine tabernacle 118 by 176 feet was built at the southeast corner of Murrell Boulevard and Broadway, containing seats for 4,800 persons. The choir contained 600 seats. An inquiry room 30 by 80 feet was built in addition. The huge building was razed following the campaign.

Assisting Dr. Mordecai Fowler Ham, the evangelist, were two prominent co-workers, William J. Ramsay, song writer and choir director, and Earl S. Rodgers, expert pianist. Dr. Ham was calm, deliberate, persuasive of manner and speech, and his discourses sparkled with rare gems of diction.

An elaborate pageant in which 270 girls participated, jammed the building and sidewalks with more than 8,000 persons on the evening of February 11.

Among the songs which proved popular were two of Mr. Ramsay's composition "My Grace Is Sufficient" and "My Heart Is Fixed On Jesus".

CHAPTER XIX

IRVIN S. COBB[1]

World-wide fame attaches Paducah as the home of Irvin S. Cobb, the author. Due to frequent references to his birthplace, the famous writer has given the city an international reputation.

Born June 23, 1876, Irvin S. Cobb was the first son and second child among four children born to Joshua Clark Cobb and Manie Saunders Cobb. An aunt suggested the name "Irvin", while the middle name "Shrewsbury" was given in honor of Captain Joel Shrewsbury, an intimate friend of the father. The boy was born in a two-story frame house on the west side of Third Street between Washington and Clark Streets, then the attractive home of his maternal grandfather, Dr. Reuben Saunders. The home was torn down in 1914.

He had hardly reached the age of three when he began drawing pictures and at four was showing amazing skill. His parents taught him the alphabet. When he was seven they sent him to Miss Mary Gould, who conducted a private school where Hotel Irvin Cobb now stands. He next attended the public schools, his teachers including Miss Nannie Clark, Miss Adah Brazelton, Miss Mary O. Murray and Miss Mary Dodson. In the fall of 1890 he went to Professor William A. Cade's Academy, part of which still stands as the Adah Brazelton School.

As a student, the lad showed proficiency in literature and history, along with drawing. He revelled in the classics. Further reading outside the class room broadened his knowledge and added to his maturity of thought. His power of memory was astonishing and he rarely forgot anything. All studies came easy except mathematics. He quit Cade's Academy in the early summer of 1892.

Eager to work through the summer, the boy got a job driving an ice wagon. As the winter approached business became slack and his father asked him how he would like newspaper work. He grew enthusiastic at the thought, and January 16, 1893, appeared at the editorial room of the Paducah Daily News for assignments. He was then sixteen. The first day he wrote only one item, as follows:

> Cal Evitts, the efficient and popular market master, says there were more rabbits brought to the local market this week than any week this winter. Molly Cottontails sold this morning for ten cents dressed or five undressed.

Within a few weeks he was gathering and writing news stories of almost every character--social notes, court proceedings, accidents, deaths and political rallies. Two years later he was made head reporter, at ten dollars a week, turning in four or five columns a day. When the managing editor went into another business in 1896, the youth was promoted to the post.

He remained in this capacity until 1898 when he joined the staff of the Louisville Evening Post. For three years he did regular reporting and in addition conducted a humorous column called "Sour Mash", which struck popular fancy.

In 1901 he came back to Paducah as managing editor of the Paducah Democrat, a new daily which merged a few months later with the Paducah Daily News. Mr. Cobb remained in this capacity until the early part of August, 1904, when he went to New York City. His first work there was on the Evening Sun, where he did "leg" work. This consisted of getting the major facts of a news story and telephoning them in to a re-write man.

The Paducahan was sent to Portsmouth, New Hampshire, the latter part of August, 1905, to write the story of the Russian-Japanese Peace Conference. For three weeks he sent back daily sidelights touched with a breadth of vision and human understanding. This series won him a place on the Evening and Sunday World, where his chief work was feature writing.

Daily stories were carried besides his humorous articles in the Sunday edition. The latter included "Live Talks With Dead Ones", "New York Through Funny Glasses" and "The Diary of Noah",

THE STORY OF PADUCAH   221

which was syndicated all over the country. Meanwhile Mr. Cobb reported the Harry K. Thaw trial, writing 600,000 words in longhand. It gave him a chance to "spread".

But his finest performance during the six years he spent on the Gotham newspapers consisted of two articles descriptive of the New York Horse Show. The word pictures were brilliant and picturesque. Humor punctuated some of the lines. In describing the women's evening costumes, he wrote: "I do not know much about this sort of thing, and when I looked at these women I did not know whether they were dressed for an opera or an operation".

Mr. Cobb took up magazine writing in 1911, joining the Saturday Evening Post staff that year. A short story appeared and then humorous articles, after which the Judge Priest[2] stories made their bow in *Words and Music*. Nearly everything Mr. Cobb wrote for the next dozen years was printed in the Philadelphia weekly before coming out in book form. In 1923 he became a regular contributor to Cosmopolitan and other well known magazines.

Ten short stories of the Judge Priest variety appeared in 1912 in a book called *Back Home*, Mr. Cobb's first volume. *Words and Music* heads the list and is followed by other well-written tales like *A Judgement Come to Daniel*, which relates the community's riddance of an undesirable character, and *Up Clay Street*, recording Judge Priest's manner of pleasing a youthful shut-in by having the circus parade pass his house. As in the case of all Judge Priest narratives, the locale is the author's home town.

Another collection came out in 1915 under the title *Old Judge Priest*. Each story treads on the heels of perfection. The first, *The Lord Provides*, tells how the old judge arranged a church funeral in keeping with an unfortunate girl's dying request. Several stray yarns of the Judge Priest type have appeared in Mr. Cobb's later books.

The Escape of Mr. Trimm, a book published in 1913, is named after the first tale in the volume, one of the best the author has done. There are three other tragic conceptions among the nine yarns--*Fishhead*, in which the three characters meet a baffling

IRVIN S. COBB.

end, *The Belled Buzzard*, and *An Occurence Up a Side Street*.

Mr. Cobb's next book of fiction, *Local Color*, also received its title from the initial story within its covers. The volume contains *The Great Auk*, which Edward J. O'Brien classed among the best short stories written in 1916. While this was Mr. Cobb's fourth volume of short stories, it was his eleventh book to date, for he had meanwhile gone into the field of humor and description.

An outstanding yarn in *Those Times and These* (1917) is called *Hark! From the Tombs*, giving an account of a New Year's party staged by darkies which very nearly results in a stampede as strange sounds are heard at the midnight hour.

Nine short stories make up the story-teller's eighteenth book, *From Place to Place*, which came from the press in 1920. It is featured with *Boys Will Be Boys*, wherein Peep O'Day looms alongside Judge Priest. The story is of exceptional merit and was well received both in printed form and on the screen.

In 1922 another full-size book of yarns appeared under the caption *Sundry Accounts*. Of the ten, *Darkness*, a finished mystery story laid in Paducah, and *A Short Natural History* take the lead. The latter is a tremendously funny account of a superstitious darky led through a dozen side-splitting situations. Two Judge Priest yarns are also wedged between the covers, *The Cater-Cornered Sex* and *Alas, the Poor Whiffletit!*

Production of *J. Poindexter, Colored*, Mr. Cobb's first novel which was undertaken in 1922, received favorable recognition all over the country.

Five years later (1927) this premiere was followed by his second full-length novel, *Chivalry Peak*, which merited even wider praise both in America and Europe. The story receives its name from a mountain in the northwestern part of the United States, which the natives had corrupted into *Shivery Peak*. A swindler fools the mountaineers into the land, and visiting the country some years later is recognized by Boone Ransom, who holds up the train as it departs and takes the grafter's valuable papers. Detectives are put on the case, including a girl, Joan, who finds Ransom at the top of Shivery Peak. There he shows her the Swindler's documents, all worthless paper. Finally, there is love on both sides.

Meanwhile he continued to prosecute the story-teller's art and his publishers brought out *Snake Doctor*, bearing the name of the initial yarn which won the O. Henry Memorial Award committee's first prize for the best short story of 1922. It is an extraordinary tale, gripping to the last degree. In attempting to get Snake Doctor's supposed fortune, Japhet Morner pricks his hand and dies from imaginary "snake-bite". Two Judge Priest narratives in the book are not likely to be neglected, --*That Shall He Also Reap* and *His Mother's Apron Strings*.

The year 1924 witnessed publication of *Goin' On Fourteen*, twenty-nine stories bearing on the adventures of the author and his boy companions around that age. Paducah and its environs offers the back ground. There are such alluring chapter-titles as *One of Those Dull Afternoons, P. T. Barnum Passes Through* and *A Lady Cat Goes on a Journey*. The latter is undoubtedly one of the funniest bits of fiction the writer has done, chronicling the lightning activities of a scared cat that found its way into a lamp store at Third and Washington Streets with a salmon can over its head. In telling how the "unbalanced thing" got started and its subsequent actions, the author says in part:

> We may safely figure that our cat's recessional only began to attract attention and comment when she reached and had entered Pettus' lamp store at the intersection of Locust and Washington Street, an outpost of the main business district. In the interim we may figure her as going with high velocity along, by alternating spells a living projectile, a blind ungovernable pouncing force, a paroxysm, a seeming violation of all natural and physical laws and, even so, absolutely unobserved. So, then, by leaps and bounds, fleetly yet erratically moving, she brings herself and us to Pettus' corner.
>
> The proprietor, Mr. O. D. D. Pettus, better known as Mr. Odd Pettus, was alone when the interruption came. The first suspicion Mr. Pettus had that anything out of the ordinary impended came as he himself stated later, when he heard--but let us give his own stirring description in his own graphic words:
>
> All of a sudden there was a kind of a scrambling, scrabbling sound out front, like as if something alive was spinning around out there, and then a showcase breaking and things beginning to smash off the shelves. Only these sounds didn't seem to be coming separately--not in succession, I mean. It was more like as if they all hap-

THE STORY OF PADUCAH

"THE DUKE OF PADUCAH" IS REMINDED OF A STORY

pened, as you might say, right together, or anyways so close together that you couldn't scarcely pick out one from the other.

"So, naturally, with that I came running out from behind to see what was the matter, and I never had such a jolt in my life. Something or other--it was moving so fast I couldn't make out then what it was, but it was about two feet long, more or less, and it was covered all over with stiff black hair and it was screeching and spitting all the time in a curious kind of a choked-up way, and it had about ten or twelve legs, seemed like, or maybe more, and there was a funny looking kind of a fancy tinware coupling capped on to one end or the other of it, but which end I couldn't tell, not at first, but I did in a minute--well, anyhow, this here crazy whatyoumaycallum was going like a streak of greased lightning along that further shelf yonder, stripping it bare as it went and knocking brand new coal oil lamps every which-a-way.

"Don't ask me where it came from, or what it was aiming to do, if anything, by cutting up all those didoes, or whatever possessed it to pick out that shelf to swarm up on, or even how it got up there in the first place. Because I can't tell you any one of those things. But I can tell you how it got down, because I saw that part myself.

"When it got through cleaning off that shelf its entire length--with me standing there, as you might say, just so absolutely dumbfounded I couldn't make a move--why, about that time it butted into a cross brace, and with that it seemed to sort of hunch up and right quick stretch out again, same as a chunk of rubber, and next minute it'd fell out and landed on top of that other showcase and cracked it across the top, too, and then dove off of there and lit on the floor and capered around a little bit more in a kind of a general direction, as you might say.

"Then, it seemed to get organized and skedaddled out of the side door, tail first, like a crawfish--only no crawfish ever traveled as fast as this varmint did--and was gone like a flash; and me left here with my mouth hanging wide open, and up to my knee joints, pretty near it, in ruin and destruction. The whole thing happened so quick that if it hadn't 'a 'been for this here mess of busted lamps and smashed lamp chimneys all over the floor and the holes in both them showcases and all, I could almost 'a 'sworn it was a dream, I could so."

Alias Ben Alibi is a series of interrelated stories about a big city editor and *Here Comes the Bride* is a collection of miscellaneous essays, drenched in humor and seasoned with wisdom. Both books appeared in 1925. The latter volume opens with a chapter in keeping with the book's title, an amusing account of weddings and the tumult preceding them. Then follow *The Funniest Thing That Ever Happened to Me*, an incident that occurred in Germany, *Who's Who at Our Zoo* and *Our National Holidays*, to mention only a few chapter headings. It is one of the most entertaining of all the books in the Cobb family.

Laughter and tears abound in the story-teller's epic of Manhattan, *On An Island That Cost $24* (1926). The contents represent first class literature and combine situations at once dramatic and true to life.

An admirable book termed *Prose and Cons* came from the bindery in the summer of 1926. It was suited to all tastes, the first part consisting of six short stories and the last half a quartet of humorous philosophies. The book leads off with *The Chocolate Hyena*, a dark-town adventure in vaudeville. Further on the author tells about his first pair of long pants, and also the thrill received from tying a tin can to a dog's tail. Encountering a funeral procession, the yelping canine continued through it, with the result that the hearse overturned and the corpse tumbled out. The delightful chapters are brought to a close with a somewhat elaborate sketch of the ages of man, wherein the author reverts to Paducah for the following story:

> The richest man I ever knew had trouble sometimes when paying his poll tax. His check would have come back from the bank, but his face was good for any amount among children: for he had mastered the art of getting old gracefully and gently--or else it came to him naturally. People were happier for his having lived among them; and he was the happier for it too.
>
> He had been a soldier, and his was the side that lost too; but I never heard him speak a harsh word or a bitter one against the winners. He belonged to no church, but he preached the broadest and the kindest and the lovingest doctrine that one might hope to hear. I do not mean to imply by this that he lacked convictions, for he had them and the courage of them; but he conceded that other people had a right to their opinions.
>
> In time those afflictions of age that Shakespeare has described came upon him. His figure, which had been arrow-straight, bent under the burden of his three-score and ten years; yet, seeing him so, you thought of the simile of a kindly old tree drooping, with each recurring season, ever nearer and nearer the earth that had nurtured it. His brain stayed clear--the old tree was not dying at the top first.
>
> His eyes grew dim, but the fires of an unquenchable youthfulness still flickered genially in them. His voice cracked, but became as certain bells that chime all the sweeter for having cracks in them. He was alone in the world, but he was not lonely. A whole community loved him.
>
> Finally one day he fell asleep. When he woke he was in the company of those kindly and tolerant old philosophers whose sayings he had so loved to repeat. I

remember that it snowed on the day of his funeral. Through the whirling white flurries the sorrowing town came to see him laid away, and the snow had covered the mound with a soft white covering almost as soon as the spade of the sexton shaped it and smoothed it. A millionaire might have envied him then, for his funeral was another one of those things that money cannot buy.

Two more books, *Ladies an Gentlemen*, made up of short stories that are humanly pathetic and mordantly funny, and *Some United States*, a series of novel articles appeared in the early part of 1927.

Humor is one of Mr. Cobb's chief roles. His contribution to this phase of American literature is notable, for he ranges all the way from a conversational jester to a book-wit. The first book to come from his pen along this line was *Cobb's Anatomy*, which like several other of his books was also published in London. It deals with "Tummies", teeth, hair, and hands and feet. In discussing "Hair", he says in part:

> Your hair gives you bother as long as you have it and more bother when it starts to go. You are always doing something for it and it is always showing deep-dyed ingratitude in return; or else the dye isn't deep enough, which is even worse. Hair is responsible for such by-products as dandruff, barbers, wigs, several comic weeklies, mental anguish, added expense, Chinese revolutions, and the standard joke about your wife's using your best razor to open a can of tomatoes with. Hair has been of aid to Buffalo Bill, Little Lord Fauntleroy, Samson, The Lady Godiva, Jo-Jo, the Dog-Faced Boy, poets, pianists, some artists and most mattress makers, but a drawback and a sorrow to Absalom, polar bears in captivity and the male sex in general.

The same year (1913) saw *Cobb's Bill of Fare*, touching on "vittles", music, art and sport, colored from his own reservoir of observation, imagination, philosophy and feeling. He recalls his adventure in a sailboat "not much larger than a soap dish" when "the waves were slopping up and down, and giving to the water that dark forbidding appearance that is so inspiring in a marine painting, but so depressing when you are thrown into personal contact with it".

Next came *Roughing It De Luxe*, word pictures describing everything from the Grand Canyon to the Golden Gate as seen through a funny-man's glasses, and *Europe Revised*, written while abroad and the most talked-of book on foreign travel since Mark Twain's *Innocents Abroad*.

228　THE STORY OF PADUCAH

The year 1915 marked appearance of his very amusing book, *Speaking of Operations--*, which followed his stay in a hospital. Although small in size, the volume is a vast wedding of wit and wisdom, and is adjudged the "funniest book in the world". The way the doctors and nurses came into his room without knocking caused him to remark that he was "not having any more privacy than a goldfish"--a felicitous figure of speech which seems likely to become the most famous of all similes.

Three other books with a humorous tang followed --*Fibble, D. D., Eating in Two or Three Languages* and *The Life of the Party*. A large book, *The Abandoned Farmers* (1920), bore on the author's retreat from the city to the farm. The next year a slender volume entitled *A Plea for Old Cap Collier* came out as a defense of the dime novel of his youth.

With comments as savory as Charles Lamb's *Dissertation on Roast Pig*, the genial Paducahan wrote *One Third Off* in 1921. It records his processes of weight reduction. Incidentally he states

SPEAKERS' TABLE AT IRVIN S. COBB BANQUET GIVEN IN HONOR OF HIS FIFTIETH BIRTHDAY.
Left to right: R.B. Phillips, Mrs. O.B. Powell, Fred G. Neuman, Mrs. R.B. Phillips, Elliott C. Mitchell, Irvin S. Cobb, Dr. O.B. Powell, Mrs. Manie S. Cobb, Robert H. Davis, Mrs. Elliott C. Mitchell, Mrs. Fred G. Neuman, Judge E.W. Bagby.

his favorite dish--hog jowl and turnip greens.

Two large books called *A Laugh a Day Keeps the Doctor Away* and *Many Laughs for Many Days* contain a part of Mr. Cobb's storehouse of jokes. These seven hundred anecdotes display his story-telling skill. Popular among after dinner speakers as well as for straight reading, the morsels of humor have furnished entertainment for all classes. Both books rate high on the nation's laugh meter.

Some United States, published in 1927, offers a variety of merriment in picturing the quirks, foibles, habits and mannerisms peculiar to geographical sections of the country. There is laughter all the way through, but atop it a sound philosophy. Seventeen distinct parts of his native land are touched by the glare of his hilarious pen. The Kentucky sketch bears witness that "from center to circumference, from crupper to hame, from pit to dome, a Kentuckian is all Kentuckian". In speaking of California, he finds one city there excels in good-looking women, closing the chapter with the declaration that "when it comes to pretty women, San Francisco is the Paducah, Ky., of the Pacific Slope".

E. V. Lucas, the English essayist, comments on the Paducahan's humorous writings in his *From An American Notebook*. He says: "Beneath Mr. Cobb's fun is a mass of ripe experience and sagacity. However playful he may be on the surface, one is aware of an almost Johnsonian universality beneath. It would not be too extravagant to call his humor the bloom on the fruit of the tree of knowledge."

Mr. Cobb has often written and spoken of the glories of the Bluegrass State. On one occasion he wrote:

Kentucky being the State where I was born and where I grew up, it is natural that I should love her. But there are other reasons than this one to make me love her. To me she is the moss rose of the sisterhood of the states. California is the hollyhock, Florida the trumpet vine, Louisiana the magnolia, Kansas the sunflower, Texas the wind-blossom. But I think of Kentucky as an old-fashioned moss rose, a bit withered, perhaps, but bringing the fragrance which conjures up pictures of a grandmother's garden, of a moonlight night and a pretty girl leaning against a porch pillar, of a gay horseman racking on a fox-trotting horse down a sandy road to see his true love.

She has her faults. Occasionally she is rent by foolish quarrels over dogmas, and frequently she is seized with spasms of political hate. But underlying these surface symptoms of passing disorders are those traits which make her distinctive among the states--the spirits of hospitality,of tolerance, of kindliness, of human charity, of compassion.

She has had a glorious past, has Kentucky. And now she is progressing out of a somewhat sleepy present into a splendid future of achievement and progress. All

230 THE STORY OF PADUCAH

the signs point to this and, as a Kentuckian, I am proud that my State is giving such unmistakable evidences of a great and a complete reawakening.

While connected with the Saturday Evening Post, in 1914, Mr. Cobb was sent to Europe to "cover" the World War. It afforded an opportunity for his tremendous writing powers to be put to the supreme test. No sooner had the articles appeared than they were gathered into a book, *Paths of Glory*. He saw the war lines from a German observation balloon--"a reserved seat for the biggest show on earth". Returning to America, he lectured on what he saw at the front.

—By James Montgomery Flagg.
OLD IRVIN COBB'S BACK HOME!

Just before he left again for the war zone in 1917, two small books came from the press, *Speaking of Prussians*-- and *The Thunders of Silence*. Upon his return, the country eagerly devoured a new volume, *The Glory of the Coming*. It was a vivid chronicle, and rainbowed his work in this field with romance and glory.

An autobiographic account soon appeared between covers, called *Myself to Date*. It deals with his youthful newspaper experiences, inside stories he "scooped" while with the big papers, and a few leaves from his thrill-book. The book is widely used as s supplementary reader in schools of journalism.

Aside from his sixty-odd books, the Paducahan has written several plays. *Funabasha*, a musical comedy, was produced in 1907 and a musical skit, *Mr. Busybody*, in 1908. Five years later he collaborated with Bozeman Bulger in writing a one-act play called *Sergeant Bagby*. He was joined by Harry Burke in writing *Guilty as Charged*, and the same year (1915) Bayard Veiller assisted in producing *Back Home*, a comedy and the most pretentious of a half-dozen attempts at play-writing. With Roi Cooper Megrue he wrote a melodrama, *Under Sentence*, produced in 1918. *Happy New Year*, a vaudeville sketch, started running in New York in 1926.

Irvin S. Cobb was married at Savannah, Georgia, June 12, 1900, to Miss Laura Spencer Baker. They have a daughter, Mrs. Elisabeth Cobb Chapman, whose first novel, *Falling Seeds* (1927), met with distinguished success. In that year she completed a second novel, *The Marvels*.

Mrs. Cobb died in 1969 and the daughter, Elizabeth expired in 1959. They are buried in Paducah, one on the right and the other on the left of Mr. Cobb in Oak Grove Cemetery.

Fond of hunting, Mr. Cobb made several excursions into the country each year, generally stopping off at Paducah to visit his mother. He was noisy and good-natured, and liked a good cigar-- one of which, incidentally is honored with his name and is manufactured "back home". Like Dickens and Kipling, he habitually had a cigar between his teeth. He played golf, evidentally to be good-natured, considering one of his remarks. He watched a baseball game with interest, took a swim when on the coast, and liked to fish.

Any number of clubs in New York City bear his name on their roster. He was a chevalier of the French Legion of Honor and major in the Intelligence Department of the Officers' Reserve Corps of the United States Army. The Confederate Veterans' Association named him a colonel, and two governors of Kentucky appointed the writer a member of their staffs. Dartmouth College and the University of Georgia bestowed upon him the degree of LL. D.

A magnificent tribute was paid the genial philosopher on April 25, 1915, when one of the biggest banquets ever tendered an individual in America was given at the Waldorf-Astoria Hotel in New York. Six hundred and sixty-nine guests were seated at the tables, representing the country's foremost men in letters, art, music, the stage and newspaper circles. Speakers included Governor Martin H. Glynn, DeWolf Hopper, and Hal S. Corbett, Paducah attorney, the latter going from Paducah for the occasion.

Three hundred and four guests gathered for a city-wide testimonial dinner at the Paducah Woman's Club auditorium April 30, 1926, in honor of Mr. Cobb's approaching fiftieth anniversary. The dinner, sponsored by the Paducah Rotary Club, was an earnest demonstration of pride from the home folks. Elliott C. Mitchell presided and Robert H. Davis, of the Munsey magazines, was among the speakers.

In a graceful response the "Duke of Paducah", as Mr. Cobb is affectionately known around town, dropped a matchless simile by saying the city of his birth "lies like a dimple in the cheek of the Purchase".

Just before the guests departed they were each presented with a leather-bound copy of "The Story of Irvin S. Cobb" (Neuman) through kindness of Matthew J. Carney (1876-1942), an intimate friend of the celebrated writer.

Robert H. Davis in the New York Herald of April 23, 1922 wrote that ten literary men--editors, critics, readers and writers--were dining together when discussion arose as to the respective and comparative merits of contemporaneous popular writers. At length each man present set down upon a slip of paper his choice in various fields of endeavor. Mr. Cobb was first choice as the best writer of humor, all-round reporter, local colorist, in tales of horror, and teller of anecdotes.

Mr. Cobb died in New York on March 10, 1944, following a three months illness. He left instructions for burial in a letter addressed to Edwin J. Paxton, Sr., Sun-Democrat editor and publisher and Fred G. Neuman, Cobb biographer, with instructions it be opened only after his death.

The letter quite lengthy read in part:

"When convenience suits, I ask that the plain canister--nothing fancy there please-- containing my ashes shall be taken to Paducah, and that at my proper planting season a hole shall be dug in our family lot or elsewhere at Oak Grove and a dogwood tree planted there and my ashes strewn in the hole to fertilize the tree roots. Should the tree live that will be monument enough for me. But should any surviving relatives desire to mark the spot further, I make so bold as to suggest that they use either a slab of plain Kentucky limestone set flat in the kindly earth, or a rugged natural boulder of Southern granite. . . . . . ."

Mr. Cobb's wishes were carried out and he was buried on the grassy island five hundred feet from the entrance at Oak Grove Cemetery. This was set aside by the city and dedicated to Cobb's memory and his ashes interred there.

A large granite boulder at his grave bears this wording:

Irvin Shrewsbury Cobb
1876-1944
"Back Home"

¹The facts in this chapter were drawn largely from "The Story of Irvin S. Cobb" (Neuman), published in 1926. Under the heading "Newspapers" in Chapter XV of the present volume, additional light is thrown on Mr. Cobb's newspaper career in Paducah.

²Characters in the "Judge Priest" stories were men and women Mr. Cobb knew while living at Paducah, with their names slightly changed for purpose of spinning the yarns. Judge William Pitman Priest, the principal character, was in real life Circuit Judge William Sutton Bishop (1839-1902). Others prominent in the tales were Dr. Lake, who was Dr. John Gaunt Brooks (1840-1915); Sergant Jimmy Bagby, who was William Gaston Whitefield (1838-1915); and Ike Felsburg and Herman Felsburg, merchants, who were Joseph Ullman (1838-1912) and Herman Wallerstein (1839-1922), respectively. Connie Lee is pictured as Jeff Poindexter, a smart darky who figures more or less in all the stories. He is the only survivor at this time (1927).

³See "Judge Priest" by Fred G. Neuman in Louisville Courier Journal roto-magazine, p.p. 8-11. November 25, 1945; also "Paducahans in History" by F. G. N.

CHAPTER XX

NOTED PADUCAHANS

GENERAL LLOYD TILGHMAN

The fourth child and only son born to James Tilghman and Ann Caroline (Shoemaker) Tilghman, Lloyd Tilghman gained the highest military rank of any Paducahan and won distinction in the Civil War. He was born in Baltimore, Maryland, January 26, 1816, moved to Paducah in 1852, and lost his life in the Vicksburg campaign when he fell mortally wounded May 16, 1863.

After attending the schools in Baltimore, Lloyd Tilghman at the age of fifteen entered the United States Military Academy at West Point. Upon graduation five years later, he was commissioned as a second lieutenant, but resigned shortly afterward to take up the duties of civil engineer on the Baltimore and Susquehanna Railroad.

He subsequently associated himself in similar capacities with other railroads, but when the Mexican War broke out in 1846 his inherited chivalry was not to be denied and he joined the American forces on the border. He was made a captain and held that title when the troops disbanded two years later, whereupon he resumed his engineering pursuits. One of his achievements in this field consisted of surveying and superintending construction of the New Orleans and Ohio Railroad in 1853, Paducah's first rail artery.

The year previous he brought his family to Paducah, taking residence in the then new two-story brick house at the northeast corner of Seventh and Kentucky Avenue. It was there that he bade his loved ones good-bye and joined the Confederacy in 1861. He organized a company of volunteers and upon leaving the city was placed at the head of the Third Kentucky Regiment, with the rank of colonel. He was promoted to brigadier-general in October, 1961.

GEN. LLOYD TILGHMAN.

Given command of Fort Henry on the Tennessee River and Fort Donelson on the Cumberland, General Tilghman's small band of 2,610 poorly-armed men was attacked by 16,000 Union soldier's on February 6, 1862. Rather than surrender his whole force, he retired the major portion to Fort Donelson and remained fighting steadfastly with a hundred men until captured. Taken prisoner, he was held in keeping six months and then exchanged.

Promptly upon release General Tilghman returned to the scene of military activities and was given charge of ten thousand exchanged Confederate prisoners in Mississippi. To reorganize these men into war units and equip them anew was no small task, but the Paducahan was a trained commander and the work moved smoothly. Like Olive, Nature made him a great soldier.

It was in the spring of 1863 that Tilghman was stationed near Vicksburg, Mississippi. On May 16 the advancing columns of the Federal forces were met with stubborn resistance at Champion's Hill, twenty-two miles from Vicksburg, where Tilghman commanded the First Brigade of Loring's Division.

As the fight waxed hot late that afternoon, the Paducah officer dismounted and took command in person of a section of field ar-

THE STORY OF PADUCAH 237

tillery. Just as he was sighting a howitzer a cannonball struck him in the hip. After three hours of suffering his labored breathing ceased and the intrepid commander exchanged immortalities. The remains were buried in Vicksburg but disinterred in 1901 and taken to Woodlawn Cemetery, New York City.

At the time of his tragic death General Tilghman was a man in the prime of life; tall, vigorous, and symmetrically formed. His head was a noble one, finely developed in the regions of ideality, and set upon broad shoulders in leonine grace. He had a wealth of dark auburn hair. Beneath the eyebrows flashed a pair of black eyes. His nice sense of personal honor and genial courtesy endeared him to all his friends.

General Lloyd Tilghman was married to Miss Augusta Murray Boyd (1819-1898) on May 26, 1843. Eight children blessed this union, of whom Frederick Boyd Tilghman and Sidell Tilghman were the last survivors. The former died in 1924 and the latter in 1927.

In token of their reverence for their father's memory these two sons of the family presented Paducah with a handsome statue of General Tilghman, which was unveiled in Lang Park on May 15, 1909. The stone base was furnished by the United Daughters of the Confederacy. Donation of the site for the Augusta Tilghman High School in 1919 resulted in the city naming that institution after the donors' mother.

In the life of General Lloyd Tilghman, consecration to duty was paramount and he never swerved from what he thought was right. His career recalls the story of the Greek boatman, suddenly caught at sea in the storm. While the terrible waves were threatening to engulf him, the ancient seaman cried out to Saturn that the god of the seas could sink or save him, but in either event he would hold his rudder true.

SENATOR ALBEN W. BARKLEY

Elected to the United States Senate in the fall of 1926 and taking office March 4 following, the Honorable Alben W. Barkley became the first Paducahan so honored and a most distinguished political figure in the history of the city. Preceding his election to the Upper House he represented the First District in Congress for fourteen years, and, before that, served McCracken County as prosecuting attorney and judge, respectively. He came to Paducah in 1899.

Born in a two-room log house at Lowes, Graves County, Kentucky, on November 24, 1877, Alben W. Barkley was the firstborn of John W. and Electa (Smith) Barkley. Four brothers and three sisters followed him.

The father, a farmer, by industry and frugal living sent the boy to school for a common education. It was a decided sacrifice for parents of meager circumstances, but they were encouraged from the beginning by a remark of the boy's first teacher. "Never let up on his education," said the teacher; "for there is something in him and you ought to do everything possible to bring it out."

As the years passed, the boy prosecuted his studies and made good headway. At fourteen he was recognized as the best debater in the country school--a talent he developed since then by application and study until it gave him national reputation.

To afford the youth better educational advantages, the family in 1893 moved to Clinton, Kentucky, and entered young Barkley in Marvin College, where he did chores in exchange for tuition. During the summer vacations he tied sacks at a thresher and once worked as a railroad section hand. Graduating at Marvin College in 1897, he attended Emory College in Georgia but returned the next year to teach in Marvin College. The following year, with only fifty-cents in his pockets, he came to Paducah. He went to work in a tobacco factory.

In his leisure Alben W. Barkley read law in the offices of Charles K. Wheeler, Judge William S. Bishop and John K. Hendrick, respectively. The job of court reporter was tendered him at-fifty dollars a month and out of this he saved enough for a law course at the University of Virginia.

Mr. Barkley returned to Paducah, was admitted to the bar in 1901, and began practicing law. Although the first years were

THE STORY OF PADUCAH 239

lean, he soon built up a substantial practice. He was married to Miss Dorothy Brower on June 23, 1903. They had three children.

The brilliant young lawyer's first venture in public service was in 1905, when he was chosen county attorney. In this capacity he strengthened his reputation for sensible and ready speech. Four years later he carried honors for county judge. He fostered a pro-

ALBEN W. BARKLEY.   LINN BOYD.

gressive road program and other beneficial measures. His attitude in regard to the improvement of highways in a day when the good roads movement was in its infancy proved him a man of vision. In 1913, the electorate sent him to Congress from the First District of Kentucky, a post he filled with distinction until named Senator in November, 1926.

An outstanding figure in the national House of Representatives, the Paducah statesman won favor as an exceptionally able orator and virile political leader. Firm, earnest and progressive, he advocated liberal principles and took front rank among the members of the Lower House. Entering the Senate on March 4, 1927, the Kentuckian at once became known in that assembly for his fearless manner, convincing speech and sound logic.

Senator Alben W. Barkley died April 30, 1956 and was buried from the Broadway Methodist Church in Paducah. He was interred in Mt. Kenton Cemetery near Lone Oak. Thousands mourned the passing of the "Veep".

A monument to his memory stands at Twenty-eighth and Jefferson Streets.

Although a Democrat of pure Jeffersonian type and distinctly different in party affiliation, Alben W. Barkley, in his career, has been strikingly similar to that other great Kentuckian, Abraham Lincoln. Both men were born and reared under like conditions, had much the same struggles for education and devoted that learning and talent to the uplift and succor of the same classes-- namely, the plain folk.

It is a peculiar fact that three such men as Abraham Lincoln, Jefferson Davis and Alben W. Barkley were born within the borders of the same Commonwealth, within only a few leagues distance of each other. Truly, that caravan which crossed the Blue Ridge and followed the Wilderness Trail after the close of the Revolution, brought with it the makings of the greatest and noblest of mankind.

HONORABLE LINN BOYD

Congressman for twenty years and Speaker of the House of Representatives through four years, the Honorable Linn Boyd was a conspicuous figure in the national capital from 1835 to 1855. His presence there brought honor both to himself and the people he represented.

The son of Abraham Boyd, a Revolutionary patriot, Linn Boyd was born at Nashville, Tennessee, November 22, 1800. His parents moved to Trigg County, Kentucky, when he was two years old, and the lad later received an elementary education in the rural schools. As a young man he was sent to the Kentucky Legislature.

His grasp of public questions was soon recognized by the people at large and in 1835 he became their choice for congressman from the First District, then more commonly known as Jackson Pur-

chase. Serving well in this capacity, he represented the district till 1855, enjoying great popularity as an orator and verbal architect. During the last four years he was honored with the speakership.[1]

In the Democratic convention which met at Cincinnati on June 2, 1856, Mr. Boyd came within three votes of being nominated for the presidency of the United States, the honor going to James Buchanan.

The brilliant statesman took up his residence in Paducah after becoming a member of Congress. He built a handsome brick residence, "Oaklands", at 1710 Kentucky Avenue, where he died December 17, 1859. The home was one of the city's landmarks. He was buried in the western part of Oak Grove Cemetery.

Linn Boyd was one of the most positive forces at Washington in the days of Clay, Calhoun and Webster, all of whom knew him well. Chosen congressman on eight occasions and then selected by that body as its presiding officer, his worth was recognized by his colleagues as well as the constituency he served so faithfully.

Boyd County, Kentucky, is named after Linn Boyd.

DR. REUBEN SAUNDERS   CAPT. JOHN LAWSON

DR. REUBEN SAUNDERS

Discovery of a remedy for cholera by Dr. Reuben Saunders, pioneer Paducah physician, gave him a wide fame during the epidemic of 1873. Dr. Saunders was the son of James Saunders, an Indian fighter and Revolutionary patriot who accompanied Daniel Boone into Kentucky on that pathfinder's expedition from North Carolina. The elder Saunders remained in Central Kentucky where Reuben Saunders was born September 6, 1808.

Reuben Saunders grew to manhood near Frankfort and then left home to study medicine. After graduating from Jefferson Medical College at Philadelphia, he practiced for several years in Alabama, but moved to Paducah in 1847. His death occurred December 13, 1891, and he rests in Oak Grove Cemetery surrounded by hundreds of fellow citizens who loved and admired him for his noble ways.

While Dr. Saunders administered to the ills of the townfolk for nearly a half a century, his chief distinction was a discovery he made in connection with the cholera terror. This revelation focused attention of the medical world on Paducah and its humanitarian.

The story of the discovery is ably told in a chapter in Robert H. Davis' book, *"Over My Left Shoulder"*.

A part of it reads:

The test of Dr. Reuben Saunders' endurance came when the cholera scourge swept from the Ganges in India in 1873, moving southwest across Italy, France and the Atlantic, creeping into the New World at New York and Philadelphia and levying its terrible toll upon the South. The death rate was appalling. One carpenter at the conjunction of the Ohio and Tennessee Rivers, where Dr. Saunders was fighting the epidemic, consumed an entire lumber yard making rude coffins for the dead. The last box contained the body of its builder.

Medical science despaired of halting the dread disease and the mortality rate was on the increase. Dr. Saunders at this juncture decided to make an experiment. He selected for the test a young negress who was in the last stage of the fever. Into her exhausted and emaciated body he injected hypodermically what he thought was one-quarter grain of morphine, but it proved to be one-quarter grain of morphine combined with atropia.

Almost immediately a change for the better manifested itself. Dr. Saunders on another visit the same day found the patient much improved. The following day he repeated the experiment upon the person of a white man with the same gratifying result. Out of six subjects he brought five of them back from the grave and they recovered.

Hopeful beyond words that he had discovered by accident a means of halting the disease and believing in his heart that he had thrown up a barrier against the terrible mortality he telegraphed the results and the prescription to his college and then sent the news out to other plague-stricken countries.

For this great discovery he was decorated by several foreign governments and cited by his own country. It was a great triumph for a frontier doctor, but he could not be won away from his own people. There he remained, raised a family and carried on.

MATTHEW J. CARNEY

No Paducahan has attained greater success in the business world than Matthew J. Carney, who came to the city as a small boy with his parents from Leitchfield, Kentucky, where he was born August 31, 1876. He was educated at St. Mary's Academy from which he was graduated in 1894.

As a youth he procured employment as traveling auditor on the Paducah, Tennessee and Alabama Railroad, and then as a reporter on the News-Democrat. He next took up publicity work for a public utility company. While in this field he heard of the Union Carbide Company and in 1899 was made selling agent for the concern in the Kansas City district.

Success followed Mr. Carney in this endeavor and two years later he became more directly connected with the company, and was made general manager of a subsidiary, with offices in Chicago. From this time on his rise in the commercial world was phenomenal until in 1927 he was leading executive in a dozen large corporations. Among these were the Prest-O-Lite Company, Incorporated, the Oxweld Acetylene Company, and the Oxweld Railroad Service Company, in each of which he was chairman of the board of directors.

Although he was a busy man, Mr. Carney visited "back home" occasionally. He also found time for golf and fishing, his favorite recreations.

HARRY M. GILBERT

Among names that stand high in American musical circles is that of Harry M. Gilbert, who was born in Paducah, November

19, 1879. Besides excelling in organ and piano, he achieved distinction for his compositions, which include anthems, selections for the violin and piano, piano solos, and a cantata, "The Vision of Music".

At the age of seven Harry M. Gilbert began studying music under a private teacher. He took up music at Cincinnati and then studied in Berlin, specializing in composition and directing under Hans Pfitzner and other great modern composers. Returning to Paducah, he spent a year at home and went to Dallas where he taught in the Bush Conservatory for two seasons.

Still less than thirty years old, he next went to New York City and became organist and choir director in leading churches there. He was with the Central Presbyterian Church for ten years and in

MATTHEW J. CARNEY.   JOSEPH L. FRIEDMAN.

1920 took charge of the choir at the Fifth Avenue Presbyterian Church. In 1922 he organized a choral society now known as The Gilbert Singers.

Mr. Gilbert gained wide note as accompanist and piano soloist with David Bispham, Maud Powell, Evan Williams, Geraldine Farrar, Mme. Nordica and other famous artists.

WILLIAM REDDICK

Eminently successful as a musician and composer, William Reddick has established a reputation that is country-wide. He is a native of Paducah and attended the public schools in this city. He was born June 23, 1890.

Mr. Reddick went to New York City in 1911 and there became known as a pianist of exceptional ability. In connection with piano instruction he accepted a position as church organist and in 1927 served as organist at the Brooklyn Music School and the Master Institute of United Arts, teaching harmony and counterpoint.

As associate artist, Mr. Reddick has toured the United States and Canada in company with such celebrities as Alice Nielson, Sophie Braslau, Riccardo Martin, Jean Gordon, David Bispham, Maud Powell, Arthur Hartmann and others.

Mr. Reddick has achieved a reputation for his effective arrangements of negro spirituals, the best known of which are "Standin' In de Need o' Prayer". "Swing Low, Sweet Chariot" and "Travelin' to de Grave". His best known compositions include "The Velvet Darkness" and "Dawn".

HARRY M. GILBERT.   WILLIAM REDDICK.

PADUCAHANS OF DISTINCTION

Proud of its native and adopted sons and daughters who have achieved distinction in various lines of endeavor, Paducah recognizes them on every occasion. Both local and former residents are equally boastful of their city and are constantly bestowing favors upon it.

Among former residents who have made a mark in literature is William R. Scott, whose masterly treatise on the evils of tipping appeared in 1916. The volume bears the title, *The Itching Palm*. Other books by Mr. Scott include *The Americans in Panama* and *Scientific Circulation Managements*.

Nature poems and other fine lyrics by Mrs. Mary Lanier Magruder, have won her much fame in addition to her novel, *Wages*, which came from the press in 1924 and presented a vivid romance of the Kentucky lowlands.

Miss Anna Bird Stewart, a former English teacher in the public schools has won success in poetry and prose, and is the author of *The Gentlest Giant*, *A Midsummer Dance Dream* and *The Laughabet*, the latter an operetta. Miss Stewart made her home later in New York.

Though born in Trigg County, Kentucky, in 1890, V. Blaine Russell moved to Paducah with his parents in 1894 where some years later he began indulging in verse. In 1912 he located in Vicksburg, Mississippi. Winged with enthusiasm, Mr. Russell's lyrics possess a homely philosophy couched in simple language, as found in "The Happy Race" and "The Noblest Profession", two of his best poems. "Huntington Row", written in 1927, recalls an avenue of two-story frame houses that stood in Paducah just west of the old Illinois Central Railroad shops, where a score of families lived--

Do you remember old Huntington Row,
With its big ugly houses--a dozen or so--
Where the honest shop men (and the dishonest, too)
Left their wives at the door as the shop whistle blew?

I said some were honest, and some otherwise,
You will find men that way though to knighthood they rise.

So you'll think of the just, and ignore all the rest,
For no caste, sect or creed as a whole is the best.

True, their hands were all dirty, but grimy from toil.
There is no job worthwhile but some fingers must soil,
For what makes the black palm sometimes makes a white heart,
And a lily-hand job oft' makes conscience depart.

They worked on big engines that clean folk might ride,
And I know of some cases where one or two died,
Who were brought home quite mangled, untimely laid low;
And the women would weep there on Huntington Row.

There was "Humpy" McGrew with gray hair on his pate,
Coming northward one evening some two hours late,
When he struck the "Y" curve like a hurricane blow,
And next day was a funeral on Huntington Row.

Ah, 'twas many a dark night the caller came'round,
And the father and children a-frolicking found,
Then they all watched him leave for the yards, in the rain;
And sometimes those child-faces he'd ne'er see again.

There was happy Claude Hazzell, the widow's young son,
Who came in one bright morn from his Illinois run;
The good mother waved as he sped down the track;
Then a trestle, a crash--and Grim Death brought him back.

Poor silent John Woolley between the cars paced,
On the search for hot-boxes, replenishing waste.
They found him one day, cut in halves, in the snow,
There were three more new orphans on Huntington Row.

But the nation must travel where business leads,
And the brighter man's garb, all the braver his deeds,
But strong hearts out from squalor quite often would go;
Some returned, and some didn't, to Huntington Row.

Some poet has said men must work and wives weep,
That the earnings are small for the many to keep;
And that muse would have found his philosophy so,
Had he gone through those homes there on Huntington Row.

Mrs. David Gamble Murrell, whose husband was formerly chief surgeon at the Illinois Central Railroad Hospital (1884-1914) in Paducah, wrote *The White Castle of Louisiana* in (1903), in which she preserves some ante-bellum customs of that state. A trip abroad furnished material for a second novel, *What Marjorie Saw Abroad* (1906). Mrs. Murrell lived in New Orleans following the death of her husband.

One of the city's foremost writers is Mrs. C. E. (Martha Grassham) Purcell, well known for her historical studies. Her books include *The Settlements and Cessions of Louisiana* and *Stories of Old Kentucky*, and a monograph entitled *Lucy Jefferson Lewis*. Aside from her literary activities, Mrs. Purcell was prominent in the club and social life of the community. She introduced a resolution in the Paducah Woman's Club prohibiting the use of public drinking cups, a measure which was adopted by the city and, later, the State of Kentucky.

Miss Eugenia Parham is the author of a charming collection of verse called *Longing and Other Poems*, written in 1906 before she removed to Mayfield, Kentucky. Colonel Henry E. Thompson, deceased, sketches the city's past in a booklet *Paducah Historically*, published in 1910. Captain Ed Farley (1842-1929) relates his Civil War experiences in a small volume, *Recollections of an Old Soldier*, which came from the press in 1917.

Assigned to the Paris bureau of the New York Herald-Tribune as first assistant to the chief editor in 1927, Joseph B. Phillips is a young Paducahan whose rise in journalism has been phenomenal since he left the editorial staff of the News Democrat in 1925. He was with Washington and New York newspapers before accepting the post abroad.

Mrs. Olive Holbert Chaffee has won wide acclaim among art lovers for her paintings. Several of her canvasses are found in Paducah homes where they have attracted much notice, particularly "Autumn Gold", owned by Mrs. Muscoe Burnett. The Paducah Woman's Club has an artistic painting from her brush called "Tranquility".

W. G. McFadden, a portrait photographer of considerable note has done some excellent paintings. Robert Wilkins has also exhibited skill with the brush; one of his finest paintings is a large canvas representing a panorama of West Kentucky, done in 1927.

The business world has witnessed the executive ability and sound judgment of not a few Paducahans. Marc Klaw, the first male child of Jewish parentage born in the town (1858), assisted in organizing the great theatrical syndicate known as Klaw and Erlanger. Lawerence B. Pierce struggled out of a Paducah boyhood to build the Pierce and Monward buildings in St. Louis. Two other Paducahans left the city in their youth and made fortunes in St. Louis--John T. Milliken and A. E. Einstein. The famous baseball magnate, Barney Dreyfuss, spent his youth in Paducah.

Miss Anne I. Baker, assistant manager of the Ayer and Lord Tie Company, ranks with the leading business women of the country. Miss Baker assisted in organizing the Business and Professional Woman's Club of Paducah, which took form in October, 1920; she served three years as its first president. Miss Baker was at the head of the state business women's organization two years.

Elevated to the office of president-general of the United Daughters of the Confederacy in 1919, Mrs. Roy W. McKinney was the first Kentucky woman to occupy this high office. Mrs. McKinney previously served a two-year term as state president. Election of Mrs. E. G. Boone as state regent of the Daughters of the American Revolution in 1915, resulted in her administration equiping the beautiful Kentucky Room in the Memorial Hall of the D. A. R., at Washington.

Prominent in club work throughout the State of Kentucky were Mrs. H. G. Reynolds, Mrs. E. G. Boone, Mrs. Andrew Campbell, Mrs. W. J. Hills, Mrs. J. A. Rudy, Mrs. Armour Gardner, Miss Emily Morrow and other Paducah women. Mrs. Josephine Fowler Post was conspicuous in both State and national activities of a patriotic nature.

The Paducah Woman's Club, organized November 15, 1906, has been eminently successful in its purposes, credit for which in a measure is due its officers. Eight women of exceptional ability have served as president, as follows: Mrs. J. A. Rudy (1906-1912); Mrs. Elbridge Palmer (1912-1914); Mrs. R. B. Phillips

THE STORY OF PADUCAH   251

(1914-1916); Mrs. H. S. Wells (1916-1918); Mrs. Roy W. McKinney (1918-1920); Mrs. W. J. Hills (1920-1924); Mrs. T. E. Elgin (1924-1927); Mrs. C. E. Purcell (1927-). Incorporated January 6, 1907, the club joined the Kentucky Federation three months later, and the General Federation in 1910. Following enlarging and remodeling, the handsome club quarters at 608 Kentucky Avenue were reopened September 24, 1925.

The Woman's Club purchased a lovely two-story buff brick residence at 1406 Jefferson Street in August 1957 and moved to the new location. This was formerly the home of Benjamin J. Billings, owner of Billings Printing Company.

Able presidents have served through the years and much has been accomplished of benefit to the city.

Mrs. Douglas Moore took office as President of the club this year (1979).

In musical talent the city has been especially fortunate. Mrs. Mayme Dryfuss Gruenebaum is highly praised for her vocal work and success as a teacher of voice and piano. Misses Krystal Smith, Courtie Puryear, May Pratt Bonds, Ruby Kolb and others are known for their distinctive methods of piano playing. Talented violinists include Misses Thalia Levy Rice and Emma Jean Fisher, and Leonard Smith.

Besides Mrs. Gruenebaum, the genuineness of method and vocal proficiency of other Paducahans is widely popular. The admirable means and clear enunciation of Mrs. Luther Carson stamp her as a vocalist of high favor. Affability in disposition adds to the vocal charm of Miss Lucille Rawleigh and Mesdames Edna Hays Lyle, Eugene E. Bell. G. Tandy Smith and Russell L. Long, to mention only a few who ranked high in the city's musical life. Miss Gladys Gross possessed a mezzo soprano voice of rare promise and displayed good schooling.

William C. Landfear, Robert H. Scott, Slavie Mall, Harold Williamson and Jack Major have clear voices, representative of the best talent among men in this part of the state. Mr. Major has made several phonograph records and has played the leading vaudeville circuits.

Unusual success was attained by Miss Gladys Coburn of Paducah, whose appearance on the screen drew national favor. Her leads, well-chosen and specially adapted to her type of beauty, were reinforced by her striking personality.

As a professional actor and traveler of note, Richard Scott has appeared with Otis Skinner and other celebrities in Shakespearean dramatics. He spent five years in Africa and toured India, China, Japan and other countries. Mr. Scott was born in Paducah in 1879 and was a graduate of the Paducah High School.

Victor Sutherland is another Paducah-born actor whose stage career has met with wide approval. He has taken leading roles in movies, as has his cousin, Richard Sutherland, who plays comedy and dramatic parts with equal success. Though born at Benton, Kentucky, Richard Sutherland came to Paducah as a boy and grew to manhood in his adopted city. For a time he was employed at the Illinois Central Railroad shops.

Success has followed Harry T. Berry as a high-class vaudeville

JAMES C. UTTERBACK.   CHARLES G. VAHLKAMP.

star. His versatility ranges from vocal and instrumental numbers to juggling and acrobatic features. His show was featured at the West Kentucky Fair at Paducah in 1939.

As a minstrel favorite, George M. Rock was among the best comedians in this part of the country.

Dr. Henry Cave prosecuted his medical studies abroad and then located in New York City, where he was a member of the surgical staff at the Roosevelt Hospital. He has performed operations on a number of prominent persons, including J. P. Morgan, Charles Dawes and the Duchess of Windsor. Dr. Harold Amoss has achieved distinction for his research work at the Rockfeller Institute in the same city. Dr. Will Rock has gained prominence in medical circles since locating in Milwaukee, Wisconsin.

Major General Richard Donovan of the United States Army won steady promotion since his graduation from the West Point Military Academy. He was born and educated in Paducah.

Prominent in banking circles were James C. Utterback, president of the City National Bank since 1917, who came to that institution at the age of sixteen as messenger; W. F. Bradshaw, president of the First National Bank since 1924 and the Mechanics Trust and Savings Bank since 1910; Richard Rudy, president of the Citizens Savings Bank since 1920, and Walter A. Blackburn, president of the Peoples National Bank since its opening October 15, 1926. Opening of the Mechanics Trust and Savings Bank occurred January 3, 1903. The City National Bank was organized January 17, 1873; The Citizens Savings Bank on May 1, 1888; the Mechanics Trust and Savings Bank in December, 1902; and the First National Bank in 1865.

Among the city's leading business men of the early 1900's were James C. Utterback and Charles G. Vahlkamp, the latter president of the City Comsumers Company. Both were active workers in any enterprise tending to Paducah's development. Although identified with a mutiplicity of business connections these community leaders were never too busy to give of their time and means for any public cause.

For a quarter century, or until his death July 5, 1913, Joseph L.

Friedman took front rank in the city's commercial activities and in various ways contributed to the growth, happiness and prosperity of Paducah. Farsighted and alert, he served as president of the old Commerical Club and was a potent factor in bringing many leading industries to the city. He was also noted for encouraging younger men and training them for larger tasks, and a score of those whose names are now associated with the business and commercial life of the community owe their start to his wise counsel and generous financial aid.

The kinds deeds of Mr. Friedman increased with the years and probably outnumbered those of any other person in the city's history. A wealthy man, he expended his means freely in making the burdens of his fellowmen lighter. He was a friend and benefactor to all and seemed to read the needs of those about him. Many Paducahans testify to his generous assistance in making possible the ownership of their homes, which was but one of his quiet, unostentatious ways of making others happy.

At a "Boys Back Home" dinner given in Paducah in 1914, Irvin S. Cobb recalled the goodness of Mr. Friedman. In concluding his remarks, Mr. Cobb said: "Let me say a word of the best friend I ever had when I needed a friend, Joe Friedman--a Jew--who possessed more of the so-called Christian virtues than any man I ever knew. Here before the people who of all the world can best understand, I want to lay one loving tribute on the ever green grave of Joseph L. Friedman."

Mr. Friedman was laid to rest in a mausoleum in Temple Israel Cemetery on the Lone Oak Road. His remains were borne from his home, The Pines, to the cemetery three miles away. Hundreds of carriages, buggies and automobiles formed a trail to the burial grounds, and the hearse reached the cemetery before all the last mourners--a community--joined the long procession. The floral tributes were legion, the greatest in Paducah's history, covering an acre of ground.

The death of Ferd Hummel, Sr., at the age of 79, (1827-1907) removed from the walks of life one whose genius marked him as a man of more than mediocre talents. A gunsmith by trade, Mr. Hummel won favorable recognition for his fine workmanship and wide renown for his inventions. He came to Paducah in the latter part of 1861. In April 12, 1886 he patented a needle or bolt movement for rifles, an idea which became universal on firearms and was superseded for U. S. Military purposes only in 1936 by the Garand rifle. In this action the breechlock took the form of a lever operated bolt. His shop at that time was at 109 North 4th Street.

Mr. Hummel's next patent was obtained on a rotating valve under the lid of oil cans, which in those days were household necessities. This boon eliminated the faulty screw top and old style thimble device, but of course, did not possess the more permanent value of his firearms improvement.

In Captain John ("Jack") Lawson, Paducah boasted a resident who was the first in this country to demonstrate the practicability of the locomotive. As a young man he came to America from England in 1829 and was engineer on an engine brought over and operated on the railroad.

The "new invention" which Captain Lawson conducted on its maiden trip ran at the rate of eighteen miles an hour. Aside from its prominent boiler, it had a high smokestack, so that fumes cleared passengers who rode in open cars.

Captain Lawson afterward superintended construction of the first locomotive built in this country, now exhibited by the Baldwins. He later took to the river and owned seven steamboats which the Union forces threatened to commandeer. Rather than surrender them to the Federals, he burned them and then joined the Confederate ranks, returning to the river after the war. The gray-haired patriarch died in 1901 and was buried in Mt. Kenton Cemetery, where a huge granite boulder marks his grave.

With the death of Captain Lawson there was brought to close a life of varied adventure and sturdy usefulness. Parting this life at the age of 97, he climbed to the high tide of the years before he found the ebb tide. An engineer and river man for nearly a century, nightfall found him in the last port seeking a landing that is safer than any other and a harbor that is eternal and secure. In the last few years of his life the old gentleman might himself have been likened to an ancient craft idly lying in a bird-haunted bay, bearing the scars of many a voyage and strange trophies of distant travels.

CHAPTER XXI

HOME-COMING WEEK, 1913

> I remember, I remember
>   The place where I was born;
> Where the morning glories twine around
>   The door at early morn.
> I've forgotten, I've forgotten
>   How long I've been away,
> But I'm glad to wander back again
>   Down the lane to yesterday.

Nothing ever drew so many former sons and daughters to its gates at one time as did Paducah's Home-Coming Week, May 19 to 24, 1913. Colonel Ben Weille originated the idea and months before the occasion preparations were made for entertaining thousands who would return to the place of their birth, or younger days.

Upon returning to the city of their love, former residents realized again and again there is something gripping about Paducah: that life here is replete with sunshine, laughter and the merriment of little children; that handclasps are a little warmer; that friends are not so far away nor so soon forgotten; that green things grow in front yards and flowers bloom wild; and, above all, that Paducah is a city of homes, a hospitable center, a capital of cordiality.

Bright, unusually bright was that Monday morning when Home-Coming Week was ushered in; the sun rose just as it did any other day but somehow one could not help but feel that it was a little brighter and the greeting of friends a little more cheerful. The whole week was a kaleidoscope of changing moods and scenes during which five thousand visiting revellers joined in the carnival festivities, a frolicsome time when cares were cast aside and people abandoned themselves to riotous pleasure.

Monster parades, pompously picturesque and without thought of expense, traversed the principal streets each night. Elaborate floats of unrivalled beauty marked the merchants' and manufacturers' parade on Thursday night. Floral displays in the amalgamated parade the next evening were gorgeous. A burlesque parade on Wednesday evening was the most laughable flourish of the week. Saturday night's festivities were enlivened by the traveling men's parade, Home-Coming closing at midnight in a blaze of glory. For six days the community re-lived part of its colorful past.

An entertaining feature was the street fair, the city fathers suspending all ordinances against obstructions of thoroughfares and licensing booths, tents and riding devices where the owners chose. Jefferson Street, for instance, was lined with everything from wheels of fortune to circus features, and a merry-go-round at Fourth Street was defiant of traffic and noisily busy sixteen hours each day during the whole week. Tony Janus in an airplane winged his way across the Ohio River and over the city each afternoon. Moving pictures were made and two weeks later the palefaces witnessed their follies on the screen.

But the crowning event was Chief Paduke's triumphant return on Tuesday evening. Coming of the chief had been heralded by shrieking factory whistles and roaring of a cannon on the river front, which gave the signal for Chief Paduke and his party to begin their trip toward the city on the steamer G. W. Robertson.

In due time James G. Wheeler, decked in paint and feathers and impersonating the chieftain, arrived at 7:45 o'clock with his party consisting of Miss Adine Corbett as princess, and Misses Ruth Hinkle and Bertha Ferguson as maids of honor. Chief Paduke, tall and astute, mounted his white steed, the party boarding a handsome float. The guests were escorted to Fifth and Broadway through a crowd that packed the thoroughfare, a colorful throng of city and country cousins imbued with a spirit of fun, neighborliness and good fellowship.

Fifteen thousand people surged about a platform erected beside the post office where Chief Paduke dismounted. Every roof top nearby held its quota and from every window protruded heads

THE STORY OF PADUCAH 259

eager for a glance at the beloved chief. As horns ceased tooting and the noise abated, Mayor Thomas N. Hazelip came to the stand and welcomed the resurrected Indian. The mayor concluded by saying, "Take Paducah; it is yours".

Calmly the old warrior stepped forward. There he stood! It had been years since he saw the spot, but memories of it were as clear in his mind as the crystal waters that flow from a Kentucky mountain spring. He knew its every nook and cranny, had drunk its waters and walked its levels; but now he stood amazed to find a bustling city at the site of his tribesman's wigwams. The tribal head spoke at some length upon the old Indian days. The Honorable W. V. Eaton closed the ceremonies.

The gala week was the merriest the city had ever known. Even the air seemed redolent with good feeling and everywhere could be heard the street greeting, "Hello, Pad". Faces were wreathed in smiles and everyone was wont to say--

> There's no place like the old place
> Where you and I were born,
> Where we lifted first our eyelids
> On the splendor of the morn.

Yet amid all the joy there was a sense of sadness in not a few hearts as visitors gazed upon some spot dear to a day long since past. It was remindful of the gay party of Virginians in John Eston Cooke's "Henry St. John"--young men and women who wrote their names with a diamond ring on the window glass and in after years came to read those names again, calling back to memory the bright morning of youth when the names were written there.

CHAPTER XXII

A GOLDEN PERIOD

With scarcely more than a century and a half elapsed since white men made their first pilgrimage to the site of Paducah, a glance at the past presents a picture of romantic interest, a panorama of changing scenes. Events of great moment have occurred and great changes are represented on the canvas.

See the removal of the red man, an ancient race, and transplanting of the pale face in his stead. The pioneer comes with his ax, cattle and plow. Then comes General William Clark and, moved by its beauty and promise, he plants a town at the confluence of two majestic streams.

Through thorny paths and over waters deep, immigrants are seen bound for the new townsite. A government is set up by honest hearts and order set in motion. Soon the valleys resound with the teeming of an industrious, ambitious people. Steamboats ply the rivers, commerce makes progress and industry thrives. Auspicious is the beginning, and strong men, fair women and happy children join in thanksgiving.

Alas! two fires sweep the business section and three record floods, 1884, 1913, and 1937 pour their ravaging waters upon the community. A battle is fought on a Good Friday and a hundred Blues and Grays fall dead and wounded in civil strife, brother arrayed against brother.

Now come the railroads, several of them, and sorrowfully the big river packets pass from view. Behold the automobile, with its advent in Paducah in 1901. Note the disappearance of horse-drawn wagons, carriages, and even streetcars in this electric age. Hear the whirr of many thousand motors--pleasure cars, comfortable busses, ponderous trucks.

Marvelously, almost overnight, a score of immense railroad structures rear themselves in Paducah's midst, skyscrapers are

THE STORY OF PADUCAH 261

built and planned, and gravelled streets become paved boulevards. Surely the sun never shone brighter!

Government statistics show a steady growth in population in Paducah since its settlement. The number of inhabitants recorded in decade 1880-1890 showed 4,761 residents were added, an increase of 37 per cent. The years 1850 to 1860 brought 2,224 new citizens, making a gain of 36 per cent over the ten years. A gain of 34 per cent was registered during the decade from 1890 to 1900, the city adding 6,649 residents.

THE CITY CONSUMERS COMPANY, AN IMPORTANT FACTOR IN DEVELOPING THE DAIRY INDUSTRY.

Year	Population	Year	Population
1830	105	1880	8,036
1840	1,328	1890	12,797
1850	2,161	1900	19,446
1860	4,590	1910	22,760
1870	6,866	1920	24,735

Caron's City Directory for 1926-1927 gave the population of Paducah as 36,090. This figure included all residents of the newly-annexed territory, the city proper covering approximately nine square miles following addition of the suburban sections.

The last annex to the city was in March 1978. Paducah now covers 16.7 square miles with a population of 34,083 inhabitants. This fact is misleading about Paducah, since hundreds live just beyond the city limits. Beautiful homes have been built in newly developed areas and many city dwellers have moved to these subdivisions.

Close bonds of friendship knit Paducahans with their country cousins, resulting in a co-operative spirit that is far-reaching in effect. With mutual interests at heart, the farmers of McCracken County and the business men of Paducah have learned the value

BROADWAY LOOKING EAST FROM SEVENTH STREET
AS IT APPEARED IN 1927.

of proper understanding, and a fine relationship exists between the two.

The rich lands surrounding Paducah have been brought to fruition by a diversification of crops, the old plan of raising only tobacco and corn having been abandoned in more recent years. No

THE STORY OF PADUCAH 263

longer does the tobacco market affect the commercial well-being of the community, although tobacco interests are still represented by the presence of large warehouses. The growing of soy beans is a major crop in this area. (1979)

Apple and peach orchards now hold a prominent part in the country's financial returns, along with many acres of strawberries. Truck gardening is becoming increasingly popular realizing profitable sums from tomatoes, peas, green beans, squash, corn, watermelons and canteloupes.

The strawberry crop, however, yielded the best return in 1927 as shown by the number of cars shipped and income, as follows:

Year	Carloads	Income	Year	Carloads	Income
1922	39	$ 53,242	1925	121	$256,000
1923	55	$ 65,774	1926	217	$401,000
1924	78	$146,000	1927	361	$550,000

The City National Bank Building was erected in 1910 at the northeast corner of Fourth and Broadway. It is ten stories in height exclusive of the basement and juts 110 feet from the ground level to the top. It is of brick and stone construction, with steel framework.

This edifice (Citizens Bank and Trust Company building) was long called the skyscraper of Paducah, but now there is one that exceeds it. It is the Jackson House Apartments. They were built for the Senior Citizens by the A.F.L.-C.I.O. labor unions. It has nineteen stories with 236 apartments, recreational facilities, beauty shop and pharmacy for the convenience of the occupants. It is located at 301 South Ninth Street and was opened February 1, 1974.

The Ritz Hotel at the northwest corner of Twenty-second and Broadway, and the Charleston Apartments at the southeast corner of Twenty-second and Jefferson Streets, were erected in 1927.

The Irvin S. Cobb Hotel at Sixth and Broadway opened April 29, 1929. It was built by Adolph Weil, Paducah capitalist, on the site of the Weil home and named for his life long friend. It contains 200 rooms.

CITY NATIONAL BANK BUILDING.

THE STORY OF PADUCAH

A joyous occasion was the opening of the Paducah-Brookport Bridge on May 8, 1929, which spans the Ohio River. The Tilghman and Washington school bands led a parade of 1300 cars across the bridge.

The bridge was begun in October 1927. Credit for success of the venture is due the Paducah Board of Trade bridge committee, composed of Richard Rudy, chairman; Charles G. Vanlkamp, W. F. Bradshaw and Harry L. Meyer. It has ten spans, measuring 4,208 feet. The longest of these, 715 feet, is at the Kentucky end. The bridge has a clearance of 53 feet above the 1913 high water mark.

The bridge cost $1,256,482 plus $10,000 for the right-of-way. The name was changed to "Irvin S. Cobb", November 24, 1943, in honor of a favorite son.

The Riverside (Lourdes) Hospital on North Fourth Street and the Illinois Central Hospital (Katterjohn Building) at fourteenth and Broadway were sold and are being used for a rest home and office building, respectively. Two new hospitals were built to care for the sick and meet the needs of approximately 650 patients.

Western Baptist at 25th and Broadway was opened in October

WESTERN BAPTIST HOSPITAL

266   THE STORY OF PADUCAH

1953. Dr. A. M. Parrish then pastor of the Immanuel Baptist Church, led in the drive for funds to build. It originally had three floors and a fourth was added later. A building adjacent was built to house a $30,000 Cobalt machine. It is no longer necessary to go to another city for treatment. The hospital has grown from 117 to 319 bed capacity.

A new addition is now under construction for a larger radiology department and addition to the coffee shop. Mr. H. E. Feezor is the capable Executive Vice President and Administrator. Approximately 850 are employed. A landing area is available for helicopter to convey patients needing further treatment to other cities.

Lourdes Hospital, owned and operated by the Sisters of St. Francis of Tiffin, Ohio, is located on the Lone Oak Road. It was opened January 18, 1973 with 259 beds available and with the addition of floor space has now six stories and facilities for 323 patients.

LOURDES HOSPITAL

A Psychiatric Unit and a C A T scanner have been added and were much needed in treatment of the ill. The hospital stands as a lighthouse on a hill. Mr. Harold R. Jenks is the administrator. There are approximately 900 employees.

Paducah has fast become a medical center with many fine doctors who specialize in certain fields of medicine as well as general practitioners. People come from miles around for treatment in Paducah.

Paducah Junior College which had its beginning at Seventh and Broadway in 1932 with seven instructors and 68 students now has a spacious campus on the Blandville Road where 2,796 students were enrolled in 1978; 1,332 in the spring term, and 1,464 in the fall.

The school library bears the name R. G. Matheson, so named in honor of a faculty member for many years.

Paducah Tilghman High School is now located at 2400 Washington Street where the school was erected at a cost of

TILGHMAN HIGH SCHOOL

$3,500,000 and opened in 1965. Located on a 23 acre site, the beautiful school has a gym which seats 3,500, auditorium, 1,700 and cafeteria 500. The Paducah Area Vocational Technical School has been added more recently. The school graduated 313 students in the year 1979.

The former school building on 1000 Clark Street became a junior high. At that time the name was changed to Jetton honoring Professor Walter C. Jetton who served as principal of the high school from 1922 to 1957.

St. Mary's High School has relocated on Kennedy Road with beautiful campus and much larger facilities than formerly.

The older grade schools have been razed and new buildings pro-

THE STORY OF PADUCAH

vided to accommodate the pupils who are now bussed to their respective schools. Some areas have been combined with one large building serving the purpose of several smaller ones. Paducah is justly proud of her school system and the instructors who serve so ably.

Fourteen mayors have guided the populace since 1927. Each of them has been well equipped and intensely interested in the well-being of the city. They are as follows:

Name	Years	Name	Years
Ernest Lackey	1928-1932	Robert C. Cherry	1952-1956
Ed G. Scott	1932-1936	George Jacobs	1956-1960
Edgar T. Washburn	1936-1940	Robert C. Cherry	1960-1964
Pierce E. Lackey	1940-1944	Tom Wilson	1964-1968
Wayne C. Seaton	1944-1948	Robert C. Cherry	1968-1972
Gene Peak(Died in Office)	1948-	Mrs. Houston McNutt	1972-1976
Stewart Johnson	1949-1952	William S. Murphy	1976-1980

ERNEST LACKEY   ED G. SCOTT

EDGAR T. WASHBURN

PIERCE E. LACKEY

WAYNE C. SEATON

GENE PEAK

STEWART JOHNSON

ROBERT C. CHERRY

GEORGE JACOBS

TOM WILSON

MRS. HOUSTON MCNUTT   WILLIAM S. MURPHY

When Governor Breathitt held office he was much concerned about having a summer festival at Paducah. Letter was received by our officials and after discussion of the possiblity of such a program, it was decided to try it. This was 1967. Mr. Tom Wilson was chosen to head the movement.

Now for several years Paducah has had outstanding programs on the river front. The city built a large stage on the river bank to accommodate the entertainers. Some are local talent and others come from some distance. It has proven very successful and large crowds each evening for a week are in attendance. The Dixie Land Band from St. Louis has furnished a part of the program several years.

The many trees which line the streets of Paducah have given it distinction and beauty. In 1977-78 a move to give Broadway between Sixth Street and the river a face lift was undertaken. In Operation Town Lift, light poles were removed, wires placed under the street, large signs in front of businesses were set back, ornamental trees were planted and flower boxes filled with plants and concrete sidewalks replaced with brick ones. New and larger street lights were added--all in all a complete change.

The Alben W. Barkley Museuam came into being through the efforts of Mrs. Evelyn Howard and Mrs. Court Neal who sponsored the Young Historians at Brazelton School. Interest grew and a larger group was formed of those whose bend was history.

A drive was begun to raise funds to purchase a building to open a museum of natural history. Mrs. Chapman Jennings, now deceased, led in the endeavor, assisted by Mrs. Neel and Mrs. Howard and a home was secured at 533 Madison Street. It proved to be a very desirable one since it is a pre-war one built in 1852. It was formerly the residence of the Honorable David A. Yeiser, Sr., who served as the seventh mayor of Paducah.

The museum contains many Barkley trophies, one of them a saddle given Mr. Barkley by General Douglas McArthur; another is a bust of the former Vice-president made by Admiral Gene Paro. The home and treasures belong to the Young Historians Association. The museum was opened in October 1970.

In 1948, the Crounse Corporation, a barge line specializing in transportation of coal was organized. The office is located at 27th and Broadway. The company operates 23 tow boats, 500 barges and employs approximately 350 people and transported 30,000,000 tons of coal in 1978.

The Louis Igert Towing Company located at 2200 South 4th Street was opened in 1925. Has grown from year to year until at present, 1979, it operates seven main line towboats on Tennessee River, mainly from Paducah to Knoxville. They also run two harbor boats in the Paducah area.

Some products carried are grain, coal, salt, chemical and petroleum. Most everyday seventy-five barges go out carrying 75,000 tons of cargo.

The fleet carries 17,000 horse power.

Providing employment for hundreds of persons in Paducah and McCracken County is the Shawnee Steam Plant, the Atomic

THE STORY OF PADUCAH 273

Gaseous Plant, Calvert City Chemical Plant and at Wickliffe, Kentucky, the paper and pulp mill.

A large and spacious Paducah Mall Shopping Center has been opened at 3200 South Beltline Highway containing 28 businesses.

The building of Interstate Highway I 24 through McCracken County and spanning the Ohio River has given easy access to the city from adjoining states.

Time marches on! Many of the leaders of yesterday who planned and ventured to build our fair city, nurtured it and brought it into being--and gave to us the advantages we now enjoy, have passed on. The lovely two--story homes that were theirs have been razed to make space for business houses, parking areas, banks, garages, restaurants, schools, etc. But as the years have passed and gone, other leaders have risen up to carry on and bring into fruition the many luxuries of this time. (1979)

With its new railroad shops, plans for a bridge across the Ohio River and bonds voted for paving arteries leading to it, the newspapers conducted a "slogan contest" in 1927 calling for a fit phrase that would express the modern Paducah and its golden period. The committee chose "Paducah: Rails, Rivers Roads--Hub" as the best slogan, inasmuch as it directed attention to the city's three-fold advantage in being a river port, a railroad center and a diverging point for State and Federal roads.

Judges in the contest selected "Paducah, Heap Much Big Chief" as second best, which, like the first, was sent in anonymously along with eight thousand others. "Paducah--Active and Attractive", was sent in by Miss Jacqueline Rieke and declared third choice. Other original slogans included "Plucky Paducah Kentucky", by Jimmie Noonan; "Kentucky's Latchstring", by C. C. Grassham, and among the hundreds that came from out of the city, Irvin S. Cobb's contribution, "The Front Door to Dixie".

The most impressive feature of the contest, aside from the rich variety of the suggestions offered, was the remarkable interest created in Paducah by the search for a slogan. A great amount of advertising resulted from the contest, and it showed the interest and love Paducahans have for the city.

For years Paducah did not have a flag to call her own. Mr. and Mrs. John Pearce Campbell IV will be remembered as the couple who designed and promoted the official flag of Paducah. It has a blue background with Chief Paduke in the center, and waves proudly with the American flag over the city hall. Mrs. Campbell passed away in 1965 and Mr. Campbell died only this year (1979). He was a descendant of the Fowler, Cobb and Saunders families.

Viewing Paducah's unrivaled blessings and manifold opportunities, Robert H. Scott, a devoted citizen, characterized the city as "Paducah the fortunate; city of promise where the waters divide!" He added that the first letter in "Paducah" stands for prosperity and the last for happines while the "u" in the middle represents unity.

Never, never in the history of Paducah has the future been so rosy. This was spoken in 1927 and it holds true today. A rainbow of fairer hue and greater majesty than ever before arches the sky and sweeps the horizon.

In the great day of assize, when empire, republic of earth, and state and city shall be gathered to judgement, and the Muse of History shall unroll the record of their good and evil, Paducah, that gem in the diadem of American cities, will be in their midst, her white vestment honorably stained by the blood of her sons, her eyes dimmed by the sorrow and suffering of her daughters. A chaplet of laurel shall encircle her brow, and a noisy trump of fame shall hail her coming; and round her fair, proud head will shine a halo of love, and others shall look on in admiration not unmixed with envy as the spirit of Paducah passes by.

INDEX

Addition, 63.
Adventist, Seventh Day, church, 215.
Airplane, 123.
Allard, John L., 99.
American Legion, 157.
Amoss, Harold, 253.
Amusements, 112.
Anderson, Fort, 151, 148.
Annexation, last, 262.
Area, 262.
Armentrout, L. V., 176.
Automobiles, 166-168.

Bagby, E. W., 173.
Bailey, J. N., mayor, 94-96.
Baker, Anne I., 250.
Banks, 67.
Baptist, First, church, 189, 190.
Baptist, Immanuel, church, 206-208.
Baptist, East, church, 208, 209.
Baptist, North Twelfth Street, church, 211.
Baptist, West End, church, 213, 214.
Barkley, Alben W., Monument, sketch of, 237-240.
Barge Lines, 272.
Baseball, 122.
Bell, Mrs. Eugene E., 251.
Bicycles, 121-123.
Birth, first, 54.
Birth rate, 180.
Bishop, William S., 234.
Blackburn, W. A., 253.
Boone, Mrs. E. G., suggests Paduke statue, 27.
Boyd, Linn, home, 103, sketch of 240-242.
Boyd, Frank, 156.
Bradshaw, W. F., 253.
Brazelton home, 106, picture 109.
Breweries, 108, 109.
Bridge, Paducah-Brookport, 265.
Broadcasting station, 176.
Brooks, J. G., 144, 234.
Bryan, Holland G., 48.
Burnett, Henry, first professional telephone, 184.
Burnett, Mrs. Muscoe, 249.
Burns, Frank N., mayor, 91-93.
Busses, 166.

Carnegie Public Library, 172, 173.
Carney, Matthew J., 244.
Carson, Mrs. Luther, 251.
Catholic, St. Francis de Sales Roman, church, 194-196.
Cave, Henry, 253.
Cemeteries, 68, 178-179.
Centennial, McCracken County, Celebration, 50.
Chaffee, Olive H., 249.
Charleston Apartments, 263.
Cholera Epidemic, 243.
Christian, First, church, 196-198.
Christian, Murrell Boulevard, church, 204, 205.
Churchill, S. B., 56.
Churches, 186-215.
Church of Christ, Broadway, 210, 211.
Circuses, First, 72, 117, 118-120.
City Hall, built, 72, third floor added 87, present, 78.

City limits, 85, 95.
City National Bank building, 263, 264.
Civil War, 143-151.
Clark, George Rodgers, exploit, 29, given land, 21.
Clark, William, plats town, 51-52, changes Pekin to Paducah, 22.
Cobb, Irvin S., birthplace, 219, life sketch and review of writings, 221-229, reporter and editor in Paducah, 220, dinners, 228, 232.
Cobb, Irvin S., quoted, theory of name Paducah, 17, 18, Wilmington, 47, sleet storm, 137-139, city's location, 229, Bob Noble inscription, 127, tribute to Friedman, 254, slogan, 273, Burial, 233.
Coburn, Gladys, 252.
Columbia Theater, 114.
College, Paducah Junior, 267.
Connolly, H. A., writes Paducah poem, 196.
Contest Street, 56.
Corbett, Hal S., 232.
Courthouse, 54-57.
Court Street, 56.
Covington, Will E., 179.
Crossland, Ed, 153.

Davis, Brinton B., 155.
Davis, Robert H., quoted, 243, 244, attends Cobb banquet, 232.
Death rate, 180.
Distilleries, 108.
Donelson, John, voyage, 30-31.
Donovan, John T., 86.
Donovan, Richard, 253.
Dorian, John J., 86, 90.
Dorian, Mrs. John J., 172.
Dreyfuss, Barney, 250.

Elevation, 133.
Elgin, Mrs. T. E., 251.
Ellsworth, C. H., 157.
Enders, Robert, 39, 61.
Episcopal, Grace, church, 192-194.
Evangelical, Unity, church, 201, 202.
Evening Sun, The, 176.

Fair grounds, 121.
Farley, Ed, 168, 226, 227.
Festival, summer, 271.
Fire chiefs, 183.
Fire departments, volunteer, 180-182, paid, 183, 184.
Fisher, Emma Jean, 251.
Fisher Gardens, 120, 122.
Fisher, John G., mayor, 75, 108.
Fletcher, Robert.
Floods, 133-135, marker, 136.
Flournoy, G. H., 54.
Flournoy, T. J., 129.
Flower, George E., 179.
Forrest, Nathan B., 151.
Fowler boats, 141.
Fowler, Joseph H., 102.
Friedman, Joseph L., 253, 254.
Fruit growing, 263.
Funeral, largest, 179.

Games, 113.
Gardner, Jesse H., mayor, 71.
Gilbert, Harry M., 244-245.
Gilberto, Don, 118, 99.
Goodman, George H., 176.
Grant, U.S., 143-149.
Gross, Gladys, 251.
Gruenebaum, Mayme Dryfuss, 251.

Hail storm, 139.
Harrison, Francis A., 37, 101.
Hazelip, Thomas N., mayor, 88-89, welcomes Chief Paduke, 259.
Hicks, Stephen G., 152.
Hills, Mrs. W. J., 251.
Home-Coming Week, 257-259.
Hook's Field, 123.
Horses, witticism about, 168.
Hospital, Riverside (Lourdes) 265, 266.
Hospital, Western Baptist, 265, 266.
House, first, 35.
Houses, Hicks burns, 153, 154.
Hummel, Ferd, Sr., 102, 254, 255.
Hummel, Ferd, Jr., 199, 213.
Hummel, W. P., 80.
Husbands, James B., 63.
Husbands, L. D. home, 105.

Irvin S. Cobb Hotel, 263.
Illinois Central Railroad, 161-164.
Industries, 99-101.

Jackson House Apartments, 263.
Jackson, Andrew, 20.
Jackson Purchase, 17-22, area, 19.
Jarrett, Mrs. Emily, rescues flag, 146, 147.
Johnson, Joseph A., mayor, 80-81.
Jones, Mrs. T. Neil, 214.

Karnes, Ernest, 156.
Katterjohn, F. W., mayor, 93-94.
Katterjohn, Ray, 123.
Keiler Field, 170.
Keiler, John W., 170.
Keiler, Leo F., Park, 127.
Klaw, Marc, 250.
Kolb, Louis C., 125, recollection of Grant, 147, 154.
Kolb Park, 125.
Kolb, Ruby, 251.

Lackey, Ernest, mayor, 89-90, re-elected, 91.
Lake View Country Club, 125.
Lamp-posts, 80.
Landmarks, 99-109.
Lang, James M., mayor, 82, 83.
Langstaff home, 105, 106.
Langstaff mill, 100.
Latitude, longitude, 17.
Lawson, John, 41-42, 107, 255.
Levee, 86, 129.
Library, Carnegie Public, 172-173.
Location, Paducah, 17.
Lutheran, St. Matthew's, church, 213.

Lutheran, St. Paul's, church, 198, 199.
Lyle, Mrs. Edna Hays, 251.

Magruder, Mary Lanier, poem, 28.
Major, Jack, 251.
Manufactories, 240, 241.
Marine Ways, 129, 130.
Market House, 53, 64.
Market House Museum, 65.
Markham Day, 164.
McCracken, Virgil, 44.
McCracken County, origin of name, 44, established, 44, area, 44, first courthouse, 47, centennial celebration, 50.
McCune, Robert C., burial, 157.
McFadden, W. G., 249.
McKinney, Mrs. Roy W., 250.
Medicine shows, 113.
Merrimac, 103.
Methodist, Broadway, church, 187, 188.
Methodist, Fountain Avenue, church, 203, 204.
Methodist, Third Street, church, 205, 206.
Methodist, Trinity, church, 206.
Methodist, North Side, church, 214, 215.
Mexican War, 142-143.
Mitchell, Elliot, C., editor, 176, toastmaster at Cobb dinner, 232.
Morrow, Emily, 250.
Mt. Carmel cemetery, 179.
Moving pictures, 115, 116.
Murray, Ed, 103.
Murrell, Mrs. D. G., 248.
Murrell, D. G., 248.
Museum, Alben W. Barkley, 272.

Neuman, F. W., 140.
Newspapers, 173-177.
News-Democrat, 176.
New Orleans, first steamboat, 31-34, 128.
Noble, Bob, park, 126, 127.
Noble, Robert H., 126, 127.
Noonan, Jimmie, 273.
Norton, William F., 63, 105.
N. C. & St. L., Ry., 82, 161.

Oak Grove Cemetery, 68, 179, addition, 87.
Oehlschlaeger, George, 154.
Operation Town Lift, 271, 272.
Owen, Valentine, 36, 37, 124, home, 104.

Paducah, genesis of name, 17-19, Indian site, 17, platted by William Clark, 51, name changed from Pekin, 46, settlement, 35-37, incorporated as town, 51, becomes county seat, 49, incorporated as third class city, 70, second class city, 85, mayors, 268-271.
Paducah, battle of, 151-155.
Paducah Country Club, 125.

Paducah, gunboat, 139, 140.
Paducah, steamer, 140.
Paducah, Texas, 23.
Paduca, 49.
Paducah Flag, 274.
Paducah, Mall, 273.
Paduke, Chief, origin of name, 17, haunts, 23, appearance, 25, marker, 27, returns to Pekin, 26, death, 26-27, burial, 27, poem, 28, impersonated, 258, statue, 27, 28.
Paine, E. A., 102, 148, 149.
Pak'tukah, 18-19.
Palmer, Mrs. Elbridge, 250.
Parham, Eugenia, 249.
Parks, 96, 83, 122, 126, 127.
Park Board, 125.
Paved streets, 85.
Paxton, E. J., 176.
Pekin, changed to Paducah, 51.
Petter, Roy, 123.
Phillips, Mrs. R. B., 250.
Phillips, Joseph B., 249.
Phonograph, first, 118.
Plants, 272, 273.
Polk, John W., 48.
Pontoon bridge, 144, 145.
Population, 262, 261.
Post, Josephine Fowler, 250.
Post office, 80.
Presbyterian, First, church, 191-192.
Presbyterian, Kentucky Avenue, church, 209.
Presbyterian, Park Avenue Cumberland, church, 211, 212.
Presbyterian, Mizpah, church, 214.
Proclamation, Grant's, 147.
Public schools, 169-171.
Public well, 62.
Pulliam, Henry A., 94.
Purcell, Martha Grassham, heads county centennial, 50, author, 249, club president, 251.

Quigley, Q. Q., procures city charter, 70, city attorney, 72, encourages railroad shops, 161.

Racing, 121.
Radio, 123, stations, 124, 176.
Railroads, 159-164.
Reddick, William, 246.
Reed, Charles, mayor, 77.
Revivals, 215-218.
Reynolds, Mrs. H. G., 250.
Rhodes, H. C., 125, 127.
Rice, Dan, gives fire engine, 117.
Rieke, Jaqueline, 273.
Ritz Hotel, 263.
Rivers, 128-141, flow, 141, floods, 133-135, freezes, 131, 132, early steamboats, 128, 129, levee, 86, 129, stages, 133, marine ways, 129, 130.

Robertson, J. D., first automobile, 167.
Robertson, Lloyd P., editor, 176.
Rock, George M., 253.
Rock, Will, 253.
Rollston, Guy, 176.
Rudy, Henry, 123.
Rudy, Mrs. J. A., 250.
Rudy, Richard, 253.
Runaways, 168.
Russell, V. Blaine, 247.

St. Mary's Academy, 172, 267.
Saloons, 62, 88, 93.
Saunders, Reuben, home, 105, discovery, 243-244.
Sauner, John W., 2nd mayor, 74, reads proclamation, 74.
Schools, 169.
Scientist, First Church of Christ, 209, 210.
Scott, Richard, 252.
Scott, Robert H., 251, 274.
Scott, William R., 247.
Shops, Railroad, 161-164.
Sidewalks, first, 66, 83.
Sleeth, Jack B., 107, 108.
Sleet storm, 136-139.
Slogan, 273.
Small, Braxton, home, 103.
Smith, Charles F., 148, 149.
Smith, James P., mayor, 87-88.
Smith, Krystal, 251.
Snow, heaviest, 131.
Spanish-American War, 155-156.
Sports, 112.
Sprague, towboat, 141.
Stables, 110.
Steamboat, first, 31-32, 128.
Stewart, Anna Bird, 247.
Stewart, P. H., 157.
Streets, names, 67, renamed, 80.
Streetcars, 164-166.
Streets, hard-surfaced, 83, total mileage, 95.
Submarine cable, 107, 108.
Sutherland, Richard, 252.

Taxes, 61.
Telephones, 184, 185.
Television, 124-125.
Temple Israel, 199-200.
Terrell, R. G., first telephone, 184.
Theaters, 114-115.
Thompson, A. P., home, 101, leads charge, 152, killed, 152-153, estimate of, 154, 155.
Tilghman High School, 170, 267.
Tilghman, Lloyd, home, 102, enlists men, 144, sketch of, 235-237.
Tobacco interests, 262, 263, 109, 110.
Tornado, 139.
Town, Paducah, 51-60.

Utterback, James C., 164, 253.

Vahlkamp, Charles G., 253.

Wallace, Lew, headquarters, 106.

Wallace Park, 122, name, 126.
Wallerstein, Herman, 234.
Walters, Grace, 40-41.
War, Mexican, 142-143, Civil, 143-151, Spanish-American, 155-156, World, 156-158.
Washburn, B. A., 157.
Water Works, 80.
Water Fountain Horses 110, 111.
Weather, coldest, 116.
Weber, John L., 157.
Weil, Meyer, mayor, 76.
Weille, Ben. 123, 257.
Well, public, 62.
Wells, Mrs. H. S., 251.
Wheeler, Charles K., 86, 139.
Wheeler, James G., 258, 157.
Wilkins, Robert, 249.
Williamson, John E., 144.
Wilmington, 46-50, marker, 50.
Wisdom, Benjamin H., 101.
Woman's Club, 250.
Woodson, Urey, 175.
Woolfolk, Angeline Owen, 104, 105.
World War, 156, 157.

Yeiser, David A., Sr., 85-86.
Young, Al, E., 90.